MORE ADVANCE PRAISE FOR
Roman Pilgrimage

"George Weigel's original, contemporary reflections on the station church liturgies of Lent and Easter are greatly enhanced by Elizabeth Lev's descriptions of the station churches and Stephen Weigel's evocative photographs. An indispensable guide."

—NOEL FAHEY,
Irish ambassador to the Holy See, 2007–2011

"The Lenten station church pilgrimage is increasingly popular in Rome, especially among English-speaking Catholics. Zealously promoted and led by the students of the Pontifical North American College, the daily Eucharistic celebrations at these earliest of the Eternal City's churches commemorate the martyrs of the first three centuries, whose witness is being emulated throughout the world today. Up to now, though, these sunrise pilgrimages have been known to few outside Rome. No more!"

—EDWIN CARDINAL O'BRIEN,
Grand Master of the Equestrian Order of the Holy Sepulcher of Jerusalem

"*Roman Pilgrimage* evokes a tradition dating back to Pope St. Gregory the Great, but it also highlights, in a remarkable way, how relevant, contemporary, and even fashionable pilgrimage continues to be today. This beautiful book is an important gift to contemporary Christians, those looking for their roots and those seeking new ways to deepen their faith. At the same time, it makes an important proposal to those who doubt and to those who got lost on the way. *Roman Pilgrimage* should be on the packing list of anyone who, setting off for the Eternal City, wants to return with something more than the usual tourist mementos."

—HANNA SUCHOCKA,
Polish Ambassador to the Holy See, 2001–2013

"*Roman Pilgrimage* is a special gift to those who cannot be in Rome for Lent, for it connects every reader spiritually to this ancient walk of faith. No one will come away from the station church pilgrimage—a unique opportunity to renew our friendship with the Lord—disappointed."

—MSGR. JAMES CHECCHIO,
Rector, Pontifical North American College

"The Roman station churches describe an itinerary with a difference. Along it, pilgrims encounter two thousand years of the masterpieces of culture while being invited to reflect on the claims of Christian faith in light of today's challenges. A great companion on a pilgrimage through the station churches, in Rome or at home."

—ANNE LEAHY,
Faculty of Religious Studies, McGill University, Montreal

"More than a historical and cultural narrative and a striking guide book, *Roman Pilgrimage* is also an inspiring reflection on the spiritual life, well-suited to an enriching retreat."

—ARCHBISHOP TIMOTHY P. BROGLIO,
Archdiocese for the Military Services, U.S.A.

"Theologically rich, spiritually inspiring, historically informative, and beautifully illustrated, *Roman Pilgrimage* takes the reader on a spiritual journey into the incarnate depths of the Christian faith. Whether we are in Rome or elsewhere, we are invited to walk with the saints and martyrs along the path of paschal renewal in Christ."

—FR. JOSEPH CAROLA, S.J.,
Pontifical Gregorian University

ROMAN PILGRIMAGE

ROMAN PILGRIMAGE

The Station Churches

GEORGE WEIGEL

ELIZABETH LEV
Art and Architecture

STEPHEN WEIGEL
Photographs

BASIC BOOKS
A Member of the Perseus Books Group
New York

Published by Basic Books
A Member of the Perseus Books Group

Books published by Basic Books are available at special discounts for bulk purchases
in the United States by corporations, institutions, and other organizations. For more
information, please contact the Special Markets Department at the Perseus Books
Group, 2300 Chestnut Street, Suite 200, Philadelphia, PA 19103, or call (800) 810-
4145, ext. 5000, or e-mail special.markets@perseusbooks.com.

Designed by Brent Wilcox

A CIP catalog record for this book is available from the Library of Congress.
ISBN: 978-0-465-02769-9 (hardcover)
ISBN: 978-0-465-07495-2 (e-book)

10 9 8 7 6 5 4 3 2 1

Martyribus Tunc et Nunc

CONTENTS

THE FIFTH WEEK OF LENT

HOLY WEEK

ROMAN PILGRIMAGE

Janiculum Hill: Pilgrims on the Sant'Onofrio steps

THE STATION CHURCHES OF ROME

To go in a spirit of prayer from one place to another . . . helps us not only live our lives as a journey, but also gives us a vivid sense of a God who has gone before us and leads us on, who himself set out on man's path, a God who does not look down on us from on high, but who has become our traveling companion.

—JOHN PAUL II, "Letter on Pilgrimage," 1999

IN VIRTUALLY EVERY TIME and place known to history, men and women have gone on pilgrimage.

In the ancient Near East, pilgrimage was a common, usually seasonal, affair: farmers brought the first fruits of the harvest, and herders culled the best of their flocks, to offer in sacrifice at a tribal or familial shrine. The Israelites adapted several Canaanite pilgrimage shrines for their worship of the God who had brought them out of Egyptian bondage and had made them a people uniquely his own. Jerusalem became a great pilgrimage destination after King David brought the Ark of the Covenant there and made it his capital. On three occasions each year, the Israelites were instructed to come before the Lord in Jerusalem: at Passover; at *Shavuot* [Pentecost], which commemorated the gift of the Ten Commandments; and at *Sukkot* [Booths, or Tabernacles], a memorial to their wanderings in the desert.

Christianity adopted the religious practice of pilgrimage from its Jewish parent. After Constantine's edict of toleration brought the Church out from under the rubble of illegality and persecution, pilgrimage to the sites associated with the life, ministry, death, and resurrection of Jesus became a staple of Christian life. Constantine's mother, Helena, was an early and influential pilgrim who encouraged the practice of Holy Land pilgrimage, as did the great patristic biblical scholar Jerome. Texts from as early as 333 A.D. speak of a pilgrimage path that led from Bordeaux to Jerusalem and then back to Europe through Rome and Milan. One of the most important pilgrimage texts of the early Church is the diary of Egeria, thought to have been an abbess or nun from Spain or Gaul, who chronicled her Holy Land pilgrimage in 395 and recorded many details of the Church's Lenten disciplines and Easter worship in Jerusalem in those days.

The pilgrimage tradition in Rome began even earlier. In times of persecution Christians made their way to the tombs of their martyrs clandestinely. Almost two millennia later, catacomb graffiti (including those found near the tomb of Peter) bear silent witness to the Christians who went on local pilgrimage to venerate the saints, many of whom they had known personally, by celebrating Mass. Foreigners came to Rome as well, including such major figures from early Christian history as Polycarp of Smyrna, a disciple of the apostle John, and Origen, the great Alexandrian theologian. Like pilgrimage to the Holy Land, the Roman pilgrimage tradition to the shrines of the martyrs grew after 313 and the legalization of Christianity; Pope St. Damasus I's restoration of the catacombs in the second half of the fourth century was one factor in putting this tradition close to the center of Roman Christian life. So many pilgrims began to flock to the tombs of Peter and Paul that, by the early sixth century, Pope St. Symmachus built three pilgrim hostels near the tombs of the two great apostolic patrons of the city and the tomb of Rome's third principal patron, St. Lawrence. This flow of pilgrims to Rome continued well into the Middle Ages.

The Roman Christian practice of visiting the tombs of the martyrs, praying, and celebrating the Eucharist at these sites is the foundation on which the Roman station church pilgrimage of Lent arose. In the early fourth century, as the practice of a Lenten pilgrimage to certain churches that had been built on, above, or around the tombs of martyrs began to be formalized, the station church pilgrimage emerged in its classic form: in a designated place on a given day, the Bishop of Rome, along with his clergy, his choir, and the Christians of the city, would celebrate Holy Mass together as their common sacred offering to God.

In those days, the Lenten fast was day-long, such that no food was taken during the working day. Toward mid-afternoon, Christians began to gather at a church known as the *collecta* [the "gathering place" or "assembly point"], where they would be joined by their bishop, the pope; the pastors of the Roman parishes; the seven deacons of the city's seven districts; and the subdeacons and acolytes of each of Rome's neighborhoods. The pope then led a procession to another church, the *statio*, or "station." The procession was considerable; as it made its way through the streets of the city, it included people from each neighborhood district, who sang the Litany of the Saints along with their priests and deacons.

At the *statio*, the pope celebrated a solemn Mass, and fractions of the consecrated bread were dispatched to the other *stationes* in Rome, underscoring that each day's Mass was the entire local Church gathered in worship around its bishop. After singing Vespers [Evening Prayer of the Liturgy of the Hours], the liturgical services concluded, and the day-long fast was broken by a communal meal. Sung and splendid, the papal stational Masses did not end with the traditional *Ite, missa est* [Go, the Mass is ended], but with *Benedicamus Domino* [Let us bless the Lord], a form of grace-before-meals.

In the station church pilgrimage's early form, some twenty-five Roman churches were assigned as pilgrimage goals for the daily processions from the designated *collecta*. Moreover, the *statio* appointed for each day was not the church building (many of which had evolved from Roman house churches), but the martyr buried at that site. Thus, the Mass of the day was always identified as, for example, "Station at St. Lawrence in Panisperna," not "Station at the Basilica of St. Lawrence in Panisperna."

The order of visitation during the Lenten station church pilgrimage in Rome was largely fixed by Pope St. Gregory the Great (590–604), although later additions filled out the program to its present form. The station church pilgrimage shaped the evolution of the Roman liturgy in several ways. The pre-1970 gospel reading for the Thursday after Ash Wednesday (Matthew 8.5–13, the cure of the centurion's servant) was almost certainly chosen because that day's station was St. George in Velabro, the site of the relics of the great soldier-saint and model of Christian chivalry. Echoes of that choice and of St. George's life can be heard in the twenty-first-century liturgy's Entrance Antiphon for that day: "When I cried to the Lord, he heard my voice; he rescued me from those who attack me. Entrust your cares to the Lord, and he will support you." The station at St. Eusebius, on Friday of the Fourth Week of Lent, was chosen because the gospel account of the raising of Lazarus was appointed for that day and the cemetery on the Esquiline Hill was near at hand; thus, in this instance, the *statio* was chosen to fit the prescribed reading of the day.

The Roman station church pilgrimage continued throughout the Octave of Easter. The structure of that week strikingly illustrates the theological and liturgical care that went into the pilgrimage's design: during the eight days of the Easter Octave, the Roman Church's liturgical prayer unfolded along a stational hierarchy of sanctity, beginning and ending at that hierarchy's pinnacle. Thus the Easter Vigil station is the Papal Archbasilica of St. John Lateran, originally known as the Basilica of Our Savior. Easter Sunday's station is St. Mary Major. On Easter Monday, Tuesday, and Wednesday, the station is at St. Peter's in the Vatican, then St. Paul Outside the Walls, then St. Lawrence Outside the Walls—the three principal patrons of Rome. Easter Thursday's station is the Twelve Holy Apostles, while Friday's is the Pantheon, the church of all the Roman martyrs and the place where many of their relics were kept. Finally, the Saturday within the Octave of Easter brings the pilgrimage back to the Lateran Basilica. This was the day before the baptized catechumens took off their white garments: the *Dominica in Albis Depositis* [Sunday of White Vestments Removed]. (The station church for the Octave of Easter is St. Pancras, a youthful martyr whose memory reminds the Church that it is ever young, and ever called to radical fidelity and witness.)

The earliest reliable textual witness to the classic form of the Roman station church pilgrimage is the Würzberg Manuscript of the mid-700s, the oldest surviving Latin lectionary, or book of Mass readings. It embodies the structure of the Roman liturgy some one hundred years before, and thus takes us within fifty years of the death of Gregory the Great in 604. Here, scholars can trace the reciprocal relationship between the Mass texts of a given Lenten day or day within the Octave of Easter and the *statio* of that day.

Other cities, it should be noted, also had a tradition of "station churches," including Paris, Vienna, Venice, and Milan. In Milan, where the Ambrosian Rite, rather than the Roman Rite, was celebrated, Fridays in Lent have traditionally been "aliturgical"—that is, days on which Mass is not celebrated. In the Roman Rite, Thursdays were aliturgical for centuries, and the institution of Mass on Thursdays in the eighth century prompted the expansion of the station churches of Rome beyond the original twenty-five fixed by Gregory the Great.

The Roman station church pilgrimage flourished throughout the first millennium, but began to die out by stages in the first centuries of the second millennium. From 1050 to 1300, the popes were frequently out of Rome for various reasons, in the Papal States or elsewhere; this was the period when popes were elected in such diverse places as Cluny, Perugia, Ravenna, Siena, and Terracina. One of the results of the eleventh-century reforms of Pope St. Gregory VII was a heightened emphasis on the pope as an administrator. Thereafter, pontiffs devoted more of their daily routine to management, and papal liturgies tended to center around the pope-administrator's enlarged court, the Roman Curia; now, the pope and his bureaucratic subalterns celebrated the liturgy together, rather than out in the city with the people of Rome. In its classic form, the Roman station church pilgrimage ceased to exist when the primary papal residence was relocated in 1305 to Avignon in the south of France.

Although the return of the popes from their Avignon exile did not usher in a revival of the classic station church pilgrimage, the Roman Missal retained the stational notation for each day of Lent and Easter, and thus the memory of the pilgrimage lived on in the liturgy. Any early modern thoughts of a revival of the pilgrimage were ended when Rome was taken by the forces of the new

Kingdom of Italy in 1870 and the pope withdrew behind the Leonine Wall as "the prisoner of the Vatican."

After the 1929 Lateran Treaty solved the Roman Question of the pope's temporal sovereignty by creating the State of Vatican City, Pope Pius XI (1922–1939) and Pope Pius XII (1939–1958) encouraged a renewal of the ancient tradition by attaching special indulgences to attendance at stational Masses during Lent. During this same period, the Vicariate of Rome (the administration of the Roman diocese, which is led in the pope's name by a cardinal vicar) encouraged local pastors to organize processions to the stations during Lent, while also urging the universities, colleges, and religious houses or residences in the city to participate. This modest revival was interrupted by World War II, particularly during the German occupation of Rome in 1943–1944, but was continued by Pius XII after the war.

On Ash Wednesday, 1959, the newly elected Pope John XXIII accelerated the contemporary restoration of the station church pilgrimage by going to St. Sabina on the Aventine Hill to receive penitential ashes. His successor, Pope Paul VI, went to the station at St. Eusebius in 1967, thereby signaling that the Lenten station church tradition had not been superseded by the liturgical reforms mandated by the Second Vatican Council—although the Concilium that implemented those reforms relied far less on the station church/Lenten liturgy nexus in fashioning the Roman Missal of 1970 than had the Missal of Pope St. Pius V, the product of the sixteenth-century Council of Trent.

In the early twenty-first century, the Vicariate of Rome sponsors daily Lenten stational Masses. Pope Benedict XVI made a practice of going up the Aventine to St. Sabina for the celebration of Ash Wednesday Mass and the reception of ashes, as did Pope John Paul II. Yet, in the last decades of the twentieth century and the first decades of the twenty-first, the greatest impetus toward a revival of the Lenten station church pilgrimage in Rome has come from the Pontifical North American College, the residential house of formation at which seminarians from the United States (and fellow-Anglophone countries such as

Canada and Australia) prepare for the priesthood while studying theology at the pontifical universities in the city.

Beginning in the mid-1970s, American seminarians and student priests began walking the pilgrim's road through Rome before dawn in order to celebrate a daily Lenten stational Mass at 7 a.m. The North American College station church pilgrimage grew, and, by the turn of the millennium, hundreds of English-speakers from Rome's universities, diplomatic posts, and Anglophone seminaries were joining in the pilgrimage and celebrating Holy Mass together at the ancient Roman *stationes*. On any given Lenten day, seminarians and student-priests from Iowa, New York, California, South Carolina, Maryland, Wisconsin, Surrey, Alberta, and New South Wales join university students from Louisiana, Minnesota, and Oregon; diplomats from Canada, Ireland, Poland, the United Kingdom, and the United States; religious sisters from Africa, Asia, Latin America, and North America; and English-speaking members of the Roman Curia in re-creating, in the first decades of Catholicism's third millennium, the experience of the Lenten stational church Mass as a unique global crossroads of faith and worship—just as it was when Rome was the center of the Western world.

The station church pilgrimage can be, and in fact is, walked on many levels, not unlike the city in which it takes place. For Rome is so deeply layered by the accumulated stuff of centuries that the roads along which one makes the pilgrimage in the twenty-first century are many meters above the roads along which Gregory the Great would have led his people from the daily *collecta* to its accompanying *statio*.

Thus, along the pathways of the station church pilgrimage (and at whatever time of year it is walked), the twenty-first-century pilgrim or visitor passes through multiple layers of the history of Western civilization and has the opportunity to ponder the rise and fall of empires—as well as the continuities of culture that endure despite radical changes of political and economic fortune. This layer of the station church pilgrimage is open to everyone, whatever an individual's religious "location" or lack thereof. It can be a deeply moving reminder of the fragility of civilization as well as of the richness of regenerative powers embedded in the West.

On another level, Christians of all denominational persuasions will find along the paths of the station church pilgrimage an *itinerarium* of sanctity and profound Christian conviction. Here walked Peter and Paul, and perhaps others of the apostles and evangelists. Here walked Leo and Gregory, two popes popularly acclaimed as "the Great"; here walked another pope, John Paul II, whom many believe history will remember with that same title. Martin Luther strode along these pathways, as did John Henry Newman, two men of genius who came to dramatically different conclusions about the place of Rome in the Christian scheme of things. Here, Ignatius Loyola and Philip Neri devised different Catholic responses to the challenges posed by the Reformation and the fracturing of Western Christianity. And here, in the late twentieth century, Orthodox and Protestant leaders began to pray in common with the Bishop of Rome for an end to the fragmentation of the Christian world.

At yet another level, the station church pilgrimage—especially when it is made during Lent—is an itinerary of conversion. For while the linkage between the Lenten liturgy and the station of the day is not so tight as it was in the past, so many elements of tangency can be found between these churches and the prayers and readings the Church prays and ponders in them that the station church pilgrimage can become an extended retreat: seven and a half weeks of reflection that synthesize the truths of Christian faith and offer pilgrims an opportunity to reflect on how well those truths have been integrated along the pathways of their lives.

Making the station church pilgrimage is also a marvelous way to discover the many faces of Rome. On the pilgrimage, one walks through the always-clogged and now-funky streets of Trastevere, crosses the high baroque Piazza Navona, breathes the early-morning aromas of the markets of the Campo dei Fiori, skirts the ruins of the Circus Maximus, and climbs up the beautiful Aventine Hill, with its unparalleled views of the city. Ascending the Caelian Hill on another day, one looks into the great ruins on the Palatine Hill, the Park Avenue or Belgravia of the Augustan Age. Climbing the gentle rise of the Esquiline Hill, one is reminded of snow miraculously falling in August 352, indicating where a church in honor of Mary, Mother of God, should be built. Americans, ascending the Capitoline Hill to another *statio*, will learn or be reminded of where the legislative seat of their federal government got its name. All those who look back to Rome as one of the foundations of their own national experience, and to Latin as a primary source of their language, can reflect, in various moods, on the glory that was classical Rome, on its enduring cultural impact, and on its inability to sustain itself indefinitely as a political community.

Along the station church way, one passes, sometimes frequently, artifacts and ruins that jog the cultural memory: the Forum, where Cicero and others argued for the superiority of law over brute force in the governing of states and peoples; the Colosseum, reminder of the perennial human attraction to sport and the perennial human temptation to cruelty; the arches of Titus, despoiler of the Temple of Jerusalem, and Constantine, who initiated a troubled relationship between Christianity and state power, from which some Christian communities have only begun extracting themselves in the past two centuries; the Temple of Saturn and *La Bocca della Verità*, reminders of the paganism and superstition that still emerge on occasion from beneath the surface of modern Roman life; and the Baths of Caracalla, once a different kind of public square, now a venue for opera.

The stones here are witnesses, if silent ones, and so are many of the buildings, streets, and artifacts encountered along the pilgrim's way, or explored after the daily stational Mass. The obelisk in St. Peter's Square once stood in Nero's Circus, and quite likely witnessed the martyrdom of Peter. The Via Lata, now the Via del Corso, was trod by Julius Caesar after he crossed the Rubicon, and by Constantine after his victory at the Milvian Bridge. Benito Mussolini, a caricature of grandeur, tried to re-create rhetorically the glory that was antique Rome by delivering harangues from the *loggia* of the Piazza Venezia, near the station at St. Mark. An Italian of the same generation, Pope Pius XII, came to the people of Rome gathered outside the stational basilica of St. Lawrence Outside the Walls after bombs had destroyed parts of their neighborhood during World War II; he distributed alms and returned to the Vatican with blood staining his white cassock. From 1962 through 1965, the marble, statuary, and mosaics inside the Vatican Basilica, St. Peter's, witnessed the four sessions of the Second Vatican Council and the Catholic Church's wrestling with the good and the evil of modernity. The stones of the square outside the basilica witnessed the greatest gathering of humanity in a generation at the 2005 funeral of John Paul II, the Polish priest who had been shot in that very square, whom the Romans had taken to their hearts as they had sometimes not done with popes of their own stock.

And through it all, Pasquino, the battered statue that symbolizes Roman wit, stood silently along one of the station church pathways, a witness to human foibles—and to the human capacity to laugh at them.

The station church walk is also an invitation to discover artistic treasures that the casual (and sometimes even the assiduous) tourist would likely miss. The apse mosaic in the stational church of Sts. Cosmas and Damian, hard by the Roman Forum, is a wholly unanticipated mid-sixth-century anticipation of twentieth-century art deco. The gemlike mosaics in the small Chapel of St. Zeno, in the completely out-of-the-way *statio* at St. Praxedes on the Esquiline, make this small space one of the most beautiful rooms on the planet. Numerous stational churches, rarely visited, have magnificent Cosmatesque floors, made by ingenious medieval craftsmen from shards of marble and other stones; the obscure station at St. Balbina, behind the drably modern headquarters of the United Nations Food and Agricultural Organization, has a splendid thirteenth-century Cosmatesque throne. The *statio* at St. Augustine houses Caravaggio's *Madonna of the Pilgrims*, one of the most strikingly earthy of his renderings of the Mother of God.

All these wonders can, of course, be enjoyed for their beauty. Yet if Swiss theologian Hans Urs von Balthasar was right—that beauty, the often-forgotten transcendental, is, in late modernity, uniquely magnetic in drawing us to experience anew the good and the true, the transcendentals often obscured by modernity—then beauty can be a unique pathway to God. Thus the discovery of unexpected beauty along the station church walk may stretch the visitor's imagination in ways that he or she never imagined possible.

For all of late modernity's confusions, the rediscovery of the ancient human instinct for pilgrimage has been a striking feature of the late twentieth century and the early twenty-first. Though it has been made possible by the relative ease of contemporary travel, this rediscovery of pilgrimage surely is not entirely attributable to the Boeing 747 and the Airbus 380. Muslims in their millions make the Hajj to Mecca. Jews, able for the first time in centuries to pray at the western wall of Herod's Temple, come to Jerusalem from all over the world. Tens of millions of Hindus participate in the Maha Kumbh Mela, a pilgrimage to the Ganges River that takes place once every twelve years. Even in religiously arid Europe, the medieval pilgrim roads to Santiago de Compostela in northwestern Spain—roads that played no small role in forging "Europe" out of a congeries of tribes—are once more trod by tens of thousands of hikers, many of whom are nonbelievers.

This late twentieth- and early twenty-first-century passion for pilgrimage, which the late nineteenth century, confident of the inexorable advance of secularism, would not have anticipated, has been a particularly striking feature of late-modern Catholic piety. Millions of Catholics make pilgrimage to Marian shrines such as Lourdes, Fatima, and Guadalupe every year. The Great Jubilee of 2000 drew unprecedented numbers of Catholic pilgrims to Rome from all over the world. Perhaps most unexpectedly, the international World Youth Days initiated by Pope John Paul II in the mid-1980s have become triennial global events of a sort that no one imagined possible in the late 1970s: young people, from all over the world, gathering for a week for religious instruction and prayer.

Amid all of this wayfaring—some of it explicitly religious, some of it searching—the Roman station church pilgrimage retains a special character, uniquely combining history, art and architecture, and distinctive religious qualities. For those of other faiths or no faith, as well as for Catholics, the themes for reflection prompted by the station churches themselves, and by the liturgical rhythms of Lent, make for a striking human experience. The station churches of Rome have a special place in the religious imagination of Catholics. They are emphatically not, however, for Catholics only.

Trastevere: Pilgrims approaching the Piazza S. Maria in Trastevere

St. Prisca: Ancient baptismal font

LENT

An Itinerary of Conversion

THE REDISCOVERY OF THE baptismal character of Lent, the ancient penitential season that precedes Easter, and the restoration of the Paschal Triduum—Holy Thursday, Good Friday, and the Easter Vigil—as the apex of the Church's liturgical year are two of the most important accomplishments of modern Catholicism.

Over the centuries, the summit of the Church's year of grace—the celebration of Christ's passing over from death to life, for which the Church prepares in Lent—had become encrusted with liturgical barnacles that gradually took center stage in the drama of Holy Week. And while some of them had a beauty of their own, such as the Tenebrae service, celebrated early in the morning of Holy Thursday, Good Friday, and Holy Saturday, the overall effect was to diminish the liturgical richness of the Triduum; the Easter Vigil's essential character as a dramatic night-watch, when the Church gathers at the Lord's tomb to ponder the great events of salvation history while awaiting the bright dawn of the Resurrection, was almost completely obscured. Similarly, Lent, which had an intensely baptismal character centuries ago, became almost exclusively penitential: a matter of what Catholics must *not* do, rather than a season focused on the heart of the Christian vocation and mission—conversion to Jesus Christ and the deepening of our friendship with him.

Now, thanks to Pope Pius XII's restoration of the Easter Vigil and the liturgical reforms mandated by the Second Vatican Council, Catholics of the twenty-first century can celebrate both Lent and the Paschal Triduum in the richness of their evangelical and baptismal character, as moments of intensified conversion to Christ and incorporation into his Body, the Church. Lent, once dreaded, has become popular: churches are full on Ash Wednesday, and the disciplines of

Lent—fasting, almsgiving, intensified prayer—have now been relocated properly within the great human adventure of continuing conversion. Celebrated with appropriate solemnity, the Paschal Triduum today is what it should be: the apex of the liturgical year, in which those who were initially conformed to Christ in Baptism, along with those baptized at the Easter Vigil, relive the Master's Passion and Death in order to experience the joy of the Resurrection, the decisive confirmation that God's purposes in history will be vindicated.

This revival of Lent in the Catholic Church has involved the rediscovery of the Forty Days as a season shaped by the *catechumenate*: the period of education and formation through which adults who have not yet been baptized are prepared to receive Baptism, Confirmation, and the Holy Eucharist, the three sacraments of Christian initiation, at the Easter Vigil. The baptismal character of Lent is not for catechumens only, however. The adult catechumenate (called the Rite of Christian Initiation of Adults) offers an annual reminder to the Church that *all* Christians are *always* in need of conversion. The Church's conversion, the Church's being-made-holy, is a never-ending process.

Baptism, the Scriptures tell us, is "for the forgiveness of sins." And while that central aspect of the sacrament is most dramatically manifest in the baptism of adults at the Easter Vigil, those who were baptized in infancy, and who, as all do, inevitably fall into sin, are also in need of forgiveness. Thus baptism "for the forgiveness of sins," which is such a prominent theme throughout Lent, reminds all the baptized that they, too, require liberation from sin: from the bad habits that enslave us and impede our friendship with Christ.

To make the pilgrimage of Lent is to follow an itinerary of conversion. Lent affords every baptized Christian the opportunity to reenter the catechumenate, to undergo a "second baptism," and thus to meet once again the mysteries of God's mercy and love.

The God of Abraham, Isaac, and Jacob—the God whom Jesus calls "Father"—is not the kind of deity imagined by twenty-first-century treatises on "spirituality," which typically treat the spiritual life as the human search for God. Biblical religion—the faith of the People of Israel and of the Church—is entirely different. As the liturgical readings of Lent insistently press home, biblical religion is about God's search for us and our learning to take the same path through history that God is taking: to follow the itinerary of conversion and salvation that God has marked out.

Biblical religion is built around what Pope Benedict XVI called, in his 2011 Lenten meditation, "the adventure of God, the greatness of what he has done for us." And that adventure consists in the fact that "God did not remain within himself: he came out from himself." The divine itinerary begins with Creation, which God sustains every day in the power of his love (for, as Thomas Aquinas taught, if God wanted to end the world, he would not have to do something; he would only have to stop doing something). The divine itinerary continues in salvation history as God enters the drama of creation and asks those whom he elects to follow his path into the future; the dramatic struggles of that elect people, Israel, to follow the divine itinerary form a consistent theme throughout the biblical readings of the Lenten liturgy, both at Holy Mass and in the Liturgy of the Hours. Salvation history, in turn, reaches its climax in the Incarnation. As Benedict XVI put it to a synod of bishops in 2010, "God . . . united himself so much, so radically, with this man, Jesus, that this man Jesus is God, and what we say about him we can always say about God as well. He was born not only as a man who had something to do with God, but in him God was born on earth. God came out from himself." And in doing so, "God has drawn us into himself, so that we are no longer outside of God, but we are inside, inside God himself."

Jesus does not live "for himself." He lives to "draw all things" to himself [John 12.32], which he does by forming a body, the Church, of which he is the "first-born among many brethren" [Romans 8.29]. This body, this Church, continues the mission of Jesus in history. Yet it is a Church that, while bearing within itself the truth of the world, is always composed of sinners. That is the reason for Lent. Lent is the journey in which the people of the Church are annually purified for their mission of witnessing to the Gospel and offering men and women friendship with Jesus.

As the Church understands it, repentance is more than a matter of moral purification, important as that is. Repentance opens the door to a Gospel-centered life, to friendship with Jesus, and to mission. Thus it is that, throughout Lent, the Church ponders the first recorded words of the Lord—"Repent, and believe in the Gospel" [Mark 1.15]—and considers the relationship of that challenge to its evangelical mission.

That mission belongs to all of the people of the Church, who are commissioned as missionaries by the fact of their baptismal incorporation into Christ. For what the Lord said to the apostles in the Great Commission—"Go, therefore, and make disciples of all nations, baptizing them in the name of the Father and of the Son and of the Holy Spirit, teaching them all that I have commanded you" [Matthew 28.19]—he says to each and every Christian. Every Christian enters mission territory every day, even in countries where the Christian imprint in lives and cultures remains visible.

The Church's mission is the same as that of the Master whose Body she is: the Church exists to proclaim the good news that "the time is fulfilled and the Kingdom of God is at hand" [Mark 1.15]. That Kingdom is "not of this world," as Jesus will tell Pontius Pilate during the drama of his Passion [John 18.36]. The Kingdom, as biblical scholar Gianfranco Ravasi once explained, is the great "design that God wants to actualize with Christ in the world and in history": it is fellowship with God the Holy Trinity here and now, in anticipation of the Wedding Feast of the Lamb that extends through eternity. And in order to become effective witnesses to God's reign, God's kingdom, among his people *now*, the people of the Church, who carry that salvific project across the centuries, must continually be converted. A people in mission is constantly called to a change of heart, a deepening of friendship with the Lord who goes before us, no longer to be touched by death.

The Bible includes three paradigmatic forty-day periods of fasting and prayer: that of Moses, who prepared for forty days to receive the Ten

Commandments, the moral code that God gives his chosen people to help them avoid falling back into the habits of slaves [Deuteronomy 9.9]; that of Elijah, who fasted "forty days and forty nights [at] Horeb the mount of God," prior to hearing the "still, small voice" of the Lord passing by [1 Kings 19.8]; and that of Jesus, prior to his temptation. Thus the "forty days" of Lent—Ash Wednesday through Holy Saturday, exclusive of Sundays (which were always exempted from the Lenten fast as the disciplines of the season became defined)—evoke two great figures from the Hebrew Bible, Moses the lawgiver and Elijah the model of prophecy, as well as the Lord's own fast in the desert, which is variously described in the gospels of Matthew, Mark, and Luke as the critical prelude to his public ministry.

In all three biblical instances, these forty days are a stepping-aside from the ordinary rhythms of life in order to be more open to the promptings of the spirit of God, and thus more deeply converted to walking along God's path through history. That "stepping aside" is a primary characteristic of Lent and, according to the ancient tradition of the Church, is embodied in almsgiving and intensified prayer as well as fasting. The three practices go together. "Giving up _____" for Lent would have little more meaning than a weight-loss program were it not accompanied by a deeper encounter with Father, Son, and Holy Spirit through prayer, spiritual reading, and reflection and a new concern for those in need. Thus the special practices of the Forty Days, like the liturgies of each day of Lent, constantly bring the Christian back to the primordial call of Christ: "Repent, and believe in the Gospel" [Mark 1.15].

These great themes—the *annual catechumenate* by which all the people of the Church are renewed in the baptismal promises they repeat at the Easter Vigil; the *adventure of God* in salvation history and in the coming of the Kingdom in the person of Jesus; and *the invitation to deeper friendship with Christ* through a more intimate embrace of his Passion and Death—shape the liturgical rhythm of Lent.

Ash Wednesday, the days immediately following, and the first two weeks of Lent are *penitential* in character. The prayers and readings of daily Mass and the

Liturgy of the Hours call us to an extended examination of conscience: How am I living as a witness to the Kingdom? Have I been the missionary of the Gospel I am called to be? What is there in me that needs purification, if I am to deepen my friendship with Jesus?

The focus shifts with the Third Sunday in Lent, which begins a three-week period that has a *baptismal* character. In this second Lenten period, Christians are called to a deeper imitation of Christ: How am I responding to Christ's thirst for my friendship in prayer, in light of Jesus's invitation to the Samaritan woman, whom he asked for a drink of water? How are my eyes being opened to the demands of my mission, by the Christ who gave sight to the man born blind? Do I, like Martha, truly believe that Jesus is the Son of the living God, with power to raise me, like Lazarus, from the bonds of sin and death? These three gospel accounts—the woman at the well, the man born blind, and the raising of Lazarus—were central to the ancient catechumenate and summed up, for those about to be baptized, the call to live the life of the Kingdom made present among us in the Lord Jesus. Today, as they are read on the Third, Fourth, and Fifth Sundays in Lent, they invite every Christian to reenter the catechumenate imaginatively, in a new season of pondering the mysteries of God's mercy and love, in order to imitate more closely Christ the Head of the Body, the Church.

Then comes Holy Week. It begins with the original celebration of Christ the King: Palm Sunday, the liturgical commemoration of the Lord's triumphant entry into Jerusalem. Monday, Tuesday, and Wednesday of Holy Week are days of preparation for the Paschal Triduum, which starts with the Evening Mass of the Lord's Supper on Holy Thursday, continues through the Celebration of the Lord's Passion on Good Friday (the only day of the year on which the Catholic Church does not celebrate Holy Mass), and concludes with the summit of the Lenten journey, the Easter Vigil.

Easter Sunday follows seamlessly from the Easter Vigil, and is celebrated by the Church for eight days, concluding on the Octave, or Second Sunday, of Easter, which Blessed John Paul II designated as Divine Mercy Sunday. Thus each day of Easter Week *is* Easter, as the Preface used in daily Mass reminds us. Here, we ponder for eight days the fulfillment of the itinerary of conversion, whose destination is the Risen Christ: Alpha and Omega, the beginning and the end, to whom all time and all ages belong, for whom all things were made, and in whom all things find their true meaning.

The great mysteries of redemption celebrated in the Church's liturgy always unfold gradually. Throughout Advent, the season of preparation for Christmas, the Church's worship slowly and steadily unfolds the mystery of God-made-man, until we see him in the flesh, born of Mary "in Bethlehem of Judea" [Matthew 2.5]. The same process of unfolding takes place during Lent, intensifying its character as a pilgrimage. The "exterior" of that process takes us, with Jesus, up to Jerusalem, where the decisive events of human history will dramatically unfold. The process has an "interior" as well: as the people of the Church walk with Jesus from his temptation in the desert to his temptation in the Garden of Gethsemane, and then to the final temptation to despair on the Cross, we see unfolding before us (and within us) a cosmic struggle between good and evil—between God's purposes and all the forces that resist the power of divine love.

Lent thus engages the deepest truths of Christian faith: truths that cannot be approached as if they were the logical results of mathematical equations, or as if they were laboratory specimens to be dissected. The deepest truths of Christian faith are always more than human logic and human cleverness can grasp. That is why the Lenten pilgrimage through the station churches of Rome, encrusted as they are with layers of legend about the saints and martyrs of old, is an opportunity to live what philosopher Paul Ricoeur called a "second naivete": not the naivete of the child, but the wonder of the adult who, on the far side of skepticism or cynicism, is grasped by the truths of legends, stories, even myths that go beyond the historically knowable facts and precisely for that reason are the bearers of deep truths—truths about light and darkness, truths about what is life-giving and what is death-dealing, truths about God and us.

This is not a journey about abstract truths, however. To walk this pilgrim way of Lent with Jesus is to confront the often mysterious darknesses of our own lives and thereby strengthen our capacity, with God's grace, to resist everything in us that impedes us from making our lives into the gift for others that life itself is to each of us. The journey is an arduous one. Its difficulties are eased when we keep our eyes fixed on the Lord, who goes before us, and when we ponder the stories of the saints who have walked this path throughout history. At the end of the pilgrim's way is Easter: the power of God vindicates the sacrificial obedience of Jesus by raising him from the dead and seating him at the Father's right hand in glory. At the conclusion of the itinerary, love proves stronger than death.

That is the good news of Lent, which is, in the final analysis, a joyful season. For, as the Church prays at Holy Mass during the Forty Days, "by your gracious gift each year, your faithful await the sacred paschal feasts with the joy of minds made pure." The Lenten itinerary of conversion—the intensification of prayer and charity—leads finally to "the fullness of grace" that the God of mercies bestows on his sons and daughters at Easter, in the New Life that is our life in the Risen Lord, life at the eternal Wedding Feast of the Lamb.

St. Clement: Apse mosaic (twelfth century)

St. Sabina: St. Catherine Chapel dome (Giovanni Odazzi, 1700)

The
FIRST DAYS
of LENT

St. Sabina: Nave and apse

ASH WEDNESDAY

Station at St. Sabina

Holy Mass

Joel 2.12–18

Psalm 51

2 Corinthians 5.20–6.2

Matthew 6.1–6, 16–18

Office of Readings

Isaiah 58.1–12

St. Clement: Letter to the Corinthians

THE ITINERARY OF CONVERSION can bring about unexpected changes in our lives.

Take, for example, Carolyn Gordon Tate, a major figure in the literary renaissance of the twentieth-century American South, who once described to an even greater writer, Flannery O'Connor, the impact her conversion to Catholicism had had on her writing. As Miss O'Connor recalled in a letter, "Mrs. Tate told me that after she became a Catholic she felt she could use her eyes and accept what she saw for the first time, she didn't have to make a new universe for each book but could take the one she found."

Catholicism, Tate recognized, is realism. Catholicism means seeing things as they are. Catholicism means finding within the grittiness of reality the path God is taking through history for the salvation of the world. What we might call "Great Tradition Christianity"—the Christianity that, in several forms, takes the truth of the Gospel with complete seriousness—is no airy idealism, detached from reality. The truths of Christianity are truths embedded in reality.

For *Things As They Are*, his fine novel about a boy growing up in early twentieth-century America, Paul Horgan took as his title a question that the young boy's parents put to him as he navigated the alarms, discoveries, and vicissitudes of childhood: "Richard, Richard, when will you learn to see things as they are?" Learning to see the world straight is no easy business. Like the Old Testament figure of Tobit, we, too, must be cured of our blindness; we, too, must learn to see things as they are. The truths of Christian faith are the prisms through which our myopia (which turns us in on ourselves) and our astigmatism (which warps our view of what we see around us) are corrected, as the mercy of God grants us sight—and genuine insight.

Lent, a relentlessly gritty season, is a good time to be reminded of all this. That is one reason why the beginning of Lent is literally gritty: the Lenten pilgrimage begins with the reception of ashes (preferably in abundance) and the reminder that we are dust and to dust we shall return. The grittiness of Lent continues for six weeks, until pilgrims enter the supreme realism of the Paschal Triduum. Four days from now, the pilgrim way will take us into the grittiness of the Judean wilderness, a harsh landscape on which the first Lenten drama, the clash between light and darkness, will be played out in the temptation of Jesus. At the end of the Forty Days, that drama will reach its climax in the Crucifixion (the first artistic representation of which is found at today's station). In between we will encounter Jesus's parched thirst, the sorrow of Lazarus's death, and many other facts of life that are often hard to see squarely. Lent is grittiness, all the way: an uphill climb embodied in today's pilgrimage walk up the Aventine Hill to the Basilica of St. Sabina.

Yet while we are reminded on this first day of Lent that we are all dust and that the grave is everyone's mortal lot, the Forty Days also point to an even greater truth: dust is not our ultimate destiny. For those who repent and believe in the Gospel, the last act of the drama is not the dustbin. The last act of the drama is quite different. It is the Wedding Feast of the Lamb in the New Jerusalem, where all things are made new and those who have washed their robes in the blood of the Lamb are, in the astonishing usage of the Fathers of the Church, "divinized."

One of the greatest artistic evocations of the grittiness of Lent is Peter Bruegel the Elder's 1564 painting *The Procession to Calvary*, which is housed in Vienna's Kunsthistorisches Museum [Museum of Art History]. *The Procession to Calvary* is a large work, five and a half by four feet, featuring hundreds of small figures, with the equally small figure of Christ carrying the cross in the center of the painting. Bruegel included certain familiar motifs in rendering the scene: the holy women and the apostle John are in the right foreground, comforting Mary; the vast majority of those involved, concerned about quotidian things, are clueless about the drama unfolding before their eyes. What is so striking about *The Procession to Calvary*, however, is that we are in sixteenth-century Europe, not first-century Judea: Christ is carrying the cross through a typical Flemish landscape, complete with horses, carts, oxen, and a windmill. Christ is carrying the cross through history—right through the grittiness of everyday life.

A man who could see things as they are, like Peter Bruegel the Elder, would want us to understand that the "procession to Calvary" is taking place in our midst, too. He would be right to do so. Lent is a privileged time for recovering the sight that lets us see and enter the passion play going on around us.

In the second reading of the Office of Readings for Ash Wednesday in the Liturgy of the Hours, Pope St. Clement I, whom we will meet in the basilica named in his honor later in the station church pilgrimage, links the repentance to which we are called to the mission that every Christian has to offer the Gospel to the world—to share with others the friendship with Jesus that we are privileged to share. As Clement wrote to the Corinthians (who were still fractious decades after St. Paul's efforts), God, throughout history, is constantly offering the men and women of this world a great opportunity: "the opportunity of repentance." This opportunity was also a recurring theme in the prophets of the Old Testament: *now* is the time, *now* is the moment when the grace of forgiveness is made available, if only we acknowledge the gritty reality of our failures, our sins, our self-love.

Yet, as the second reading of today's Mass (also addressed to those cantankerous Corinthians, this time by Paul himself) reminds us, repentance is not for the penitent only. True repentance leads to mission: to be "reconciled to God" means to be "ambassadors for Christ," for without mission, we may "receive the grace of God in vain."

The pilgrimage of Lent, just begun with the ashes, should lead us into mission territory. And mission territory, as Bruegel's painting testifies, is all around us.

St. Sabina: Marble intarsia
(fourth century)

THE BASILICA OF ST. SABINA crystallized Roman Christianity's vision of the perfect church. Built on the Aventine Hill between 422 and 441, the new structure transcended the cumbersome basilicas of the previous century in a perfect synergy of light, space, and decoration.

Peter of Illyria, a contemporary of St. Jerome, who was also Illyrian, built St. Sabina in one of Rome's most luxurious neighborhoods. Soaring above the city's most important port, the Aventine (once the cause of an ultimately fratricidal dispute between Romulus and Remus as to where the city should be founded) sheltered the Roman working class until the imperial period, when it was gentrified by senators and knights. By the third century, the hill was dominated by palaces. St. Jerome's Aventine circle, including Sts. Marcella and Paula, met here before Jerome, Catholicism's first great biblical scholar, moved to the austere deserts of Judea. Yet the Aventine's wealth became its curse when the Visigoths sacked the city in 410. The villas were looted, and Marcella died at the hands of the invaders. Peter of Illyria decided to build his church in this devastated area, raising hope from despair.

The exterior of Peter's church was striking for its sheer size, but compared to the marble façades, bronze pediments, and granite porches of the extant pagan temples, St. Sabina's simple brick more resembled a *horrea*, or warehouse. The interior, however, tells an entirely different story.

High windows flood the basilica with light, which shines off the bold dedicatory inscription. Two female figures flank the metered Latin verse, representing the convergence of Gentiles and Jews toward the Truth, which is Christ. While holding books that call to mind the Hebrew Bible and the New Testament, both figures fold their fingers in the ancient Christian gesture indicating belief in the two natures of Christ and the three Persons of the Trinity.

The twenty-four matching columns in white marble are perfectly proportioned and support springing arches that confer a sense of weightlessness on the walls. Meticulously laid marble veneers decorate the spandrels between the arches, leading the eye to the apse, which once glittered with mosaics. The choir and pulpits are from the ninth century, while a floor mosaic of the tomb of Muñoz de Zamora attests to the eight hundred years the Dominicans have cared for St. Sabina; both Dominic and Thomas Aquinas lived, prayed, and studied here in the thirteenth century.

A last treasure may be found on the church's porch, where the original cypress doors have survived the wear and tear of sixteen centuries with most of their carved panels—depicting Old and New Testament stories—intact. In the upper-left-hand corner, a small panel contains the oldest known representation of the crucified Christ between two thieves. Jesus, the largest of the figures, appears against the Cross with his arms raised, proclaiming both his death and Resurrection in a single image. Ash Wednesday's station church thus points pilgrims toward the summit of the Lenten journey, the Paschal Triduum. [E.L.]

St. George in Velabro: *Baldacchino* and apse fresco (Pietro Cavallini, 1298)

THURSDAY AFTER ASH WEDNESDAY

Station at St. George

Holy Mass

Deuteronomy 30.15–20

Psalm 1

Luke 9.22–25

Office of Readings

Exodus 1.1–22

St. Leo the Great: Sermon 6 on Lent

ODAY'S OFFICE OF READINGS in the Liturgy of the Hours opens a four-week-long meditation during which the Church reflects upon Israel's enslavement in Egypt, the miracle of the Exodus, and Israel's forty years of wandering in the desert. In this reading cycle, the story ends, not with the death of Moses and Israel's entrance into the Land of Promise, but with the revolt at Meribah and the raising up of the bronze serpent—a fitting transition to the next cycle of readings in the Liturgy of the Hours, in which, through two weeks of texts from the Letter to the Hebrews, the Church ponders Christ the High Priest, lifted up on the Cross for the salvation of the world.

While there are many tales in the Old Testament of God's gracious interventions in the history of his chosen people, the Hebrew Bible rightly considers the Exodus as *the* paradigm of redemption. From slavery and bondage, a people consecrated to the Lord is formed by the miraculous experience of liberation from their oppressors; a motley crew of slaves becomes, through God's saving work in history, the People of God on pilgrimage to the promised land of milk and honey. In Christian tradition, this liberating Exodus experience becomes universal and available to all through the "passing over" of Jesus, the new Passover Lamb, from death to life.

Thus the Church prescribes that the Exodus story be read every year at the Easter Vigil. The liberating work of God, manifested dramatically in Israel's miraculous crossing of the Red Sea, is brought to its fulfillment in the new Passover that is the Paschal Triduum: Jesus's Passion, Death, and Resurrection. The history-defining truth of the paradigm of God as liberator is confirmed by the Resurrection, in which humanity is liberated from its fear of death as the unavoidably absurd end to the human story—our individual stories, and the story of humanity. History, like Israel in the desert, has a destination: eternal life with God, in the Wedding Feast of the Lamb.

Through these four weeks of readings from the Book of Exodus, the Church will relive, along with the people of Israel, the problem of their liberation: What does it mean to be a free people whom a liberating God has chosen as his own? What, in fact, is the meaning of "liberation"? Is it a matter of "free to be/ you and me," as the children's song has it? Or is there a nobler, richer, deeper meaning to the freedom for which Israel, and all who profess faith in the God of Israel, have been set free?

The liberation of Israel in the Exodus is the beginning of the history of the people of Israel as a political community—a commonality organized for purposeful action in history. Yet, as the Israelites will discover in their desert wanderings, there is far more to their liberation than the defeat of their oppressors and their own national independence. The freedom for which Israel has been set free is not just political; it has spiritual and moral dimensions. Israel is to become a community of true worship and a righteous nation.

And that is a major challenge.

For more than four hundred years, Israel was enslaved in Egypt. Over four centuries, people in slavery develop a lot of bad habits: the habits of being slaves. Those habits will bedevil Israel in her wilderness wanderings. And because the Exodus paradigm is, in truth, a paradigm of the entire human condition, those same habits bedevil us.

The first bad habit of these former slaves is the habit of worshipping false gods, and particularly the false god of the self. To become a community of true worshippers means losing the habit of self-worship to which Israel, dancing around the golden calf, succumbs in a slavish festival of self-congratulation. To become a community of true worshippers is to recognize that the God who liberates us does so of his own gracious will and out of the superabundance of his love. He is not a god we can manipulate, as we can manipulate, indeed manufacture, a golden calf. Neither is he a god we can fashion in our own image (that golden calf again, which for more than three millennia has represented the perennial bad habit of fashioning a manipulable deity according to our liking). To become a community of true worshippers means to listen for that "still small voice" [1 Kings 19.12] by which the God of the Exodus made himself known to Elijah, and to worship him, and him alone, "in spirit and in truth" [John 4.23].

The bad habits of slaves include bad moral habits as well. That is why, during their desert wanderings, the God of the Exodus gives Israel the Ten Commandments: a moral code intended to help Israel resist falling back into the bad habits it internalized over four centuries of bondage. Yet here, too, the God of the Exodus works with the materials at hand. As he first formed his chosen people out of a rag-tag gang of slaves, he now gives those liberated bondsmen a moral code that was written on the human heart before it was written on tablets of stone, as Pope John Paul II said at Mt. Sinai in 2000. The God of the Exodus gives Israel, and through Israel, the world, a moral code that expresses the longing for goodness—the desire to live with an undivided heart—that has been built into men and women "from the beginning."

In the twenty-first century, this summons to live in the fullness of integrity is given a special character by the ancient charge of Moses to the Israelites in the first reading of today's Mass: "I have set before you life and death, the blessing and the curse. Choose life, then, that you and your descendants may live, by loving the LORD, your God, heeding his voice, and holding fast to him" [Deuteronomy 30.19–20]. A liberated people, free to choose the spiritual and moral nobility made possible by the grace of a liberating God, will resist the encroachments of what Blessed John Paul II called the "culture of death" and will build a culture of life, defending the dignity of the human person at all stages of life and in all of life's circumstances and conditions.

Blessed John Henry Newman, the great nineteenth-century English convert and theologian, was named a cardinal by Pope Leo XIII in 1879 and given as his Roman parish, or "title," the Basilica of St. George in Velabro, today's station church. On his tombstone, Newman had inscribed the Latin motto *ex umbris et imaginibus in veritatem* [From shadows and phantasms into truth]. That poetic image summed up Newman's idea of the itinerary of conversion, the Christian life of faith: from shadowy false gods to the true God; from the fantasy of self-worship to the truth of worshipping the Father through the Son in the power of the Holy Spirit; from the illusion of the autonomous, self-defining self to the truth of the self-giving self. The passage *ex umbris et imaginibus in veritatem* is an Exodus pilgrimage. Its guide and its goal is the liberating God who frees men and women for a genuine freedom. St. George, the knight-martyr who embodies the cardinal virtue of courage in Christian iconography, is an apt companion on the way.

St. George in Velabro:
Portico and campanile

AT FIRST GLANCE, ST. GEORGE in Velabro might seem to be the twin of St. Sabina: springing arches lighten the walls; fretwork windows filter light; two slender side aisles flank a wide nave covered by a wooden ceiling with painted stars. Yet St. George is decidedly the more rugged of the two, irregular in both shape and décor.

Even its placement is humbler, for St. George sits in the swampy valley of the Forum. "Velabro" is derived from the Latin *velum* [marsh], and Roman tradition has it that here, at the base of the Palatine, when the Tiber was in flood, the infants Romulus and Remus were deposited in their basket, a first moment in the founding of the city.

The church rests above the Cloaca Maxima, ancient Rome's great sewer, and faces the Arch of Janus, built around 325 as a threshold to the meat market next door. To the left is another arch, erected in 204 in honor of Emperor Septimius Severus by the Roman money-changers. St. George is thus settled amid docks and markets, inviting blue collar locals and visiting foreigners to discover Christianity in the midst of the trappings of business. Founded in the fifth century as a deaconry where anyone could find welfare assistance from the Christian community, the church seems at home among the workers of Rome: even its columns and pavement are *spoglia*, stones recouped from other, older buildings.

In 683, Pope Leo II dedicated the church to St. George and St. Sebastian. Sebastian, a Roman soldier, was martyred in this area, and his corpse was thrown into the Cloaca Maxima. George, however, hailed from the eastern part of the empire. Like Sebastian, he was a soldier who refused to sacrifice to the emperor; both men were tortured before being killed by their comrades-in-arms. Roman recognition of St. George coincided with the dedication of new Roman churches to Eastern saints such as Cosmas and Damian; this was the age when Byzantium nominally ruled Rome, and the Velabro became the neighborhood of Greek-speaking monks and merchants.

In the ninth century, Pope Zachary donated the relic of St. George's head to the church, but the height of its glory came during the Crusades, when the Cappadocian soldier-martyr became one of Christendom's most celebrated heroes. In those days, a handsome porch with four Ionic columns was donated by Stefano Stella, who records in the inscription that he offered it "for the salvation of his soul"; the sturdy bell tower also dates from this time. The church was once lined with frescos; only the apse decoration, by Pietro Cavallini, Rome's answer to the Florentine genius Giotto, remains. His *Christ Flanked by Mary and Sts. Peter, George, and Sebastian* has been heavily restored but adds a splash of color to the simple space.

The high altar contains a splendid shrine of inlaid stone in the Cosmatesque style; the shrine guards the reliquary with St. George's head. Fragments along the walls suggest that, like St. Sabina, the church once contained a marble choir.

A 1993 bomb attack by the Italian Mafia devastated the thirteenth-century porch, which was promptly restored. [E.L.]

Sts. John and Paul: Apse fresco, *Christ in Glory* (Cristoforo Roncalli, 1588)

FRIDAY AFTER ASH WEDNESDAY

Station at Sts. John and Paul

Holy Mass
Isaiah 58.1–9a
Psalm 51
Matthew 9.14–15

Office of Readings
Exodus 2.1–22; 18.4
St. John Chrysostom: Homily 6 on Prayer

O N THESE FIRST SEVERAL days of the Lenten pilgrimage, the liturgy invites reflection on the three classic penitential disciplines of the season—fasting, almsgiving, and intensified prayer—and their interrelation. The liturgical texts for today, and the traditions surrounding the two Roman martyrs of today's stational church, offer material for pondering these linkages on this first Friday of the Lenten season.

V ery little is known to history of two fourth-century Roman knights, John and Paul, although they were so highly esteemed in Rome from the fifth century on that their names appear in the first Eucharistic Prayer, the Roman Canon. The preconciliar breviary describes them as "men of mercy, two olive trees, two shining lampstands before the Lord," who gave away their personal fortunes to the city's poor "in order to begin unencumbered their journey to eternity." That journey began with their martyrdom under Julian the Apostate (361–363), the emperor who sought to restore the old pagan deities, whose cult had been in decline since Constantine's embrace of Christianity a half-century or so previously. The house of John and Paul is beneath the current basilica; the site later became the official home of the Roman deacons, who were charged with the care of the city's poor, homeless, and neglected.

Sts. John and Paul, and their station, thus embody the word of the Lord as it comes through the prophet Isaiah in the first reading of today's Mass—a sharp critique of fasting detached from prayer and concern for the oppressed:

> Behold, in the day of your fast you seek your own pleasure, and oppress all your workers. Behold, you fast only to quarrel and to fight and to hit with wicked fist. . . . Is such the fast that I choose, a day for a man to humble himself? Is it to bow down his head like a rush, and to spread sackcloth and ashes under him? Will you call this a fast, a day acceptable to the LORD?
>
> Is not this the fast I choose: to loose the bonds of wickedness, to undo the thongs of the yoke, to let the oppressed go free, and to break every yoke? Is it not to share your bread with the hungry, and bring the homeless poor into your house; when you see the naked, to cover him, and not to hide yourself from your own flesh?
>
> Then shall your light break forth like the dawn, and your healing shall spring up speedily; your righteousness shall go before you, the glory of the LORD shall be your rear guard. Then shall you call, and the LORD will answer; you shall cry and he will say, "Here I am."

This passage from Isaiah highlights the role of the Hebrew prophets as heralds of justice. "Prophecy," in the Old Testament, was not primarily a matter of forecasting, a kind of preview of coming attractions (or, more typically, distractions). Rather, the prophet, rightly understood, was a man with a keen insight into the here-and-now and a particular sensitivity to injustice. For the classic Hebrew prophets, injustice was a form of apostasy; to act unjustly was to break the covenant sealed with the LORD at Sinai. For the people of the Exodus to live unjustly was to fall back into the habits of slaves. Injustice was "Egypt"; the Land of Promise should be a land of justice.

Some contemporary Christians have juxtaposed justice and charity, to the diminishment of the latter; theirs is a sound instinct taken to an extreme that warps both justice and charity. The sound instinct is to understand, with Isaiah, that there are structures of injustice in the world, not just unjust people. Racism, codified in law such that some people are second-class citizens, is an obvious example. Cultures of religious prejudice and political systems that do not acknowledge religious freedom, the first of human rights, are warped by injustice in a systematic, not merely individual, way. Christians are baptized into the prophetic mission of Christ as well as into his priestly and kingly missions. Thus work against injustice—the injustice in our hearts, as well as unjust social systems—is an evangelical imperative.

At the same time, the example of John and Paul, and Isaiah's call to a "just" fast of righteous living, remind us that justice divorced from charity is cold and impersonal. Misunderstood, the quest for justice that does not reach out in charity to correct injustices can end up being a new form of arrogant oppression. "Whom you would change, you must first love," taught Martin Luther King Jr., wisely.

Similarly, work for a more just society does not absolve us from the simpler, more personal forms of charity: from the kind word to the depressed colleague; the solace of a friend with a sick relative; the attention paid to a spouse or child we have neglected because of our busyness. Monetary charity is another essential part of the discipline of Lent, too. A daily gift of money to the poor and oppressed, however small, can be a useful Lenten discipline, whether it's done through the organized Lenten campaigns of various church-affiliated charities or through more imaginative efforts; in Lent 2011, for example, the seminarians of the Pontifical North American College took up a collection at the daily English-language stational Mass in Rome for the use of the hard-pressed Catholic Church in Iraq.

The traditional disciplines of Lent are intended to make us "a perfect dwelling place for the LORD," St. John Chrysostom teaches, so that the God whom we follow on the Lenten pathways of conversion may be, for each Christian, "enthroned in the temple of your spirit." The great Eastern Doctor of the Church also reminds us today of the essential linkage between almsgiving and other charitable works and prayer: "Our spirit should be quick to reach out toward God. . . . [When] carrying out its duties, caring for the needy, performing works of charity, giving generously in the service of others, our spirit should long for God and call him to mind, so that these works may be seasoned with the salt of God's love, and so make a palatable offering to the LORD of the universe."

Lent is an opportunity to practice prayer, fasting, and works of charity in an intensified way. These traditional Lenten disciplines are not for Lent only, however. In different degrees at different times, each practice ought to shape the character of Christian life throughout the year. And the three, as today's station reminds us, are interwoven within the fabric of the life of grace. How well or poorly we have been living them over the past year is a key part of the seasonal examination of conscience to which the first period of the Forty Days summons us.

Sts. John and Paul: Cosmatesque pavement

THE BASILICA OF STS. JOHN and Paul illustrates the transformation of the urban fabric of Rome during the early Christian era. For this site was not only the home of two holy brothers, but also the place of their martyrdom and burial: a striking density of testimony in a single spot. Poised on the Caelian Hill between the Circus Maximus and the Colosseum, the church and its patrons are emblems of Christian vigilance.

John and Paul, born into Rome's wealthy knight class after Christianity's legalization in 313, served Emperor Constantine's daughter Constantia and, according to their legend, were responsible for converting her husband. In 361, Constantia's cousin, Julian, determined to restore the old pagan ways, came to power. The brothers refused to serve the apostate emperor and were put to death. Contriving to keep the murder of two popular, high-ranking Romans out of the public eye, Julian ordered that they be beheaded and buried in their home on June 26, 362. Despite the imperial attempt at secrecy, however, the tomb of John and Paul was soon transformed into a martyr-shrine that received the relics of other saints.

Below the Cosmatesque floor lie the remains of several buildings, which date from the republican through the imperial eras: a private home, an apartment building, a multistory villa, and a bath complex. The apartment building, with its ground-level shops, was adapted into a Christian space, perhaps a house church, early in the fourth century, and contains a fresco of an *orante*, a person at prayer. After the martyrdom of John and Paul, the building was again modified with a *confessio*, constructed in the staircase under which the martyrs' bodies were kept; the *confessio*'s window allowed pilgrims to look into the tomb below and is framed by late fourth century paintings depicting the two saints and the martyrdoms of Sts. Crispus, Benedetta, and Crispianus, who were also buried in the shrine. In the first years of the fifth century, St. Pammachius, a Roman senator and friend of St. Jerome, transformed the cluster of buildings into a basilica, of which only the granite columns of the nave remain; by 595, the church was known as Sts. John and Paul.

After the Normans sacked Rome in 1084, the bell tower, porch, and Cosmatesque doorway were added; the bell tower's base is made of travertine blocks from the Temple of Claudius. The colorful disks speckling the brick tower are copies of Moorish ceramic tiles brought from Spain in the twelfth century. The present interior dates from the neoclassical renovation done in 1715–1718. The apse paintings of the *Martyrdom of St. John*, the *Martyrdom of St. Paul*, and the *Conversion of Terenziano* were executed by a team of Italian painters in 1726 and serve to frame the porphyry urn under the altar that contains the remains of the two patronal martyrs.

The first two chapels flanking the entrance contain important relics: the fourth-century martyr Saturnius rests on the right; eleven martyrs from Carthage, killed in 180 after refusing to hand over one of St. Paul's letters, are entombed on the left. [E.L.]

St. Augustine: Stational Mass

SATURDAY AFTER ASH WEDNESDAY

Station at St. Augustine

Holy Mass
Isaiah 58.9b–14
Psalm 86
Luke 5.27–32

Office of Readings
Exodus 3.1–20
St. Irenaeus: Against Heresies

TODAY'S GOSPEL READING, the station at St. Augustine, and the artist who created one of the basilica's magnificent paintings all prompt an early Lenten reflection on the meaning of conversion, which the Glossary of the *Catechism of the Catholic Church* defines in these terms: "A radical reorientation of [one's] whole life away from sin and evil, and toward God. This change of heart of conversion is a central element of Christ's preaching, of the Church's ministry of evangelization, and of the Sacrament of Penance and Reconciliation." Conversion defines the human drama of Lent, and its various dramatic elements suffuse the fourth of the Forty Days.

As the Catholic Church understands it, *metanoia*, or conversion, touches every aspect of our lives: conversion is a lifelong journey in which we are converted to the new life of grace in our minds, our wills, and our hearts.

The conversion of our minds means putting aside the blinders of empiricism and recognizing that the world grasped by our senses is not all the world there is: there is a supernatural world that makes itself present through the world as we perceive it. That supernatural world—the world of divine love—is the really real world. Thus what we call the "real world" is not so much a boundary as a membrane.

Moral conversion, or the conversion of the will, takes place along the frequently stony path by which we learn to choose what is truly good, and to do so freely and as a matter of habit. This is the life of growth in virtue (the medieval synonym for "habit") and into true freedom. For freedom is not a matter of doing what we like (which is a slavish habit), but of freely choosing what truly makes for an authentically human life.

The conversion of our hearts is that lifelong process by which we disentangle ourselves, emotionally and psychologically, from unruly passions and disordered affections so that our hearts and wills are drawn, like iron shavings toward a magnet, to what is truly good, true, and beautiful: God, the Holy Trinity.

A Christian's "first conversion" takes sacramental form at Baptism, in which the Holy Spirit bestows the gifts of faith, hope, and love. The "second conversion," which all maturing Christians undergo, unfolds along the fullness of life's pilgrimage and is completed at death: the moment at which each of us can offer the entirety of a life to the merciful Father, whose Son will purify into gold the dross that remains in us.

The call and conversion of Matthew the tax collector (the "Levi" of today's gospel) is a striking biblical paradigm of conversion. The Lord sees the despised agent of Roman authority (who made his living by gouging a premium on top of the taxes he collected for the hated occupying power) but calls Matthew to discipleship; Matthew "left everything, and rose and followed him." Here, conversion is instantaneous and seemingly unreflective: a dramatic change of heart, effected in an instant, which changes the entire trajectory of a life. The power (and surprise) of the moment is beautifully caught by Caravaggio, whose *Madonna of the Pilgrims* is found in today's stational church. In Caravaggio's *Calling of St. Matthew* (which can be seen in the nearby church of St. Louis, known locally as S. Luigi dei Francesi), the startled tax collector, seated at a money table, is bathed in light, while Christ, "the true light that enlightens every man" [John 1.9], remains somewhat in the shadows of the room. Yet the hand of the Lord, pointing to and seemingly directing light onto Matthew, is illuminated—and is modeled on the hand of God the Father at the moment he created Adam, as rendered by Michelangelo on the Sistine Chapel ceiling. Creation, wounded by human wickedness, is healed and, in a sense, completed by redemption: by the sinner's conversion of mind, heart, and will.

St. Augustine, patron of today's stational church, is the classic model of a different, more protracted form of conversion, recorded in the first great autobiography, his *Confessions*. There, Augustine painstakingly recalled the slow process by which he grew from skepticism to faith while passing through various intermediate stages along the way. And as the greatest of the Western patristic Doctors of the Church reflected back on the long process by which he came to know the liberating mercy of God in Christ, Augustine neatly captured in one limpid Latin sentence the bond between conversion and happiness: *Tu nos fecisti ad te et cor nostrum inquietum est donec requiescat in te* [Thou has made us for Thyself and our hearts are restless until they rest in Thee].

Augustine's itinerary of conversion was accompanied, often at a distance, by his mother, St. Monica, whose relics are venerated in today's station. Throughout the decades of Augustine's wanderings, which included an extended love affair and the birth of a son, Adeodatus, Monica never ceased praying that her supremely gifted son would, in his brilliance, come to know the God of the Bible, who is the Truth that makes all other truths make sense. Sometime after Augustine's conversion, Monica took ill at the Roman port city of Ostia as she and her son were preparing to return to their North African home. As Augustine recorded in the *Confessions*, his mother was unconcerned about where she would be buried: "Only remember me at the altar of God, wherever you are." A life of prayer for conversion ended with a reaffirmation of the deep and unbreakable linkage between conversion and prayer—including prayer for the dead.

Conversion-as-liberation-into-truth is also a theme in today's Office of Readings, where Irenaeus of Lyons, contesting with the protean heresy of Gnosticism, noted that "Our Lord, the Word of God . . . freed those made subject to him. He himself testified to this: 'I do not call you servants any longer, for a servant does not know what his master is doing. Instead I call you friends, since I have made known to you everything that I have learned from my Father'" [John 15.15]. Gnosticism has taken many forms over two millennia, and the form it takes today is not quite the same as the form it took in second-century Gaul, where Irenaeus was bishop of Lugdunum (today's Lyons). Gnosticism today typically involves the claim that the human condition is utterly plastic and malleable. According to today's Gnostics, there is no *givenness* to our lives, and those aspects of our humanity that early generations considered fixed and defining, such as our maleness and femaleness, reveal nothing important about us; they are merely social or cultural constructs that can be altered at will. This is, of course, yet another form of slavery, another form of bondage to the self-creating, self-authenticating self—the god of Me. Against that refusal to take "things as they are" seriously stands Caravaggio's *Madonna of the Pilgrims* in today's station church, with its unmistakably womanly Virgin Mary, presenting her Child to two pilgrims with very grubby bare feet: a powerful reminder of the grittiness of Lent, itself another antidote to the temptations of modern Gnosticism.

St. Augustine: Cavaletti Chapel, *Madonna of the Pilgrims* (Caravaggio, 1604)

T HE BASILICA OF ST. AUGUSTINE was built in 1483 to replace an ancient, nearby shrine dedicated to St. Tryphon, formerly the station for this day.

The travertine stone of the façade was recouped from the Colosseum, which partially crumbled after the earthquake of 1349, by Pope Sixtus IV (1471–1484), who was determined to restore Rome to its former grandeur, starting with its churches. In Sixtus's mind, "If any city should be clean and beautiful, it should indeed be the one which . . . holds primacy among all others because of the throne of St. Peter."

Because St. Augustine's was intended for pilgrims, Sixtus situated the church on the principal route from the heart of town to St. Peter's Basilica. The relics of St. Monica, mother of St. Augustine, once housed in St. Tryphon, were translated here and placed in the chapel to the left of the high altar (today, her original sarcophagus from her burial at Ostia Antica is affixed to the wall).

Fifty years after St. Monica was laid to rest in the basilica, another devotion began here. Jacopo Sansovino's *Madonna del Parto*, carved in 1521, was placed at the back of the church in a shrine shaped like a Roman triumphal arch—and in a world where 10 percent of women died in childbirth and 50 percent of children died before age two, devotion to the *Madonna of Safe Delivery* grew quickly. Sansovino carved Mary's visage with calm fortitude, ready to face the pains of childbirth or the challenges of childrearing. Every October 9, the expectant mothers of Rome come here to pray; silver votive hearts attest to thousands of graces received.

In true Renaissance fashion, this devotion-rich church is a visual feast, its elegant vaulted nave and two side aisles complemented by a scallop-shaped trimming of side chapels along either side. Pietro Gagliardi painted the prophets on the pillars along the nave, but one in particular, at the second pillar on the left, stands out: Isaiah, painted by Raphael in 1512, turns in space as he waves his scroll to command attention. Giovanni of Goritz commissioned this fresco as part of a tomb arrangement, composed of an altar surmounted by a marble group of St. Anne, Mary, and the Christ Child by Andrea Sansovino, Jacopo Sansovino's teacher: from the Old Testament to the Incarnation to the hope of resurrection, the monument expressed fundamental Christian beliefs in the most aesthetic terms.

(continues)

(continued)

The high altar boasts a pair of angels by Gian Lorenzo Bernini, while other famous artists frescoed the side chapels; reformed courtesans and curial humanists attended Mass here. But the church itself silently chastens Renaissance glamour. The Blessed Sacrament Chapel contains relics from the catacombs of Callistus, the remains of martyrs who did not die in stylish surroundings. Caravaggio's 1604 *Madonna of the Pilgrims* is even more challenging. Two pilgrims kneel at the threshold of Mary's home; their dirty feet, bared in penance, bear silent witness to the hardship of their travels. In the doorway, the Virgin Mary seems to alight weightlessly, holding the infant Christ in her arms. Jesus leans toward the pilgrims, leaving visitors to peer into the shadows for a glimpse of his face. Caravaggio's painting relegates its wealthy, educated parishioners to the side-lines; humility and childlike faith are required to gaze upon Christ's face. [E.L.]

St. John Lateran: St. Peter (Paul Monnot, 1708)

The
FIRST WEEK
of LENT

St. John Lateran: Presentation of a model of the basilica (1287)

THE FIRST SUNDAY
IN LENT

Station at St. John Lateran

Holy Mass

[A]	[B]	[C]
Genesis 2.7–9; 3.1–7	*Genesis 9.8–15*	*Deuteronomy 26.4–10*
Psalm 51	*Psalm 25*	*Psalm 91*
Romans 5.12, 17–19	*1 Peter 3.18–22*	*Romans 10.8–13*
Matthew 4.1–11	*Mark 1.12–15*	*Luke 4.1–13*

Office of Readings

Exodus 5.1–6.1

St. Augustine: Exposition on the Book of Psalms, 60.2–3

SUNDAYS IN LENT REMAIN *SUNDAYS*: the day on which the Church marks history's axial point, the Resurrection of the Lord. Even in Lent, Sundays are the Easter of every week, and on each of those days the Church celebrates Christ's victory over sin and death. Thus fasting on Sundays is generally unknown in Christian penitential practice; some scholars suggest that Sunday fasts were actually forbidden on occasion by Church authorities concerned with a too-rigorous asceticism.

The station churches of the Sundays of Lent reflect the grandeur that is always Sunday and include both major and minor basilicas: the Papal Arch-basilica of St. John Lateran, the pope's cathedral church as Bishop of Rome, is the station of the First Sunday in Lent and Palm Sunday, while the intervening Sunday stations include St. Mary in Domnica, St. Lawrence Outside the Walls, Holy Cross in Jerusalem, and St. Peter's in the Vatican.

The Lectionary also affords a deservedly special place to Sundays in Lent by highlighting gospel narratives that closely link the themes of conversion, Baptism, and the life-giving character of the divine mercy to our pilgrimage toward Calvary—and, ultimately, to the empty tomb and the appearances of the Risen Lord.

O n the First Sunday in Lent, in each of the three years of the Lectionary cycle, the Church proposes for reflection one of the Synoptic evangelists' telling of the story of the tempting of Jesus—the overture, as it were, to his public ministry, and thus the beginning of what will unfold as the itinerary of the Cross. These temptation narratives are perhaps the most dramatic evocation of the grittiness of Lent, for the temptations themselves have a sharp-edged quality to them, and they begin in a gritty place, the Judean wilderness. Yet each evangelist's rendering of the story has a distinctive quality.

Mark, as is his wont, keeps the narrative spare; all we are told is that Satan tempted Jesus in the desert amid "wild beasts" and ministering angels.

Matthew, the evangelical portraitist, fills out the story by rendering the temptations in the sequence that has become most familiar. First, there is the temptation to indulge the flesh by turning stones into bread. The temptation to test divine providence and divine favor follows, as Jesus is asked to throw himself from the pinnacle of the Temple. The series concludes with the temptation to worldly power, which can be attained by worshipping a false deity.

Luke's account of the temptations, however, drives the story even deeper into the gritty soil of history by inverting the sequence of the second and third temptations. Thus the last and gravest temptation takes place in Jerusalem, the holy city to which Luke's entire gospel is oriented. Here, in Jerusalem, Jesus faces the temptation to refuse the destiny the Father has appointed for him—to be the world's savior by stripping himself of himself on the cross. Here, truly, we are at history's crossroads. What will Jesus do? Gianfranco Ravasi put the stakes neatly in a commentary on Luke's temptation narrative: Jesus, in "the supreme test of his identity as Messiah," respects "the sovereign freedom of the plan of salvation to which he has been devoted, pronounces his definitive 'Yes' to the Father, and abandons himself completely to his destiny." And this abandonment is not an abstract matter, a decision that could be taken anyplace, anytime. Jesus gives himself entirely to the Father's will *here*, in *this* place and at *this* time: here, in Jerusalem; here, amid the history with which Luke began his Christmas narrative, with its references to the days when Augustus was emperor and "Quirinius was governor of Syria" [Luke 2.2].

The tempting of Jesus has its primordial analogue at the very beginning of the Hebrew Bible, in the tempting of Adam and Eve: the Old Testament reading for the First Sunday in Lent in Lectionary Cycle A. Although perhaps not immediately apparent, the parallels between this familiar story of the Fall and the stories of Jesus being tempted in the wilderness are striking for their joint evocation of a constant threat to progress along the itinerary of conversion.

What is the "fall" of Adam and Eve? Their fall consists in an act of egotism and self-assertion: Adam and Eve will decide for themselves what is good and what is bad for them, rather than accepting the gift of God's specification of good and evil. Egotistical, self-centered self-assertion is the primordial sin. And in its consequences—the quest for control, which ineluctably flows into the quest for power, understood as my capacity to impose my will on my own life, on others, and on the world—self-asserting pride prepares the ground for the rest of the catalogue of death-dealing sins.

The previous chapter of Genesis offers a contrasting portrait of the human condition. In Chapter 2 of the first book of the Bible, Adam lives in harmony with God, with Eve (and thus with the one who is like him), and with the natural world. This harmony reenters the world in the New Adam, Jesus the Messiah, who lives to do the Father's will, as St. Paul writes to the Romans in the second reading of the First Sunday in Lent in Cycle A. But now there is a difference. Jesus the Christ does not simply restore a disturbing imbalance in things. The merciful will of God is to do much more than rebalance the scales, for despite the fact that "sin increased" after Adam and Eve, "grace abounded all the more," such that one man's "act of righteousness leads to acquittal and life for all men." Through the New Adam, men and women are enabled to become the true sons and daughters of God, and to enter into the mystery of the divine life itself.

All of this is made possible for us by Jesus's decision, at that hinge-point of history described in Luke's gospel, to abandon himself and conform his will to divine providence. Abandonment of self opens up an infinity of possibilities. This is not the paradox it may at first seem; it is a central truth of the life of faith. And that truth is a profound countercultural challenge to twenty-first-century Western culture, replete as it is with the siren songs of self-absorption and willfulness.

The Jesus whom we follow into the wilderness teaches us, there, the necessity of self-giving and of abandonment to divine providence. By conforming those who are his brothers and sisters to the pattern of his own life, the Risen Lord renders that self-gift liberating in the fullest sense of liberation: He, the first of many brethren, opens the path to eternal life with the Holy Trinity and thereby creates the Communion of Saints. Creation, fallen into disorder, is reordered—and not only reordered but magnified by the redemption, the fulfillment of God's purposes, that lies on the far side of the wilderness of temptation.

St. John Lateran: Façade
(Alessandro Galilei, 1735)

THE MODERN FAÇADE of St. John Lateran—a mighty travertine porch, built by Alessandro Galilei in 1735—may seem to evoke the spirit of John Soane's Bank of England building or Karl Schinkel's "New Theater" in Berlin more than the humble origins of Christianity. Yet that grand exterior opens into the ancient site where the Christian community laid its first permanent roots in Rome on November 9, 324—a date commemorated in the Church's liturgical calendar. As the first church and home of the Bishop of Rome, St. John Lateran is the cathedral church of the Eternal City. Thus the façade inscription proclaims its ancient title, "Mother and Head of All the Churches in the City and the World." For all its history, though, there is little of antiquity here. Instead, the façade represents the Church's mission to be always and everywhere confident and strong in its proclamation, even in trying times.

Pope Clement XII commissioned the new façade, and that of St. Mary Major, at the dawn of the Enlightenment. Throughout Europe, intellectuals denigrated the Catholic Church as ignorant and superstitious; yet these same cultured despisers of religion flocked to Rome as tourists. Uninterested in the tombs of Peter and Paul, they only wanted to see the vestiges of the ancient Roman civilization they deemed superior to the Christian civilization that supplanted it. In response, the pope restored the Lateran basilica, a church built by a Roman emperor who recognized the supremacy of the God of the Christians over the pagan deities of the Pantheon: the grandeur of Galilei's façade, crowned with statues of Christ and his apostles, might make skeptical Enlightenment tourists reconsider their assumption that they were visiting the headquarters of a ramshackle sect whose glory days were in the distant past.

The battered bronze panels of the processional doors leading from the porch into the basilica, encased in frames of acorns and stars in honor of Pope Alexander VII (who commissioned the portal in 1658–1659), are from the ancient Roman Senate building. That august body, which once ratified decrees of Christian persecution, was no more; but the Christians they endeavored to eradicate still worshipped here. Thus the arcaded entrance to the basilica, similar to a triumphal arch, proclaims victory: the victory of the thousands of martyrs whose witness helped persuade an empire to convert. The source of their strength and courage is embodied in the smallest set of doors in the porch, the Holy Door, evocative of those jubilee years that commemorate humanity's redemption by the Cross of Christ.

Through the threshold the nave is bathed in light by high clerestory windows, a Christian innovation in the architecture of worship space. Francesco Borromini, who redesigned the basilica for the Jubilee of 1650, rounded the entrance wall and constructed giant pilasters embellished by undulating niches and colorful aedicules to contain statues of the twelve apostles. The luminosity of the interior of Rome's cathedral church, St. John Lateran, originally known as the Basilica of Our Savior, suggests Christ as light: the Christian idea of enlightenment. [E.L.]

St. Peter in Chains: Reliquary of Peter's Chains

MONDAY OF THE FIRST WEEK OF LENT

Station at St. Peter in Chains

Holy Mass

Leviticus 19.1–2, 11–18

Psalm 19

Matthew 25.31–36

Office of Readings

Exodus 6.2–13

St. Gregory Nazianzen: Sermon on Love of the Poor

THE VENERATION OF RELICS is an aspect of Catholic piety that sometimes confounds other Christians and other believers, and rather completely mystifies nonbelievers. Yet like other forms of popular piety, the respect and honor paid to the relics of the saints, when accompanied by intensified prayer, "prepare us to receive grace and dispose us to cooperate with it," as the *Catechism of the Catholic Church* teaches. Relics are not magical talismans. Relics are among those quotidian things through which we perceive the extraordinary that lies just beyond the ordinary.

The principal relic at today's station invites us to relive imaginatively, with the apostle Peter, his imprisonment in Jerusalem (from which he was miraculously freed by an angel) and at the Mamertine Prison in Rome (from which he was led to crucifixion in Nero's Circus, just outside the Vatican Basilica today).

Peter's chains also invite a reflection on a deeper form of binding: obedience to the will of God for our lives. The "chains" of a freely accepted vocation are an integral part of the Christian life. The distinctive character of this spiritual form of Peter's chains teaches us something important about Peter's unique role in the apostolic band and about the continuation of that mission by Peter's successors, the Bishops of Rome.

At the very end of John's gospel, the Risen Lord meets his disciples in Galilee on the shore of the Sea of Tiberias. After the Risen One feeds his friends breakfast from the miraculous catch of fish, he asks Peter three times, "Do you love me more than the rest of these? . . . Do you love me? . . . Do you love me?" Peter, chagrined, thrice answers, "Yes, Lord, you know that I love you," after which he is commanded to feed the Master's sheep, the people of the Church. Commentators and preachers, reflecting on the parallel between Peter's three denials during the trial of Jesus and three affirmations in this lakeside drama, often suggest that the Risen Christ is rather twitting Peter, who, having made three denials, is now being compelled to make three professions of faith.

Cardinal Karol Wojtyła, whom the world would come to know as Pope John Paul II, had a different, and arguably deeper, insight into this Johannine passage. In a sermon preached just before his election as pope, he noted that the Risen Lord was pressing a stunning, even frightening, question on this most human of his apostles. Peter was being asked whether he was open to being completely emptied of himself, "more than the rest of these," in order to be the shepherd of the Lord's flock; he was being called to a more radical self-giving, a more passionate love.

And when Peter answers, "Lord, you know everything; you know that I love you," he is told that "when you are old, you will stretch out your hands, and another will gird you and carry you where you do not wish to go." The evangelist notes that the Lord said this "to show by what death [Peter] was to glorify God" [cf. John 21.15–19]. Yet the same question, the memory of which is carried through the centuries by the chains of Peter in this station church, is asked of every pope, every successor of Peter: Will you be bound in this distinctive way?

The lesson of the chains is not for popes only, though. By freely accepting the chains of obedient, radical love, a Galilean fisherman from the far outskirts of the Roman empire—a man of no account as the world counts greatness—was led to the center of world imperium: and from there to death, to immortal fame, and, most importantly, to eternal life. That kind of binding and being-bound is available to all the baptized. Reflection on how well or poorly we have taken up the chains of a more demanding love is an integral part of the examination of conscience to which the Church calls her sons and daughters during this first period of the Forty Days.

Another way to ponder that question is to ask, "Am I becoming a saint?" Sanctity is not just something the Church officially recognizes in certain extremely holy souls, the canonized saints. Sanctity is every Christian's vocation, a calling conferred in Baptism. We are baptized into Christ, who lives and reigns forever within the light, life, and love of the Holy Trinity. The pilgrimage of the Christian life is a preparation for being able to live forever with God, and to do so . . . comfortably.

That may seem an odd way to put it. But as C. S. Lewis once wrote, most of us, snatched up to heaven *right now*, would likely feel a bit out of place. We'd be a bit uncomfortable. Saints, he suggested, are those who have learned in this life (and, the Catholic Church would add, who have been purified through or after death) to be comfortable at the Wedding Feast of the Lamb. Thus, being a saint is every baptized person's Christian destiny. Being a saint is not something optional; being a saint is an imperative. Yet it's not something we can achieve by an act of will. Sanctity is something into which we grow by the superabundant grace of God.

The difficulties we have in accepting that offer of grace are highlighted in the Exodus selection in today's Office of Readings, where the Israelites cannot hear the call to freedom, coming from God through Moses, "because of their broken spirit and their cruel bondage." The habits of slaves, acquired over the years (as in our lives) or over the centuries (as in the lives of the Israelites), can be difficult to lose. And until they are lost, they are an obstacle to hearing the liberating word of God. That word calls us to freedom—the freedom that is to be found in freely choosing the good and being bound to the truths of living nobly. This call to freedom is found in today's Mass readings, both in the Levitical "Law of Sanctity" and in Jesus's description of the works of mercy that help to sanctify us.

Given the quotidian difficulties that every Christian encounters in living the life of grace, it can sometimes be difficult to believe that our baptism (a central theme of the Lenten itinerary of conversion) makes us what the responsory to the first lesson in today's Office of Readings tells us we are: "a chosen race, a royal priesthood, a holy nation, God's own people" [1 Peter 2.9]. The chains of Peter and Michelangelo's magnificent *Moses*, two focal points of this station church, remind us that the grace of God transforms lives in unexpected and dramatic ways, turning ordinary men and women into extraordinary witnesses—into saints.

The true alternative to slavery, in its spiritual forms, is sanctity. Slave or saint? Another question, posed daily along the path of the Forty Days.

St. Peter in Chains: Tomb of Pope Julius II,
Moses (Michelangelo, 1516)

THE BASILICA OF ST. PETER in Chains perches on a spur of land at the base of the Esquiline Hill in what was, 1,600 years ago, the residential quarter of the rich and powerful of imperial Rome. This was also the site of the Prefectura Urbana, where many Christians were tried and condemned to death. The earliest notice of the church dates from 431, when it was dedicated to Sts. Peter and Paul. The pairing recalls the tradition that the two died on the same day, June 29, according them the same birthday in heaven. Dedicated to the twin pillars of the Church of Rome, the church looked toward the Palatine Hill, where Romulus and Remus had long ago first founded the city.

St. Peter was imprisoned twice: once in Jerusalem and then in the Mamertine Prison, a stone's throw from this site. While Rome preserved the chains of his last detention, the other fetters long remained in the Holy Land. Then St. Juvenal, Bishop of Jerusalem, gave them to the imperial family, and Empress Eudoxia presented the Jerusalem chains to Pope St. Leo I (440–461), who rebuilt the original church in honor of Peter's shackles.

A pious tradition holds that the two segments fused together when brought into contact with each other. Filings from the chains were Rome's most popular take-home relic, and, as Rome's Petrine pilgrimage itinerary evolved, St. Peter in Chains became the second most important pilgrimage site, after St. Peter's Basilica. The relics, along with a piece of the chains of St. Paul, are now kept in a reliquary in the *confessio* built by Pope Pius IX.

Medieval pilgrims visited a church laden with marble; Greek columns from the Portico of Octavia still line the nave. Many of those pilgrims prayed at an altar dedicated to St. Sebastian, built after a plague epidemic in 680. Its blue-ground mosaic can still be seen on the left side of the church: in this second oldest extant image of the martyr, Sebastian is not represented as a young athlete, but as *Magister Militorum*, "trainer of soldiers," with white hair and tunic.

During the Renaissance, two of the church's cardinals-titular became popes. Under Pope Sixtus IV (1471–1484), Cardinal Niccolò da Cusa restored the roof; a beam bearing his name and the date 1475 is visible along the wall. But we owe the basilica's most famous work of art to Sixtus's nephew, Pope Julius II (1503–1513), who hired Michelangelo in 1505 to build a colossal free-standing tomb for him in the new St. Peter's Basilica. Pride and politics ended that project, and in 1545 a simple wall tomb was finally completed here, featuring Michelangelo's monumental *Moses*. Carved in 1513, *Moses* embodies age with his long flowing beard and wisdom with his horns (from St. Jerome's translation of the Hebrew word for "rays"), which recall his time in God's presence. Although he sits as lawgiver on a throne, the poised foot, the sharp turns of the arms and head, and the piercing gaze into the distance proclaim an energetic readiness to rise and follow the Lord's will, anywhere. [E.L.]

St. Anastasia: Stational Mass

TUESDAY OF THE FIRST WEEK OF LENT

Station at St. Anastasia

Holy Mass

Isaiah 55.10–11

Psalm 34

Matthew 6.7–15

Office of Readings

Exodus 6.29–7.25

St. Cyprian: Treatise on the Lord's Prayer

TODAY'S GOSPEL READING, St. Matthew's account of the giving of the Lord's Prayer, prompts a reflection on our understanding of prayer as part of the annual Lenten examination of conscience that shapes these first of the Forty Days.

The gift of the Lord's Prayer is at the literary center of the Sermon on the Mount. Before teaching the crowds how they should pray, Jesus offers a prefatory admonition: "And in praying do not heap up empty phrases as the Gentiles do; for they think they will be heard because of their many words." Another translation renders "Gentiles" as "pagans," which perhaps brings the matter into sharper focus.

The deities of the ancient world had any number of unsavory characteristics. The gods and goddesses of Greece were manipulators, heavenly competitors toying with human lives on a terrestrial gaming board; in the face of the gods of Olympus, even the strongest and seemingly most-favored of humans, such as Achilles, are, finally, mere playthings. The gods of ancient Canaan, such as Moloch, were bloodthirsty tyrants who demanded—and got—the sacrifice of children.

Prayer under these circumstances was a matter of manipulating the gods, conning them, or appeasing their bloodlust. The God of Abraham, Isaac, and Jacob came into this world as a deity of a very different sort. This God did not manipulate. This God did not toy with men and women for his amusement. This God did not demand blood; rather, his prophets, who claimed to speak in the name of the Lord, railed against the ancient practice of child sacrifice and harshly condemned those who indulged in it.

This God came into the world as a liberator.

Jesus's injunction against praying like the pagans do is thus a reminder of the truth about the God of Abraham, Isaac, and Jacob, the Father to whom his disciples are to pray. Pagans try to control their gods. Jesus's disciples are to pray as if returning a gift to its giver, for our very desire to pray rightly ("Lord, teach us to pray" [Luke 11.1]) is a reflection of God's love for us, manifest in the divine spark within us. Christian prayer recognizes that fact, as it also recognizes God's sovereignty—which is why, as part of his admonition, Jesus reminds his disciples that "your Father knows what you need before you ask him." Christian prayer does not consist in giving God information and then asking God to take appropriate action in a situation previously unknown at the Throne of Grace. Christian prayer consists in acknowledging divine providence and then asking that our wills be conformed to the divine will.

Thus our Lenten examination of conscience might ask, "Do I pray like a pagan or a semi-pagan? Or do I pray like a Christian?" Is my prayer an unconscious attempt at manipulation or control? Or does my prayer reflect the four classic modes of Christian prayer: adoration, contrition, thanksgiving, supplication?

The disciples' request to be taught how to pray is answered by the gift of the Lord's Prayer, which the second-century theologian Tertullian described as "the summary of the whole Gospel." Two centuries later, Augustine agreed: "Run through all the words of the holy prayers [in Scripture] and I do not think that you will find anything in them that is not contained in the Lord's Prayer." Thomas Aquinas, for his part, underlined the difference between the prayer of petition that is rooted in an acknowledgment of God's sovereignty and praying "as the pagans do" when he wrote, in the *Summa Theologica*, "The Lord's Prayer is the most perfect of prayers. . . . In it we ask, not only for the things we can rightly desire, but also in the sequence that they should be desired. This prayer not only teaches us to ask for things, but also in what order we should desire them."

Thus, citing these and other classic witnesses, the *Catechism of the Catholic Church* describes the Lord's Prayer as "the quintessential prayer of the Church." Every day, the Church prays as the Lord taught her to pray at Holy Mass. The Church prays the Lord's Prayer at Lauds and Vespers, Morning and Evening Prayer, the two temporal hinges of the liturgical day. The gift of the Lord's Prayer is an essential part of the instruction of catechumens, as it is an essential part of the liturgies of Baptism and Confirmation. "*Our* Father . . ." is the prayer of the community of believers: even when we pray the Lord's Prayer privately as individuals, we do so as members of the Church.

We are not alone, in praying as Jesus taught us to pray.

Reflecting on the gift of the Lord's Prayer in today's Office of Readings, St. Cyprian, the third-century bishop of Carthage and one of the great Latin Fathers of the Church, links this special gift of prayer to the gift of life itself: "The Lord . . . has given us life, and with his accustomed generosity, he has also taught us how to pray." The instinct for prayer and worship seems to be built into the human condition. The question is whether that instinct attaches itself to false gods or to the one true God, to base ends or worthy ends.

And here is another point for reflection along the Lenten itinerary of conversion: Is my instinct for worship—are the things I cherish—in the right order? Do I cherish some things to the point where those things (or persons) become competitors to God? Has my commitment to living within the ambit of divine providence given me a Christian sense of detachment, so that, while enjoying all the benefits God has bestowed on me in family, friends, and the good things of this world, my appreciation of those gifts is not a matter of clinging desperately to them, but of receiving them daily as the gifts that they are? Am I prepared to leave everything and follow the Master, like Simon, James, and John by the lake of Gennesaret [see Luke 5.9–11]? By cultivating that habit, or virtue, of detachment, we prepare ourselves to make the final gift of our life, its return back to God, its source, at our death: "Father, into thy hands I commit my spirit" [Luke 23.46].

The station "at St. Anastasia" is one of the oldest in Rome and is unique in its location at the foot of the Palatine Hill, at the center of the ancient city. Devotion to the martyr Anastasia, whose liturgical feast day is December 25, may have antedated Christmas being fixed on that date. Still, the reverence in which Anastasia was held was such that, in the 1962 Missal, the Mass at Dawn on Christmas included a second Collect commemorating her, and her name remains in the Roman Canon.

There is a suggestive decorative feature on the floor in front of the recumbent marble statue of the martyr, beneath the basilica's main altar: a small mosaic duplicate of the great loaves-and-fishes mosaic in the Church of the Multiplication at Tabgha, on the northwest shore of the Sea of Galilee. This mosaic link between the Holy Land and Rome reminds us that the Eucharist, whose institution at the Last Supper was prefigured by Christ's feeding of the 5,000 at Tabgha, is not only *Viaticum*, food-for-the-journey when we die. The Eucharist is our daily food-along-the-way, the miraculous bread that sustains us on the itinerary of conversion. Through the Eucharist, we are given the courage to pray "Our Father, . . ." and to suffer, if necessary, for the truth of God in Christ.

St. Anastasia: Pavement detail

NESTLED AMONG THE REMAINS OF the Circus Maximus and the imperial palace on the Palatine Hill, the Basilica of St. Anastasia—a name derived from the Greek word for "resurrection"—challenges the glories of a long-gone empire with the enduring witness of the Christian martyrs.

With its broad brick façade and unadorned piazza, the church looks decidedly less glamorous than her pagan neighbors. Here, pilgrims used to gather with the pope on Ash Wednesday to begin the walk to St. Sabina on the Aventine Hill. The class struggles between the working-class Aventine and the aristocratic Palatine were aired in the Circus Maximus, wedged between the two. In the unity of the Christian faith, these two hills are now joined through prayer and penance.

St. Anastasia is believed to have been the daughter of a Roman noble, Praetextatus, and was born in modern-day Serbia during the era of Diocletian. Her *Passio* recounts that St. Chrysogonus was her catechist and that she was martyred on the Ligurian Island of Palmaria on December 25.

The church was already famous by the end of the fifth century. St. Jerome is reputed to have used St. Anastasia as his parish: the ancient altar on the left is believed to have been his, and the church also claims to have a chalice used by this Doctor of the Church. Pope St. Damasus (366–384) commissioned an apse fresco in honor of the saint, and a few years later a baptismal font was incorporated into the church, the first of its kind documented in Rome. The church was embellished by successive popes with mosaics and frescoes.

Only a few repairs were made to the building during the Middle Ages and the early Renaissance, however; thus, the resurrection of St. Anastasia began in the Baroque period, when Pope Urban VIII rebuilt the façade in 1664 and commissioned his team of artists to embellish the interior. The high altar was moved to its present position, and Ercole Ferrata, a close collaborator of Gian Lorenzo Bernini, sculpted the image of St. Anastasia at the moment she departed this life for heaven. The chapel of relics contains frescoes showing the lives of Sts. Charles Borromeo and Philip Neri; Domenichino was hired to paint the image of St. Jerome.

Portuguese cardinal Nuno da Cunha restored the church again in 1722, adding soft pastel colors to the nave and vault to lighten the effect of the heavy piers that had been added to support the structure. He commissioned Michelangelo Cerruti to paint *The Martyrdom of the Saints* on the ceiling.

The church has experienced another revival in the twenty-first century, serving as a sacristy during World Youth Day 2000, when 700,000 consecrated hosts were reserved here for Eucharistic celebrations in the Circus Maximus. In 2001, St. Anastasia became the first Roman church to hold perpetual Eucharistic adoration. The initiative spread from here to different parishes throughout the world. Lodged amid ancient architecture, modern mementos connect Eucharistic adoration at this site to the same devotion in Colombia, Peru, Sri Lanka, Tanzania, Uganda, and other far-flung places. [E.L.]

St. Mary Major: Triumphal arch and apse mosaic (Jacopo Torriti, 1295)

WEDNESDAY OF THE FIRST WEEK OF LENT

Station at St. Mary Major

Holy Mass

Jonah 3.1–10

Psalm 51

Luke 11.29–32

Office of Readings

Exodus 10.21–11.10

Aphraates: On Circumcision

THE BASILICA OF ST. Mary Major, built to honor the definition of Mary as *Theotokos* [God-Bearer, or Mother of God] at the fifth-century Council of Ephesus, is the first and greatest of the thousands upon thousands of Christian sites dedicated to the memory of Mary of Nazareth. At a moment in history when Marian piety is typically focused on such pilgrimage shrines as those at Lourdes, Fatima, or Guadalupe, and on the miraculous events not infrequently recorded at these and other locations of Marian apparitions, today's stational pause at the prototype of Marian shrines is a good moment to reflect on the unique role of Mary in the history of salvation.

In his 1987 Christmas address to the Roman Curia, Pope John Paul II borrowed a set of images from the Swiss theologian Hans Urs von Balthasar to remind his collaborators of the ways in which the Church, two millennia into its history, is still being shaped by the great figures of the New Testament. Through-out its temporal pilgrimage, the Pope said, the Church is formed and re-formed in the "profiles" of certain paradigmatic biblical personalities. Thus the Church of proclamation and evangelization is constantly formed and re-formed accord-ing to the "Pauline profile" created by the Apostle to the Gentiles and his mis-sionary journeys. Similarly, the Church of contemplation is shaped over the centuries by the "Johannine profile" of the Beloved Disciple, who rested his head on the Lord's breast at the Last Supper. The Church of authority and jurisdic-tion, so evident in Rome, is formed and re-formed according to the "Petrine profile," the image of the apostle to whom the Lord gave the keys of the king-dom. All of these "profiles" are constantly at work in the rich, complex tapestry of proclamation, worship, contemplation, witness, charity, and service that is the one, holy, catholic, and apostolic Church.

Yet there is another, more primordial "profile" to which John Paul II wished to draw special attention: the "Marian profile," in which the Church is formed and re-formed in the image of Mary, whose *fiat*—"Let it be to me according to your word" [Luke 1.38]—created the paradigm for the entirety of Christian dis-cipleship. Mary's *fiat* made her, we might say, the first of her son's disciples. And while it is one profile among many, this "Marian profile," John Paul insisted, enjoyed a certain priority within the plurality of New Testament images from which the Church is formed and re-formed. For everything else the Church does—be that Pauline proclamation, Johannine contemplation, or the Petrine exercise of authority—is intended to foster discipleship.

The Church, John Paul taught, is most fundamentally formed in the image of a woman and her "yes" to the divine purpose in her life.

If the station at St. Mary Major prompts a reflection on one of the first of Mary's words in the gospels, it also draws us imaginatively toward the last of her recorded words in Scripture: a word that reminds us that all true Marian piety is ordered to Christ and, through Christ, to the Holy Trinity.

The scene is the wedding feast at Cana in Galilee and the story is a familiar one: the wine has run out, the hosts are about to be embarrassed, and Mary steps into the breach to suggest that her son do something to salvage the occasion. Despite his seeming rebuff ("My hour has not yet come"), Mary confidently instructs the waiters, "Do whatever he tells you" [John 2.4–5]. The water in the ceremonial washing jugs is turned miraculously into wine, and not just any wine, but the best wine of the day.

Working with this text, preachers often concentrate on the "whatever," stressing that this was "the first of his signs," which "manifested his glory" such that "his disciples believed in him" [John 2.11]. The stress, in other words, is on the miracle. Yet there is another way to approach Mary's last words in the New Testament, and that is to concentrate on the pronoun: "Do whatever *he* tells you." Mary's final word to history is to point us toward her son. And because her son is both son of Mary and Son of God, Mary—by pointing us toward him throughout the ages—points us into the Godhead, the Trinity of Father, Son, and Holy Spirit.

All true Marian piety, in other words, is both Christological and Trinitarian. Mary's paradigmatic discipleship is one of bearing witness to the two central mysteries of Christian faith: the Incarnation and the Trinity.

The Mass texts of the day are also a reminder of the true relationship between faith and the miraculous—and thus a reminder of the truths about worship that were part of yesterday's Lenten examination of conscience. Jesus cites the story of Jonah's successful call to repentance in Nineveh in his admonition to the crowds who were seeking a "sign"—a bit of wonder-working—as a warrant, even a pretext, for their belief in him. Jesus will have none of it: as Jonah was to the Ninevites, Jesus himself will be the sign, and a sign greater than Jonah, for he is the final, unsurpassable "sign" of the divine mercy, which he makes present in himself, his preaching, and his works.

Jesus does not trade miracles for faith. In the New Testament, faith precedes every miraculous cure: attention to the words of the Lord precedes the miraculous feeding of the multitude; the centurion's act of faith comes before the cure of his servant; Martha's confession of faith precedes the raising of her brother, Lazarus, from the dead. Faith leads to the unexpected and the miraculous. And while Jesus's miracles and the cures performed by his disciples under his tutelage are signs of the Kingdom of God coming into history and into human hearts, the miraculous cannot and must not be reduced to the magical. Moreover, as the Lord's evocation of the story of Jonah reminds those with ears to hear, then and now, the faith that makes for the miraculous is always accompanied by conversion, by a profound change of heart, by repentance and a new way of life.

"Seek first his kingdom and his righteousness, and all these things shall be yours as well" [Matthew 6.33]. That basic conversion was at the heart of Mary's vocation as disciple, as it was at the heart of her mission of pointing us to her son, and thus to the Father and to their Holy Spirit. For those blessed by them, the medically inexplicable cures and other miracles that we associate with Mary's maternal intercession flow from that first conversion, from decisions to live the Kingdom life and its righteousness.

St. Mary Major: Melchizedek *emblema*
(fifth century)

ST. MARY MAJOR, atop the Esquiline Hill, is a kind of zenith: the summit of Rome's most exclusive imperial neighborhood; the climax of paleo-Christian art; the apex of Marian devotion. Throughout its 1,600-hundred year history, the basilica has borne constant witness to the Roman love affair with Mary. Its legendary founding is one of the city's most cherished tales, that of a miraculous snowfall on August 5, 352, that showed Pope Liberius where a Marian church should be built. Although this story remains unsubstantiated by written or archaeological proof, the basilica celebrates its dedicatory feast every August 5 with white rose petals dropping from the ceiling to simulate the miracle. Documentary evidence, however, tells us that, in 431, a year after the Council of Ephesus declared Mary *Theotokos*, Pope St. Sixtus III, one of the great papal builders, constructed a Marian basilica suited to its elegant surroundings. The temple of Juno (goddess of childbirth) and a market built by the empress Lidia were nearby; St. Mary Major would soon overshadow her pagan neighbors in majesty.

Sparkling through the travertine arcades on the upper story of Fernando Fuga's eighteenth-century entrance is Filippo Rusticci's thirteenth-century mosaic façade, beckoning the pilgrim into the surprising interior.

The spatial harmony of St. Mary Major is striking. Thirty-six white marble Ionic columns (the rarest order in Rome) articulate the nave. The proportions build through a rhythmic system of modules based on the columns' width to create an effect of serene grandeur. Every surface emanates light or color. The coffered ceiling, gilt with the first gold from the New World, crowns the Cosmatesque floors, and the nave mosaics are capped with Renaissance frescoes.

The mosaic panels lining the nave have captivated pilgrims for centuries. *Emblemae*, small transportable sections of floor mosaic in the *domus* of a Roman aristocrat, were the jewels of ancient art, found in Pompeii, the Imperial Villa in Tivoli, and in homes on the Esquiline. Where a Roman noble might have had one or two, St. Mary Major boasted forty-two when first built, depicting Abraham, Jacob, Moses, Joshua, and other Old Testament figures. Their stories are told with exquisite detail: armor and weapons clash on battlefields; Melchizedek offers a basket filled with loaves of bread and an amphora of wine.

The stories point toward the altar: each patriarch was given a covenantal promise by God, and the mosaics lead the visitor toward the fulfillment of those promises. Thus the sanctuary arch mosaics recount the coming of Christ, the New Covenant, and in deference to the church's Marian dedication, the stories culminate in the Lord's birth and infancy.

(continues)

(continued)

The cycle starts with the Annunciation: Mary, wearing royal robes, is surrounded by angel attendants as she receives Gabriel; the closed doors of her house allude to her virginity. To the left, an angel appears before Joseph, in the first representation of that saint in the history of art. There is no Nativity scene, only an expectant throne surmounted by symbols of the evangelists, flanked by Peter and Paul.

The story continues on the right with Christ's presentation in the temple. Mary, still wearing regal robes, carries her son like an heir apparent, standing under the arcades of a basilica—the royal audience hall of antiquity—as all incline toward her, the Mother of God.

The next register portrays Herod, interrogating the Wise Men and sending soldiers to massacre the innocents. The Magi wear the most startling garb, their brilliant hued, polka-dot costumes indicating that they are ambassadors from the exotic East.

While the mosaics of God-made-man emphasize glory and majesty, directly below them lies the *confessio*, with its relic of Christ's crib, brought to the church in the eighth century: an architectural and aesthetic rendering of the divine descent from the heavenly throne to a simple wooden manger. [E.L.]

St. Lawrence in Panisperna: Altar with relic of St. Lawrence's gridiron

THURSDAY OF THE FIRST WEEK OF LENT

Station at St. Lawrence in Panisperna

Holy Mass
Esther 12.14–16, 23–25
Psalm 138
Matthew 7.7–12

Office of Readings
Exodus 12.1–20
St. Asterius of Amasea: Homily 13

ACEDIA, A TERM PERHAPS not immediately familiar, is arguably *the* characteristic spiritual malady of the twenty-first-century Western world. Variously defined by different philosophers and theologians, *acedia* may be described as the kind of world-weariness that comes, not from spiritual detachment, but from boredom: a lack of interest in life born of cynicism rather than asceticism. In its more advanced forms, *acedia* can lead to depression and even suicide. Given the pervasiveness of cynicism in postmodern Western culture, the milder forms of *acedia* are a perennial temptation, surrender to which is a point on which consciences might well be examined in this first stage of the Forty Days.

In the gospel reading for today's Mass, the Lord asks Lenten pilgrims to rid themselves of *acedia* by remembering the divine generosity that surrounds us. A poignant scene from Evelyn Waugh's *Unconditional Surrender*, the third volume in his World War II trilogy, *Sword of Honor*, brings the challenge that Jesus poses into sharp relief. The protagonist of Waugh's trilogy, Guy Crouchback, a decent man and reasonably devout Catholic for whom nothing ever seems to work out, suffers from a mild, but nonetheless debilitating, case of *acedia*. That this ancient malady has warped his spiritual life finally becomes clear for Guy at the funeral of his father, Gervase, a wise man who, just before his death, had written to his son mildly rebuking him for lassitude:

"I'm worried about you," his father had written in [a] letter . . . that Guy regarded as being in a special sense the conclusion of their rather reserved correspondence of more than thirty years. His father had been worried, not by anything connected with his worldly progress, but by his evident apathy; he was worrying now perhaps in that mysterious transit camp through which he must pass on his way to rest and light.

Guy's prayers were directed to, rather than for, his father. For many years now the direction in the *Garden of the Soul*, "Put yourself in the presence of God," had for Guy come to mean a mere act of respect, like the signing of the Visitors' Book at an Embassy or Government House. He reported for duty saying to God: "I don't ask anything from you. I am here if you want me. I don't suppose I can be of any use, but if there is anything I can do, let me know," and left it at that.

"I don't ask anything from you"; that was the deadly core of his apathy; his father had tried to tell him, and was now telling him. That emptiness had been with him for years. . . . Enthusiasm and activity were not enough. God required more than that. He had commanded all men to *ask*.

Which is precisely what Jesus commands, gently, in today's gospel reading: "Ask, and it will be given you; seek, and you will find; knock, and it will be opened to you. For everyone who asks receives, and he who seeks finds, and to him who knocks it will be opened. . . . If you, then, who are evil, know how to give good gifts to your children, how much more will your Father who is in heaven give good things to those who ask him?"

The Christian vocation includes the duty to *ask*. When that instinct to approach the Father in confidence atrophies, so does a sense of vocational responsibility in the world. This linkage between asking and vocation, and the damage that had been done to his soul and his life's work by cynical world-weariness, were also brought home to Guy Crouchback while he knelt at his father's funeral Mass and gained new insight into the meaning of Christian vocation:

> In the recesses of Guy's conscience there lay the belief that somewhere, somehow, something would be required of him; that he must be attentive to the summons when it came. . . . He saw himself as one of the laborers in the parable who sat in the market-place waiting to be hired and were not called into the vineyard until late in the day. . . . One day he would be given the chance to do some small service which only he could perform, for which he had been created. Even he must have his function in the divine plan. He did not expect a heroic destiny. . . . All that mattered was to recognize the chance when it was offered. "Show me what to do and help me to do it," he prayed.

*A*cedia, and the cynicism from which it typically grows today, is a self-inflicted diet of the "bitter herbs" that the Israelites are commanded to eat during the Passover dinner in today's Office of Readings. Bitter herbs and unleavened bread—the "bread of affliction"—have their place in the spiritual life. The constant self-imposition of bitterness, however, can seep into the soul and do serious damage, both to the joy with which Christian life ought to be lived and to one's sense of vocation in following the Risen Lord: the source and cause of our joy and the enabler of true detachment, which is the opposite of *acedia*. Blithe indifference to Hamlet's "slings and arrows of outrageous fortune" can be a sign of Christian maturity, of a certain *joie de combat* in the spiritual life. Not giving a damn is never a Christian attitude. Neither is sprinkling bitter herbs on life out of their proper season.

The act of faith in a God who commands us to *ask* is an act of filial confidence that enables us to live comfortably with the pace of the divine plan as it unfolds in our lives. In the short reading in Midafternoon Prayer in today's Liturgy of the Hours, the author of the Letter to the Hebrews offers a useful Lenten admonition on this front: "Therefore do not throw away your confidence, which has a great reward. For you have need of endurance, so that you may do the will of God and receive what is promised" [Hebrews 10.35–36]. They serve who also stand and wait, as Guy Crouchback finally came to understand.

Another point for a Lenten examination of conscience today comes from the second reading in the Office of Readings, where the patristic writer Asterius teaches us not to indulge in that form of *acedia* that is despair about others. Reflecting on the parable of the good shepherd who brings back the lost sheep without admonition or coercion, the bishop-saint commends the patience of Christ: "We should not look on men as lost or beyond hope; we should not abandon them when they are in danger or be slow to come to their help. When they turn away from the right path and wander, we must lead them back, and rejoice at their return, welcoming them back into the company of those who live good and holy lives."

Today's station at St. Lawrence in Panisperna, traditional site of the martyrdom in 258 of one of Rome's great patrons, is the first of four Laurentian *stationes* in the station church pilgrimage. The courage of the third-century deacon in confronting the public authorities during the Valerian persecution—asked to produce the riches of the Church, Lawrence brought into court the poor he served—and the humor attributed to Lawrence during his gruesome death-by-roasting on a gridiron—"Turn me over; I seem to be done on this side"—are two dramatic manifestations of confidence in the Father, and two expressions of a life of high spiritual adventure devoid of *acedia*.

St. Lawrence in Panisperna: Christian sarcophagus
(third century)

ROMANS DISPLAY THEIR pride in the great martyr Lawrence through the vast Laurentian itinerary that extends across the city. Honored by thirty-two churches and countless altars, St. Lawrence is surpassed in devotion only by Christ, Mary, John the Baptist, and St. Peter. One Laurentian church stands on the site of his trial, another on his tomb; yet another, St. Lawrence in Fonte, rests upon his prison. Today's station, St. Lawrence in Panisperna, recalls the place where the deacon Lawrence was roasted alive on a grill; the church's intriguing name comes not from the eponymous street, but from the practice of distributing bread and ham, *pane et pernis*, here on August 10, the feast of St. Lawrence.

Jubilee years have been particularly important for this church. Pope Boniface VIII rebuilt it in 1300, when he declared the first Holy Year. The church was generously restored by Cardinal Guglielmo Sirleto, its titular pastor, for the Jubilee of 1575. Pope Leo XIII, who was ordained bishop in the basilica, gave it to the Poor Clares, who added the front stairs and the statues of St. Lawrence and St. Francis for the Jubilee of 1900.

Steep steps from today's modern street lead into a peaceful seventeenth-century courtyard; the carved wooden doors also date from this period and open into a squat nave lined with six side chapels. The chapels are arranged discreetly, compelling one to focus on the altar. There, in a golden frame supported by stucco cherubim, is a giant fresco of Lawrence's martyrdom in 258. The seventh of Pope Sixtus's deacons, stretched out on his grill directly above the altar, looks toward heaven, from which an angel descends with the crown of victory. The clever use of perspective makes the physical world of his tormentors recede into space; Valerian, the emperor who ordered his torture and death, is a mere detail in the distance.

Under the portico is the oven held to be where St Lawrence was killed; above, decorating the vault, is the image of St Lawrence in glory. Here, the end is the beginning.

The second chapel on the right commemorates Sts. Crispin and Crispinian, two Roman brothers who were missionaries in France. Settling in Soissons, they plied their trade as cobblers before being denounced to the governor, Rictus Verus. Fifty years after Lawrence's martyrdom, they were tortured, like the Roman deacon, with beatings and fire before being beheaded; their relics were then brought back to Rome, where they rest under this altar.

The second chapel on the left celebrates a woman born a millennium later: St. Bridget of Sweden, who came to Rome during the Jubilee of 1350, frequented this church, and prayed before the same crucifix that rests on the high altar today. After her death, her body lay for five months in the ancient marble sarcophagus of the chapel before it was transferred to Sweden. [E.L.]

Twelve Holy Apostles: *Confessio*

FRIDAY OF THE FIRST WEEK OF LENT

Station at the Twelve Holy Apostles

Holy Mass
Ezekiel 18.21–28
Psalm 130
Matthew 5.20–26

Office of Readings
Exodus 12.21–36
St. Aelred: Mirror of Love

THE LITURGY OF THE WORD in today's Mass begins with a passage from Ezekiel that is particularly apt on this Friday of the first full week of the Forty Days. Ezekiel was one of the great prophetic voices of Israel's Babylonian Exile, which began in the early sixth century B.C. And while contemporary Christian circumstances are not often as dramatic as those faced by the deported Israelites, all Christians of all times and places are, in a sense, exiles, or (as the second-century *Letter to Diognetus* puts it) "resident aliens": for our true home is with the Lord in the Kingdom come in its fullness. Ezekiel's reassurance to the exiles of Israel thus resonates in the Christian spirit throughout the ages.

And in today's text, that reassurance has to do with the great biblical truth that conversion is always possible. As the Lord says to Ezekiel: "If a wicked man turns away from all his sins which he has committed and keeps all my statutes and does what is lawful and right, he shall surely live. . . . Have I any pleasure in the death of the wicked, says the Lord God, and not rather that he should turn from his way and live?"

Now, as then, the superabundance of the divine mercy can be a hard saying for those who, while living upright lives, have seen wickedness rewarded. Like the Israelites, twenty-first-century Christians can say, "The way of the Lord is not just."

However understandable psychologically, that complaint bespeaks a kind of spiritual pettiness. The answer to it remains the same today as more than two and a half millennia ago and poses a caution against the kind of pride that cannot imagine falling into sin: "Hear now, O house of Israel: Is my way not just? Is it not your ways that are not just? When a righteous man turns away from his righteousness and commits iniquity, he shall die for it; for the iniquity which he has committed, he shall die. Again, when a wicked man turns away from the wickedness he has committed and does what is lawful and right, he shall save his life." The passage continues, and this section of Ezekiel concludes, with a distinctively Lenten theme: "Cast away from you all transgressions . . . and get yourselves a new heart and a new spirit. . . . For I have no pleasure in the death of any one, says the Lord God; so turn and live." All of those who follow the God of the Bible are always in need of conversion, of turning toward the Lord more fully.

The ever-present possibility of making that "turn" and being converted anew is also an apt theme for this station at the Twelve Holy Apostles. For, as the gospels record with remarkable frankness, the apostles were a dodgy lot, who constantly needed converting. They were obtuse at times; they were truculent on occasion; most of them took off in panic at the arrest of Jesus, and only one could bring himself to stand at the foot of the Cross. Yet these men changed the course of history by their preaching and their witness and became, according to the Book of Revelation, the foundation stones of the New Jerusalem. These changed lives are a powerful testimony to the historicity of the Resurrection, for what else but a wholly unprecedented experience—encounters with the Risen One—could have turned sinful, cowardly, and ill-educated men from the fringes of civilization into heroic missionaries and heralds of a new civilization? Their radical conversion also testifies to the transformative power of the blood of the Lamb of the New Covenant, prefigured in the Passover lamb of sacrifice that the Israelites are instructed to eat in the first reading of today's Mass.

The radical conversion of life to which every Christian is called is a life-long process, and for virtually everyone there are numerous potholes along the road. Falling into those potholes breeds the sense of guilt of which the psalmist speaks in the responsorial of today's Mass: "If thou, O LORD, shouldst mark iniquities, LORD, who could stand?" Moreover, the commands that Jesus lays down in today's gospel reading seem to multiply exponentially the inevitability of falling into various "iniquities." The disciples of Jesus are not simply to avoid murder, but to avoid anger. Perhaps even more demandingly, the friends of Jesus are to clear the decks of hostility before even approaching the altar for worship: "So if you are offering your gift at the altar, and there remember that your brother has something against you, leave your gift there before the altar and go; first be reconciled with your brother, and then come and offer your gift." The Church's tradition of beginning every Mass with a confession of sins and a plea for the divine mercy comes into clear focus here: we seek the Lord's forgiveness before we offer the sacrifice of the New Covenant and receive the Lord in Holy Communion, not to make ourselves feel better, but because we have been commanded to do so.

The demands of Kingdom living—in which the righteousness of Jesus's disciples must be greater than that of those who scrupulously followed the Law in their time (as the Lord begins today's gospel instruction)—are addressed to the heart as well as to the mind and the will. They are, as the twelfth-century Lincolnshire abbot, Aelred, writes in today's Office of Readings, an invitation to Christians to enlarge the horizon of their love, and of their loves. In an encounter with the divine love that invites us to fellowship with the Holy Trinity, we are empowered to love others, even to the point of embracing enemies. Reflecting on the mystery of our own forgiveness, despite our sins having been laid bare in the sight of God, we can, through the "fire of divine love," extend to those who would harm us "the embrace of true love."

In doing so, here and now, Christians continue to be fitted by grace to become the saints we must be and to enter the company of those who, like the Twelve Holy Apostles of today's station, can live happily at the Throne of Grace. This station *at* the Twelve Holy Apostles is a powerful reminder that the Church does not "make saints"; through the process of beatification and canonization, the Church recognizes the saints God has made. There is no more telling example of God's saint-making than the stories of the apostles. And however wrapped in legend some of them may be, the *statio* today, with its relics of St. Philip and St. James the Less, bears witness to the incontestable fact that lives were radically transformed by an encounter with Jesus of Nazareth—and that those lives then changed the world.

God is no less generous in saint-making today than in the past. The *statio* at the Twelve Holy Apostles invites us to try and recognize the saints who are all around us, in whatever the contemporary equivalents might be of the very improbable cast of characters—illiterate fishermen, a Roman collaborator, a political agitator, a teenage boy—whom the fire of divine love, present in the Risen Lord, forged into the saints on whom the Church was built, and on whom the Church still rests.

**Twelve Holy Apostles (cloister):
Monument to Michelangelo
Buonarotti (1823)**

THE BASILICA OF THE TWELVE Holy Apostles is difficult to distinguish from the aristocratic *palazzi* that surround it, fitting so easily into its surroundings that one might expect its portico to shelter, today, an upscale café.

The first church on this site, about ten feet below present street level, was built by Pope Pelagius around 560 to celebrate the defeat of the Goths at the Battle of Mons Lactarius: it was in the basilica form, with nine columns per side and an apse. Its most interesting feature was a raised altar, lifted almost nine feet from the floor, with a special cavity for relics. Still extant under the present altar, it houses the relics of the apostles Philip and James the Less, whose remains were later joined by others from the catacombs on Via Latina.

Pope Hadrian I praised the church for its size and its fine mosaics in a 795 letter to Charlemagne, but the building was destroyed in 1349 by an earthquake. It remained in ruins until Pope Martin V was elected in 1415, ending the Great Schism and effectively returning the papacy to Rome. One of the Colonna pope's first projects was to restore the church, as his family estate stood next door.

The basilica was given to the Franciscans in 1463, and when the general of the order, Francesco della Rovere, was elected Pope Sixtus IV in 1471, he began a major restoration. Twelve new chapels lined the nave, most of them endowed by members of the della Rovere family. Sixtus also commissioned his *pictor papalis*, Melozzo da Forlì, to fresco the apse with the *Ascension*. Sixtus's nephew, Giuliano della Rovere, the future Pope Julius II, lived next door, but the elegant entrance portico is his only extant contribution to the church.

Today's grand structure was the early eighteenth-century work of Pope Clement XI. The fifteenth-century portico, sunk slightly into the ground, opens onto a soaring nave frescoed with the *Triumph of the Order of St. Francis* by Baciccia, disciple of Gian Lorenzo Bernini. Antonio Canova's first Roman work, the tomb of Pope Clement XIV, graces one of the aisles.

Over the sanctuary, angels seem to tumble out of the heavens in an illusionist fresco by Giovanni Odazzi. The altarpiece, among the largest in Rome, shows the martyrdom of Sts. Philip and James and was painted in 1715 by Domenico Muratori. The Baroque profusion of figures contrasts with the silent simplicity of the crypt below: redecorated in the nineteenth century as the catacombs were being rediscovered, it evokes these early Christian burial spaces.

Many great men and women have been laid to rest in the Holy Apostles, if only briefly. James III, the Stuart "Old Pretender," died in Rome after decades of exile and was laid out in state here before being interred in St Peter's. When Michelangelo, who lived nearby, died on the night of February 18, 1564, his body was brought to the church to be clothed in a habit before burial because he was a Third Order Franciscan. His nephew, however, recovered the body from the portico flanking the church and brought Michelangelo home to his beloved city, Florence. [E.L.]

St. Peter: *St. Peter* (Arnolfo di Cambio, 1300)

SATURDAY OF THE FIRST WEEK OF LENT

Station at St. Peter

Holy Mass

Deuteronomy 26.16–19

Psalm 119

Matthew 5.43–48

Office of Readings

Exodus 12.37–49; 13.11–16

*Second Vatican Council: Pastoral Constitution on
the Church in the Modern World, 9–10*

T ODAY'S *STATIO*, THE SECOND of the Petrine stations during the Forty Days, takes place in one of Christendom's most famous pilgrimage sites: the Vatican Basilica, dedicated to the Prince of the Apostles, and, throughout the twentieth century, the stage on which the drama of the papacy was played out before the entire world. The basilica is a great world cultural treasure, a center of Catholic worship and a great many other things besides. It is the parish church of the entire Catholic world, where the Church's universality is most visible. It is the setting for some of humanity's greatest artistic, architectural, and engineering accomplishments. It is an enormous papal mausoleum, for beneath it or within it are buried 91 of the 266 Bishops of Rome, including every pope elected since Leo XIII. The decision to build "New St. Peter's" to replace the fourth-century Constantinian basilica on this site was one of the causes of the sixteenth-century Reformation; yet, in the providence of God, the basilica was also the place where the Catholic Church fully embraced the quest for Christian unity at the Second Vatican Council, and where great ecumenical liturgies have been celebrated ever since.

The *statio* "at St. Peter" and the texts assigned for the day prompt several reflections: on Peter himself, whose bones are thought to rest beneath the papal altar and Gian Lorenzo Bernini's great bronze *baldacchino* (canopy); on the teaching office in the Church, which is borne in a special way by Peter and his successors; and on the relationship between the papacy and the Lord's summons to radical holiness in the gospel reading for today's Mass.

Numerous legends surround St. Peter, but on a Lenten Saturday in Rome, perhaps the most compelling is the story of the *"Quo vadis, Domine?"* [Where are you going, Lord?], which in twentieth-century form helped Henryk Sienkiewicz win the Nobel Prize for Literature. According to the tradition, Peter, who had come to Rome from his first episcopal "chair" at Antioch (where "the disciples were for the first time called Christians" [Acts 11.26]), fled Rome at the beginning of the fierce persecution launched by Nero. (The persecution is established historical fact, and may have involved Nero's attempt to scapegoat the unpopular Christians for a great fire that had swept the city.) Striding out the old Appian Way, today's Appia Antica, Peter, accompanied in Sienkiewicz's novel by a friend, Nazarius, meets Jesus; the Polish novelist, in his rather ornate style, captures the essence of the encounter:

> The traveling staff fell out of Peter's hand. His eyes were fixed immovably ahead. His lips were open, and his face reflected unbelievable surprise, immense joy, and rapturous exaltation.
>
> Suddenly he threw himself on his knees, his arms uplifted and stretched to the light, and his lips cried out: "Christ! O Christ!" His head beat against the dust as if he were kissing the feet of someone only he could see. Then there was silence.
>
> *"Quo vadis, Domine?"* his voice asked at last, punctured by his sobbing. "Where are you going, Lord?"

Nazarius heard no answer. But a voice of ineffable sweetness and abundant sorrow rang in Peter's ears. "When you abandon my people," he heard, "I must go to Rome to be crucified once more."

The apostle lay still and silent with his face pressed into the dust. Nazarius thought he had either died or fainted, but he rose at last, picked up his pilgrim's staff, and turned again toward the seven hills.

"*Quo vadis, Domine?*" the boy asked, like an echo of the apostle's cry.

"To Rome," Peter murmured.

There, Peter met his fate, crucifixion upside down in Nero's Circus: and in that act of complete abandonment to the Master, Peter fulfilled his vocation. He had, once again, denied that vocation; he had, once again, been called back; and he had, once again, responded. Conversion is always possible. No one lies outside the ambit of the divine mercy. All that is required is the response of faith—the courage to live out that response will follow, as another gift of grace.

The second reflection at today's *statio* is prompted by the *Altar of the Chair*, Gian Lorenzo Bernini's bronze masterpiece in the apse of the basilica. Within the bronze *cathedra*, or episcopal chair, fashioned by Bernini, tradition holds, is the wooden "chair" of Peter. What is perhaps most striking about the composition of the piece, however, is its theological deftness. Peter's *cathedra*, symbol of Christ's promise to preserve the Church in truth through the teaching authority bestowed on Peter and the college of bishops, is held aloft by four great teachers of Christian truth: Ambrose and Augustine from the West, Athanasius and John Chrysostom from the East. The bronze figures of these Doctors of the Church are colossal; yet, rather than supporting the Petrine chair as if it were an immense weight, they support it with their fingertips: Bernini's sculptural way of reminding centuries of Christians that the truth is not burdensome—"Take my yoke upon you, and learn from me; for I am gentle and lowly in heart, and you will find rest for your souls. For my yoke is easy and my burden is light" [Matthew 11.29–30].

In the twenty-first-century world, the *Altar of the Chair* is deeply countercultural, and not simply because there is an enormous gulf of sensibility between the sculpture of Bernini and that of, say, modernist Henry Moore. The depth of the gap is theological rather than stylistic. In a culture that values autonomy above all else, the notion of the truth that liberates even as it binds is not easy to grasp. Yet that is what Bernini, and the Church, ask us to reflect upon at this *statio*: the truth that the truth, freely embraced, is light; and that, in its lightness, it frees us to be the sons and daughters of God we were born to be.

The third point of reflection at today's station comes from hearing the gospel instruction—"You, therefore, must be perfect, as your heavenly Father is perfect"—in this particular place. It is no secret that the Church has had sinful popes; as one old and wise Vatican official once put it to a *National Geographic* team preparing a book on the glories of the Vatican, "God has been very good to us. We have not had a wicked pope in centuries." The wickedness of some popes inevitably brings to mind the failings of the Church and its leaders in the late twentieth century—indeed, the failings of the Church throughout history.

Blessed John Paul II insisted that the Church confront those failings and confess before God the sins of her sons and daughters in order to enter the third millennium of Christian history with renewed evangelical energy. Thus on the First Sunday of Lent in 2000, the Pope led the world Church in a "Day of Pardon," in which sins and failures were publicly acknowledged and forgiveness sought from God. This was not a form of papal political correctness; this was repentance, in the sure hope of an outpouring of mercy from the Father of mercies. History tells us that this pattern of sin-repentance-confession-forgiveness is one of the enduring rhythms of the Church's pilgrimage through time. Christians are not yet perfected, and do not yet fully embody the perfection of the Father to the world.

The story of Peter, however, powerfully illustrates the capacity of grace to overcome the failures of the Church, its leaders, and its people. Those failures will remain until the New Jerusalem. So will the Lord's promise of preserving the Church in the truth that sets humanity free.

St. Peter: *Pietà* (Michelangelo, 1500)

Lıke the arms of Gian Lorenzo Bernini's colonnade, the golden glow of dawn on the façade of St. Peter's invites us into the heart of the Roman Church.

Nearly two millennia ago, Peter was crucified here, his corpse consigned to a pauper's grave hastily dug in the Vatican Hill. In throwing Peter's body into the earth, however, the apostle's Roman persecutors planted the most fertile seed in the Eternal City.

Jealously guarded for centuries, Peter's tomb was first transformed into a church by Constantine, who built a colossal structure around the grave of the Prince of the Apostles, complete with the rich ornament characteristic of imperial works. The Constantinian basilica—"Old St. Peter's"—was demolished in 1506 to make way for "New St. Peter's," one of the world's most recognizable monuments.

Donato Bramante, the new basilica's first architect, proposed a design that combined two structures of ancient Rome, the Pantheon dome and the Basilica of Maxentius in the Forum; thus New St. Peter's would outshine the greatest examples of ancient architecture. Bramante's plan took 120 years, twenty popes, and numerous architects (including Michelangelo, who stepped into the breach at age seventy) to execute. Still, work on what we know as St. Peter's was not yet finished when the Bramante/ Michelangelo design was completed in 1590. The new basilica could not contain the ever-increasing number of pilgrims coming to venerate the apostle's tomb. So in 1601, Carlo Maderno extended the church by three bays, turning a Greek cross plan into a Latin cross and adding the current façade.

Four of the porch's five bronze doors date from the twentieth century. The central processional doors, with reliefs of the martyrdoms of Peter and Paul, were cast in 1440 by Filarete. Past these doors, the vast space of the nave stretches 613 feet toward the altar; the baby angels, affectionately dubbed *putti* in Italian, that support the holy-water fonts stand six feet tall. Soft light beckons to the right, toward the first side chapel and Michelangelo's *Pietà*.

Carved in 1500 and intended for a small chapel in Constantine's basilica, this masterwork, its power undiminished, has been distanced from viewers by glass since a 1972 attack by a man with a hammer. Mary holds her lifeless son in her arms, but Christ's body bears few marks of suffering: he seems like a classical statue; only the lifted shoulder and dangling arm indicate lifelessness. The piece combines the beauty of a Greek divinity with the reality of a dead body: God and man, sculpted as one.

(continues)

(*continued*)

Mary's calm expression recalls the *fiat* given to God at the Annunciation; as she said "yes" to the angel Gabriel, she maintains her faith in this darkest hour. Her hand opens to offer the luminous body of Christ and reminds pilgrims entering the basilica of the price of humanity's reconciliation with God.

The next chapel contains the tomb of Blessed John Paul II; the Blessed Sacrament Chapel follows. Leaving it and turning back into the nave offers the visitor a new vision of the basilica. Michelangelo's façade stood here, for he intended that the pilgrim on entering would first confront the massive dome covering Peter's grave.

Bramante's plan called for a dome sitting atop a drum, like the dome of the Pantheon, a pagan temple built for people who believed that men became gods: thus the dome was fused to the drum, and its equal height and width expressed a pagan aspiration. Michelangelo recalculated the dome's weight and placed the 137-foot span of masonry on a high drum pierced with massive windows that flood the space with light. Michelangelo's dome appears weightless. It is resting on a cushion of luminosity: man does not fuse heaven to earth; heaven chooses to hover over Peter's tomb.

That tomb is sixty feet below the altar, but the life-size statue of the apostle, placed against the right pier, makes him seem accessible. Cast by Arnolfo di Cambio for the Jubilee of 1300, it depicts Peter as a teacher, with full beard and the robe of a Greek philosopher, the *chiton*. One hand is raised in blessing; the other holds the keys to heaven. The sandal and toes on one foot have been rubbed away, the metal worn down by human hands over the centuries: a silent, bronze witness to the number of pilgrims who have laid their petitions at the feet of St. Peter. [E.L.]

St. Mary in Trastevere: *Assumption* (Domenichino, 1616)

The
SECOND WEEK
of LENT

St. Mary in Domnica: Triumphal arch and apse (ninth century)

THE SECOND SUNDAY IN LENT

Station at St. Mary in Domnica

Holy Mass

[A]	[B]	[C]
Genesis 12.1–4a	*Genesis 22.1–2, 9a,*	*Genesis 15.5–12, 17–18*
Psalm 33	*10–13, 15–18*	*Psalm 27*
2 Timothy 1.8b–10	*Psalm 116*	*Philippians 3.17–4.1*
Matthew 17.1–9	*Romans 8.31b–34*	*Luke 9.28b–36*
	Mark 9.2–10	

Office of Readings

Exodus 13.17–14.9

St. Leo the Great: Sermon 51

I N THE STORY OF the Transfiguration of the Lord, Holy Mass for the Second Sunday in Lent offers pilgrims who are walking the itinerary of conversion a glimpse of the journey's end.

The scene is set by the Entrance Antiphon, taken from Psalm 27: "Thou hast said, 'Seek ye my face.' My heart says to thee, 'Thy face, LORD, I do seek.' Hide not thy face from me." The psalmist expresses here a universal human longing for transcendence: for something beyond the here-and-now that brings the here-and-now into clearer focus and infuses meaning into our daily lives. As the Fathers of the Second Vatican Council put it in their Pastoral Constitution on the Church in the Modern World, human beings understand, instinctively if not always reflectively, that "there is no limit to [their] aspirations and that [they are] called to a higher kind of life"—and this, despite our quotidian experience of our "many limitations" as creatures with a finite life-span in this world. Human beings are, as the social critic Irving Kristol once described himself, "theotropic": an instinct to seek the divine face is built into us, even as finding and seeing what we seek can be a startling, even shattering, experience.

The complexities of this instinct are on full display in the story of the Transfiguration, the focal point of today's liturgy and the literary pivot of the three Synoptic gospels of Matthew, Mark, and Luke. In each of these accounts of the life and ministry of the Messiah, there are three testimonies to the divine sonship of Jesus: at his baptism in the Jordan; at the Transfiguration; and on the Cross. In the first two instances, the voice bearing witness to the Son is the Father. On Calvary, the voice is that of the Roman centurion, who affirms in the last extremity what the Father had declared at the River Jordan: that this innocent man was the Son of God.

Each of the three evangelists also structures the narrative in the same way: there is a vision, which links the New Covenant in Jesus to God's covenant with the People of Israel, represented by the great figures of Moses and Elijah; there is a voice, testifying to the filial relationship between Jesus of Nazareth and the God of Moses and Elijah; there is the divine instruction to "listen to him"; there is fear and confusion on the part of Peter, James, and John; and then the disciples continue, with the Lord, along the path that will take them up to Jerusalem, where Jesus will meet the destiny he discusses with Moses and Elijah on the Mount of Transfiguration. Luke gives this last phase of the narrative a special character by using the Greek word for "exodus" to refer to the Lord's passage toward Jerusalem, prefiguring the final "exodus" of the Lord into glory at the Ascension while harkening back to that paradigmatic divine act of liberation, the Exodus from Egypt.

Both the vision and the voice in the story of the Transfiguration have a distinctively Lenten quality. The call, as always, is to conversion of life: *"Listen to him,"* to the beloved Son with whom the Father is well-pleased; to the Messiah who calls for repentance and belief in the Kingdom breaking into history here-and-now. And, as is often the case, Peter (whose human foibles anticipate those of the brethren whom he and his successors will later be instructed to strengthen) doesn't quite get the idea: rather than listening, he is all business and busyness, eager to set up camp. That conversion begins with a radical, interior turn toward the Lord, in which contemplating the Holy Face resplendent in glory takes precedence over busyness, is a lesson to be learned over and over again along the pathways of the Lenten journey, and of a lifetime.

Yet the journey is made easier by the knowledge that the disciples of the Son—those who are configured to him by repentance and conversion—will be like him: an assurance given in a particularly dramatic way in the Transfiguration. They, too, will shine resplendently. Or, as Pope St. Leo the Great puts it in today's Office of Readings, the Lord, in the Transfiguration, "was also providing a firm foundation for the hope of holy Church." Through reflection on this dramatic episode, the whole body of Christ was to understand the kind of transformation it would receive as a gift. The members of that body were to look forward to a share in that glory which first blazed out in Christ, their head.

That this vision of human possibility can be disconcerting, even frightening, as well as inspiring and comforting, seems clear from the reaction of Peter, James, and John, who are described as being, respectively, "filled with awe" (Matthew), "exceedingly afraid" (Mark), or just simply "afraid" (Luke). The Lord responds in words that would become the signature challenge of Pope John Paul II: "Be not afraid." Or, as the Matthean account has it, "Rise, and have no fear." Set out, again, along the path of conversion. It will lead to Jerusalem and to the Cross. But now the climax of the story and the end of the journey have been revealed: the cross will not be a cause of shame; death will not have the final word; the divine purpose, whose archetypal witnesses among the People of Israel were Moses and Elijah, will be completed by the death of the Messiah and his ultimate vindication in the Resurrection to glory; all those conformed to him will share that glory and will be like him—shining in the new and eternal Jerusalem.

Today's *statio* at St. Mary in Domnica is one of the most ancient of the Roman stations. According to the early twentieth-century liturgical scholar Ildefonso Schuster, the name comes from the Latin *Dominicum*, the "Lord's House," and thus links the transfigured Messiah to his mother, the first of disciples and the pattern of discipleship in the Church. That close bond is neatly embodied in another great European pilgrimage site, the Holy Land shrine of Kalwaria Zebrzydowska near Kraków. An annual outdoor passion play there helped shape the early spiritual life of Karol Wojtyła, the boy who would become Pope John Paul II and who returned to the beautiful woodland sanctuary near his hometown for prayer and reflection throughout his life. Located in the foothills of the Carpathians, Kalwaria Zebrzydowska unfolds over two trails that link dozens of chapels, each intended to embody architecturally an event in the lives of Jesus and Mary. The two pilgrim pathways, the "Path of Our Lord" and the "Path of Our Lady," intersect at one chapel: the Chapel of the Assumption.

In seventeenth-century Poland, Mary's assumption into heaven was understood to have been the first manifestation of the promise implicit at the Transfiguration—all who conform their lives to the will of the Father made visible in the Son will, like the Son transfigured on the mount with Moses and Elijah, shine resplendently by the power of the Holy Spirit. The fact that Transfiguration Sunday, this pause for refreshment along the Lenten journey, is linked to an ancient Marian title in Rome is thus entirely appropriate, for it reminds us that discipleship, the pattern for which is set in Mary, is a journey to glory.

**St. Mary in Domnica:
Ceiling detail (1566)**

ST. MARY IN DOMNICA is one of the small bouquet of churches stemming from St. John Lateran at the top of the Caelian Hill. Tradition claims that it was built over an older Christian structure belonging to St. Cyriaca, a Roman matron who assisted St. Lawrence, gathered his remains for burial, and then suffered martyrdom herself. In this early *diaconia*, or place serving as a center for charitable works, Lawrence would have distributed alms and preached.

The present church is first documented in the eighth century. Later, Pope St. Paschal I (817–824) completely rebuilt the basilica. Paschal, who also restored the basilicas of Sts. Cecelia and Praxedes, seems to have had a particular devotion to Rome's female martyrs.

The origin of the church's name is disputed. Is it a derivative of *dominicim* (the pre-Constantinian term for "church")? A respectful reference to the Latin translation of Cyriaca's name, which means "of the Lord"? Or does it allude to the surrounding imperial land given to the Christians? Its other name, St. Mary in Navicella, is more obvious: in the sixteenth century, Cardinal Giovanni de Medici, who became Pope Leo X in 1513, restored a marble boat statue that once stood in the area, turning it into the ship fountain outside the church. The son of Lorenzo the Magnificent, Cardinal Giovanni was a knowledgeable art patron and hired Andrea Sansovino to design the harmonious arcaded entrance portico; the airy arches are reminiscent of the loggia in the Apostolic Palace that Raphael would later design for him.

Inside, a triumphal arch frames the apse mosaic. The Blessed Virgin stands at the center of the composition, regally holding the Christ Child, as tiers of saints approach her. Her robe, a deep, mesmerizing blue, envelopes the Child; this, and the white kerchief in her hand, betray the influence of Byzantium, then a growing artistic influence in Rome. The candid white robes and azure halos of the saints, arranged in a primitive perspective pile-up, highlight the Mother and Child. The garden is planted with poppies, the red spots alluding to the blood shed by the martyrs. Pope Paschal, in the blue nimbus of the living, kneels to kiss the Virgin's slipper. A mosaic frieze crowns the arch with a rhythmic procession of apostles walking toward the seated Christ.

Leo X hired Perin del Vaga, of Raphael's studio, for the fresco decoration. The trompe-l'oeil band of lions alludes to the church's papal patron; the subdued ornament extends around the clerestory, framing the windows with garlands. The wooden ceiling continues the naval motif from Pope Leo's fountain outside: churches and baptisteries, symbols of the barque of Peter, float above waves.

Modern restorations were not kind to St. Mary in Domnica, but one chapel, home to the tabernacle, escaped the heavy-handed renovation. Here, angels hover against a golden ground encircling a Renaissance-era image of the Virgin, while saints gather below in various attitudes of awe.

St. Mary in Domnica offers a taste of Florentine Renaissance art: simple, subdued, and a respite from Rome's often overwhelming grandeur. [E.L.]

St. Clement: Choir and apse

MONDAY OF THE SECOND WEEK OF LENT

Station at St. Clement

Holy Mass
Daniel 9.4b–10
Psalm 79
Luke 6.36–38

Office of Readings
Exodus 14.10–31
St. John Chrysostom: Catecheses, 3

I N TODAY'S SELECTION FROM the Book of Exodus in the Office of Readings, the Israelites are in a panic. The Egyptians, having realized their mistake in letting their chattels go free, are about to overtake them—and, as so often happens in this drama, the Israelites revert to the habits of slaves, saying, "It would have been better for us to serve the Egyptians than to die in the wilderness." To which Moses, who appeared yesterday on the Mount of Transfiguration with Jesus, responds as Jesus did to the terrified disciples who hid from his glory: "Be not afraid." Or, as one translation has it, "Fear not, stand firm, and see the salvation of the LORD, which he will work for you today."

The occasions on which we are called to "stand fast" are likely not so dramatic as those faced by Israel, caught between Pharaoh's chariots and the sea, or Peter, James, and John, confronted with an inexplicable vision of the transfigured Jesus and told by the voice of the Father to "Listen to him." At the beginning of this second full week of the Forty Days, however, the call to "stand fast" can inspire an examination of conscience on a far more mundane challenge: our response to petty aggravation or general obnoxiousness.

The patience to live with, and perhaps even change, the kind of person whom those of a Franciscan sensibility might whimsically call "Brother Jackass" is one that many Christians face every day. The *Catechism of the Catholic Church* lists patience as one of the traditional fruits of the Spirit, the "perfections that the Holy Spirit works in us as the first fruits of eternal glory," and ranks it with those other fruits of which St. Paul wrote to his rowdy and troublesome Galatians: "love, joy, peace . . . kindness, goodness, faithfulness, gentleness, self-control" [Galatians 5.22–23]. The development of our capacity for patience, in other words, is an index of how well we have listened to the transfigured Lord, whose glory is a foretaste of the glory that will be his disciples'.

Today's station, at St. Clement, bears witness to the universality of the Church as embodied in the Bishop of Rome and exemplified by St. Cyril, one of the Apostles of the Slavs, whose tomb is in the basilica. According to the historical conventions, Clement was the third successor of Peter and led the Roman Church from about 91 A.D. until his martyrdom a decade or so later. He was an important subapostolic author whom others, like Irenaeus of Lyons, regarded as having received his teaching from the apostles themselves. Historian J.N.D. Kelly noted that third- and fourth-century Christian scholars, such as the theologian Origen, the historian Eusebius, and the biblical scholar Jerome, identified today's Clement with the Clement whom St. Paul cited as a fellow-worker for the Lord in his Letter to the Philippians. Kelly regarded Clement's Letter to the Corinthians as the most important first-century Christian text outside the New Testament and noted that some Christians received it as a canonical text.

Clement, too, had to learn to live patiently with obstreperousness. His epistle was written to the Church at Corinth, which was still embroiled in controversies a generation or two after St. Paul tried to calm things down there. Clement's fraternal but firm reminder of the Church's proper structure, evidently a disputed point in Corinth at the time, is the earliest extant example of Rome intervening authoritatively to still the roiled waters of another local church.

Then there is St. Cyril, brother of St. Methodius, whose sarcophagus is in the middle level of the three-tiered structure known to the twenty-first century as the Basilica of St. Clement. Cyril, too, was an exemplar of Christian universality: he and his brother created the first vernacular liturgy, which was in the language of the Moravian Slavs they were sent from Constantinople to convert; in doing so, the holy brothers created the Cyrillic alphabet, still in use among the eastern Slavs. Exhausted by his missionary labors and his efforts to keep lines of communication open between Rome and Constantinople, Cyril retired from the active ministry and took the monastic habit; when he died in Rome, his funeral was celebrated "as if he had been a pope," according to the *Old Slavonic Life of Constantine* (Cyril's baptismal name), part of which is read in the Liturgy of the Hours on his feast day, February 14. Orthodox Christianity honors Cyril and Methodius with the title "Equal to the Apostles." In 1980, Pope John Paul II declared the brothers from Thessaloniki copatrons of Europe with St. Benedict: Benedict, founder of Western monasticism, was one of the saviors of Western civilization during the so-called Dark Ages; Cyril and Methodius laid the religious and literary foundations of the Slavic culture that would shape eastern Europe. (Methodius is buried in the Moravian town of Velehrad, in today's Czech Republic.)

According to a long-standing tradition, Clement, Bishop of Rome, was exiled to the Crimea and martyred there by being drowned in the Black Sea with an anchor around his neck: thus the anchor motif on the *baldacchino* surmounting the high altar of today's *statio*. Then, the story continues, Cyril and Methodius discovered the relics of Clement in the mid-ninth century, took them to Moravia, and then later brought them to Rome, a gesture of solidarity deeply appreciated by the Roman Church. The twenty-first-century Greek Catholics of Ukraine have a special devotion to the Roman bishop, Clement, who, they believe, was martyred in exile in their land. At today's *statio*, pilgrims can venerate the memory of Cyril and Clement and ponder the universality of the Church, in which liturgical diversity can serve the cause of Christian unity. The remembrance of two great saints, one from the Latin Christian West and one from the Greek Christian East, is also an invitation to reflect self-critically on whether our lives have contributed to healing the breaches among Christians and to recomposing that unity which Christ bequeathed to the Church at the Last Supper.

The scandal of Christian division, especially between Rome and the Orthodox Churches of the Christian East, is an obstacle to the Church's manifesting the glory of the Lord's transfigured countenance in her own life. As such, it is something that calls for repentance and prayer.

There is one further element of the station at St. Clement that is especially appropriate for Lenten meditation: the great apse mosaic of the upper church. Here is the artistic embodiment of the antiphon recited or sung at the Office of Readings on the First Sunday in Lent: "See how the cross of the Lord stands revealed as the tree of life." At Calvary, the world sees death and utter destruction at the end of the Lord's journey to Jerusalem. At Easter, the truth is revealed, and the Cross, symbol of torture and degradation, now appears as that great arbor from which the New Life, proclaimed throughout the Easter season, bursts forth: an important image to keep on mental file as the itinerary of conversion unfolds over the next five weeks.

Here (to return to the theme of patience), we can ponder with Peter, in the canticle at Second Vespers of the Second Sunday in Lent, the warrant for our forbearance and charity toward those who are offensive. That warrant is nothing less than the patience of Jesus himself: "Christ also suffered for you, leaving you an example, that you should follow in his steps. He committed no sin; no guile was found on his lips. When he was reviled, he did not revile in return; when he suffered, he did not threaten; but he trusted to him who judges justly. He himself bore our sins in his body on the tree, that we might die to sin and live to righteousness. By his wounds you were healed" [1 Peter 2.21–24].

St. Clement: Mithraeum

THE BASILICA OF ST. CLEMENT is a site of great historical density. Emperors and martyrs, saints and invaders punctuate its 2,000-year history: an extraordinary cast of characters and unexpected turns of events, each leaving its mark on the passage of Rome from its pagan origins to its Christian flowering.

In antiquity, this gentle rise of the Caelian Hill was densely packed with homes and temples. After Nero set Rome ablaze in 64, he cleared the area and began construction of his mammoth residence, the Domus Aurea. Roman riots and Nero's death halted work in 68, but the property remained an imperial possession. In 70, Vespasian began building his amphitheater a few blocks down the street, along with the gladiator barracks situated next door to the present basilica.

The remains of two buildings dating from this era lie two stories below St. Clement's Cosmatesque floor. The decorations are faded and the rooms are dank, but two millennia ago, these spaces were busily occupied by two rival religions. The first rooms housed a cult dedicated to the Persian god Mithras; the ceremonial area, with its altar to a deity beloved by Roman soldiers, remains. Next to the Mithraeum, and distinguishable by its tufa walls, is a sturdier, more cumbersome structure, often identified as an imperial ministry. Another persuasive argument, however, suggests that the property was built by T. Flavius Clemens, Vespasian's nephew-in-law, who, having converted to Christianity with his wife Domitilla, gave the site to their freedman Clement, the third pope after St. Peter. If this version of the story is true, these musty chambers were once a kind of proto-Vatican. (What is known is that T. Flavius Clemens and Domitilla were executed by Domitian as Christians.)

The legalized Christian community quickly built a church on this site, suggesting that it was already in Christian use. Built in the same sprawling style as St. John Lateran (then under construction a few blocks up the street), it was dedicated to Pope St. Clement, who, like many of the early Bishops of Rome, was also a martyr.

The vast nave of this church contains remnants of fresco decoration. The oldest painting, in a little niche in the north wall, depicts *Maria Regina* [Mary Our Queen], dressed in imperial regalia typical of the sixth century. Faded scenes from the life of St. Clement, painted in the eleventh century, line the nave. One, almost slapstick, recounts the failed attempts of a Roman governor to arrest the pope, as an imperial henchman, struck blind, nevertheless tries to apprehend the saint. (This fresco also contains the first written Italian, unfortunately less than edifying.) Another mural depicts the miracle, after Clement's martyrdom by drowning, of a boy saved from the same cruel death; its close focus on the mother and child hint at a new aesthetic spirit that will eventually grow into the art of the Renaissance.

The ancient church of St. Clement was destroyed during the Norman Sack of Rome of 1084, and a third construction was built in the twelfth century upon the walls of the earlier buildings. The sixth-century marble choir, given by Pope John II, was salvaged from the lower church and is still used today. The crowning glory of the new basilica is the apse mosaic, featuring the oldest extant image in Roman art of the lifeless Christ, the *Christus Patiens*. The inscription records that the work conceals a piece of the True Cross. [E.L.]

St. Balbina: Stational Mass

TUESDAY OF THE SECOND WEEK OF LENT

Station at St. Balbina

Holy Mass

Isaiah 1.10, 16–20

Psalm 50

Matthew 23.1–12

Office of Readings

Exodus 16.1–18, 35

St. Augustine: Exposition on the Psalms, 140

ISAIAH'S STRIKING CALL TO repentance, addressed to the princes of Sodom and the people of Gomorrah in the first reading of today's Mass, is a remarkable affirmation of how the divine mercy extends even to those prototypically wicked cities: "Come, then, let us reason together, says the LORD: though your sins are like scarlet, they shall be as white as snow; though they are red like crimson, they shall become like wool." In calling us to repentance, the Father of mercies does not ask us to do anything unreasonable, but rather to conform our lives to the instinct for good that is built into us and remains within us, however dulled it may become by sin.

In the gospel reading of the day, Jesus, having chastised the false piety of religious leaders who do not take up the burdens they lay on others, reminds both the crowds surrounding him and the disciples who are his closest followers that "you are all brethren," and "you have one Father, who is in heaven."

Who is this Father, who can make things aright, even in Sodom and Gomorrah? Who is the Holy One whom the disciples of Jesus are to call "Father"?

Christians have been debating this question for two millennia. The answers at which the settled teaching of the Church has arrived, which are perhaps most concisely expressed in the Nicene-Constantinopolitan Creed that many Christians recite every Sunday, take us into what Dominican theologian Aidan Nichols called the "deep mind" of the Church—which is no bad place to spend a moment or two during the pilgrimage of Lent. For the itinerary of conversion involves stretching the mind as well as disciplining the appetites.

The notion of God-as-Father (which dates back to the very origins of the Church) has become controverted in recent decades. Feminist theologies have abandoned the usage as culturally conditioned, retrograde, and an obstacle to perceiving the fullness of God's attributes and qualities. One problem with this approach, Father Nichols argued in his book *Criticizing the Critics*, is precisely that it imagines fatherhood as "the attribution of certain qualities to the divine nature." But when the Church's creeds, following the Church's Lord, call the Holy One "Father," this is, Nichols taught, "not only, or even mainly, a statement about the provident care and tender mercy of One who knows every sparrow that falls to the ground, and considers human beings of far more worth than any sparrow—though, to be sure, the Gospels include such affirmation." Something more—something greater—is being confessed.

The People of Israel knew about God's tender care. The New Life in Christ, manifest most dramatically in the Resurrection of Jesus and the gift of the Holy Spirit to the followers of the Risen One, does more than confirm the Old Testament's teaching about God. What happens at Easter, as Father Nichols put it, is "a veritable explosion of divine glory." A previously shaky company of Jewish men and women—who had a true if incomplete grasp of the reality of God through their faith in the God of Abraham, Isaac, and Jacob—"were suddenly confronted with a super-abundance of fresh meaning." The wholly unprecedented and category-shattering experience of the Resurrection gave these men and women a new and deeper experience of the reality of God, an experience that was world-changing, *redemptive*, in its power.

Jesus, whom they had thought a dead failure, was now radiantly present to them in an entirely new way: a presence they tried to describe as his lordship over nature (he had conquered death) and history (he had reset the course of time so that all time was now a pilgrimage to glory). Who had done this? Who had shown Jesus, the Risen One, to be the divine Son? The God who, in the very same revelation of the true Person of the Son, "reveals *himself* to be quintessentially the divine Father." *Now*, in the light of the Resurrection, the injunction of Jesus to call *only* this Holy One "Father" begins to make radical sense.

This is not all, however; the Easter experience of the first believers in the Risen One was even richer. For those first Christians came to understand that it was through the power of the Holy Spirit, once promised and now sent upon them by the Father through the resurrected and ascended Son, that they had been "born again." They were forgiven, as Isaiah taught was possible. And, most astonishingly of all, they were now empowered by the Spirit to enter into the love of Father and Son through adoption as the sons and daughters of God.

This "founding happening of the Christian tradition," Father Nichols concluded, is not simply an extension of the providential care that God extends to his chosen people in the Hebrew Bible. Easter is something more, something different, something utterly and amazingly new: Easter gives birth to "the life-transforming impact on us of the supreme truth that the saving God is the Holy Trinity." And within that trinity of divine persons, "Father" is not a time-conditioned metaphor chosen by Jesus because of the cultural circumstances of his time. *Father* is a "proper name," revealed by the Son who is begotten of the Father from before all time and through whom everything is brought into being.

The life, death, and resurrection of Jesus, the incarnate Son, have far more than exemplary value; the Risen One is far more than a good moral example. In this "founding happening of the Christian tradition" toward which the entire Lenten journey of the Church is directed, the world has been made anew, things have been set aright, and the true destiny of human beings has been revealed.

We are made by God, but we are also made *for* God: for life within the light and love of the Holy Trinity.

To hold firmly to God as *Father*, and to do so knowing that this is a proper name that reveals the deep truth of the Holy One so named, is certainly countercultural in a unisex world. To compound the problem, that unisex world has learned from such paradigmatic moderns as Nietzsche and Freud that the very notion of "God the Father" is oppressive politically and likely to lead to irrational guilt-complexes, personally. Which is perhaps one reason why it is good to ponder the "deep mind" of the Church at today's station. For St. Balbina, according to tradition, was a consecrated virgin who dispensed charity to the distressed members of the Roman Church who were poor, sick, or imprisoned. Balbina spent her life as an embodiment of today's gospel truth that all the people of the Church are brethren. That truth makes ultimate sense only if God is Father.

St. Sabina: *The Crucifixion*

St. Sabina: Dedicatory Inscription

St. Peter in Chains: *Baldacchino* and Apse

St. Anastasia: *The Death of Anastasia*

St. Lawrence in Panisperna:
The Glory of Saint Lawrence

St. Lawrence in Panisperna:
High Altar and Apse Fresco

Twelve Holy Apostles:
Nave Frescoes

Twelve Holy Apostles:
Fresco Fragments

St. Clement: Triumphal Arch, *Baldacchino*, and Apse Mosaic

St. Balbina: *Crucifixion of Peter*

St. Cecilia in Trastevere: *Saint Cecilia*

St. Cecilia in Trastevere: Undercroft Chapel Ceiling

St. Balbina: *Christos Pantokrator*
(tenth century)

PERCHED ON THE EDGE OF THE Aventine Hill, the Basilica of St. Balbina is a study in steadfast simplicity. Located a stone's throw from the Via Appia (the busiest road of ancient Rome), next to the cisterns of Caracalla's *thermae* (a massive bath complex that could accommodate 1,600 people), it is also just a few steps away from Rome's oldest public space, the Circus Maximus (which held well over 100,000 spectators, as well as the first obelisk transferred from Egypt by Augustus). The neighborhood boasts of the might of the empire; this tiny church honors a Roman tribune and his daughter who honored Christ above the emperor.

Pious tradition holds that Balbina was the daughter of a tribune, Quirinus, who was afflicted by an unsightly illness. Pope St. Alexander I (106–115) told Balbina to find the chains that had bound St. Peter in Rome in order to cure her father. Balbina discovered the chains; she and her father converted to Christianity; and the Feast of Peter's Chains was added to the old liturgical calendar on August 1. Quirinus and Pope Alexander were martyred; Balbina dedicated herself to a life of perpetual virginity. Father and daughter were buried in the catacomb of Praetextatus.

The church's history is also linked to Lucius Felix Cilonus, urban prefect under Septimius Severus (193–211) and consul in both 193 and 204. Severus gave land to Cilonus next to the site where Severus's son, Caracalla, would construct his bath complex. The magnificent villa Cilonus built was later adorned with a large rectangular hall, which would in turn become the church of St. Balbina.

Today's church displays many early architectural features, including a long apsidal hall with niches carved into the walls. The wooden traves of the roof are exposed: a rarity in modern Roman churches but the norm in paleo-Christian worship spaces. Pope Leo III made substantial repairs during the Carolingian period and built the bell tower and adjacent monastery. St. Balbina's glory years came when pilgrims began flooding the city in anticipation of the first jubilee year, 1300. An episcopal *cathedra* in Cosmatesque stonework now graced the apse. Two of the side altars contain frescos by the studio of Pietro Cavallini, which was active in the late thirteenth century; Cavallini's signature *Madonna and Child*, seated on a throne draped with brocade and surrounded by saints, is visible in the third chapel on the right.

Other niches contain remains of an older, Byzantine-influenced decoration of Christ blessing with three raised fingers (symbolizing the Trinity), the thumb and ring finger bent toward each

(continues)

(continued)

other (evoking the two natures of Christ). Some have speculated that this is the "image of our Lord behind the altar, painted by no human hand, portraying Our Lord in the flesh," that was mentioned in the *Mirabilia Urbis*, a guidebook for learned pilgrims published at the end of the twelfth century.

A dilapidated porch fresco of the coat of arms of Pope Innocent VIII underscores the massive works undertaken here in the Renaissance, including the high porch with three elegant archways built by Pope Sixtus V, and a substantial restructuring that involved closing niches and converting windows into small circular openings. At the same time, several works were brought here from Old St. Peter's, among them the image of the crucifixion in the Blessed Sacrament Chapel.

Under the high altar, a casket holds the remains of St. Balbina, St. Felicissimus, and several martyrs. The apse above opens to a radiant fresco of St. Balbina in glory, painted by Anastasio Fontebuoni for the Jubilee of 1600. [E.L.]

CAPIT·
SANCT·
PETRI·

St. Cecilia in Trastevere: Apse mosaic (ninth century)

WEDNESDAY OF THE SECOND WEEK OF LENT

Station at St. Cecilia

Holy Mass
Jeremiah 18.18–20
Psalm 31
Matthew 20.17–28

Office of Readings
Exodus 17.1–16
St. Irenaeus: Against Heresies

"WHAT HAS ATHENS TO do with Jerusalem?" asked Tertullian, the first major Christian thinker to write in Latin. What has the Good News of the Kingdom to do with the metaphysical speculations of the Greeks? Who are Plato and Aristotle compared to the Lord Jesus? As the providence of God would have it, "Athens" had a lot to do with "Jerusalem," for the philosophical grammar that had evolved over centuries of Greek thought gave the early Christian Church the conceptual tools with which to turn confession ("Jesus is Lord") into creed and dogma. It made a great deal of difference that Christianity's first "inculturation" was in the intellectual world of classical antiquity, where, for example, the principle of noncontradiction (that something cannot be and not-be at the same time) was secure. In a different circumstance—if Christianity's first "inculturation" had been in an intellectual environment comfortable with contradiction (such that the two statements, "Jesus is Lord" and "Jesus is not Lord" could both be considered true)—it would have been very difficult, and perhaps impossible, for the Church to develop the doctrinal scaffolding that has sustained it for two millennia.

Still, Jesus was not a logician. And the "logic of the Kingdom" that we confront in today's gospel account of the ambitions of the sons of Zebedee and their mother is not the logic taught by Aristotle. It is a different logic, but it is coherent, and it is true. It can also be difficult to grasp and even more difficult to live.

At this stage of Matthew's gospel, the disciples have been with Jesus for some time. They have heard the Sermon on the Mount and its messianic inversion of expectations—the poor in spirit have the Kingdom already among them; the meek will inherit the earth; turning the other cheek, not seeking revenge, is the path of righteous living; so is loving one's enemies. They have seen the Lord walking on water and driving out demons. They have been taught to pray; they have been instructed by the parables of the Kingdom; they have witnessed the miraculous feeding of the multitude; three of them have been present at the Transfiguration.

And still they don't get it.

Rather than helping their mother understand that what she seeks for them—power—is not what the Kingdom is about, James and John, the two sons of Zebedee, assure the Lord that they're quite up to a task they basically misconstrue. Moreover, the other disciples are now upset that James and John are angling for positions of preferment in the new dispensation that they all sense is imminent because of Jesus. So, once again, the Lord has to remind them of a basic truth of the Kingdom: that "whoever would be great among you must be your servant, and whoever would be first among you must be your slave." Why? Because this is the logic of the Kingdom. And it is first made manifest in the herald of the Kingdom, in whom God's Reign is already erupting into history: "the Son of Man [who] came not to be served but to serve, and to give his life as a ransom for many."

This distinctive logic of the Kingdom is given a different name in today's Office of Readings, where the patristic author Irenaeus, confronting the intellectual confusions of the late second century A.D., writes of the history of divine providence as "the harmonious song of salvation." That metaphorical evocation of music is particularly apt for today's station at St. Cecilia, for the martyr whose relics are venerated here is the patroness of musicians and of Church music. That a young woman should be judicially murdered for her religious convictions, as Cecilia was, strikes the modern mind as a cruel absurdity, and from one point of view it is: to uphold religious freedom as the first of human rights is necessarily to deplore religious persecution and violence in the name of God (or the gods, as was the case with Cecilia).

Yet, in the logic of the Kingdom, martyrdom is an integral part of the "harmonious song of salvation." According to ancient and settled Christian tradition, the witness of the martyr, in which the Kingdom-logic of self-gift is played out in its most dramatic form, is the highest form of Christian testimony. Here at today's *statio*, in the marble statue of Cecilia the martyr, is an invitation to contemplate martyrdom as the ultimate gift of self in fidelity to the truths for which one has lived—and to the Truth who composed those truths in the "harmonious song of salvation." Far from being an assertion of personal autonomy (as playwright Robert Bolt tended to misconstrue Thomas More's defiance of Henry VIII in *A Man for All Seasons*), martyrdom expresses in a uniquely complete way the Kingdom-logic of self-gift that the disciples missed in today's gospel episode.

The warrant for martyrdom, like the warrant for service-rather-than-power, is ultimately the Lord himself, as we see in the selection from *Against Heresies* in the Office of Readings appointed for this day. There, Irenaeus evokes St. Paul, who in turn evokes the drama at Horeb described in the first text in today's Office of Readings, where Moses strikes the rock and the people's desert thirst is satisfied: "They drank from the supernatural rock which followed them, and the Rock was Christ" [1 Corinthians 10.4]. The miraculous rock at Horeb, St. Paul suggests, was a type that prefigured the Lord Jesus. He is the Messiah who will give living water that slakes every thirst. He is the Suffering Servant from whose pierced side will flow water and blood: signs of Baptism and the

Eucharist, the sacraments that empower the new People of God to live the logic of the Kingdom, even to the gift of their lives in martyrdom. Peter is the Rock on which the Church is built. But before Peter there is the Lord Jesus, the Rock of living water and the font of the sacramental life.

All of which is neatly captured in the responsory to the passage from Exodus in the Office of Readings, which combines texts from the prophecy of Isaiah and the gospel of John in another example of the harmonious song of salvation:

> With joy you will draw water from the wells of salvation.
> And you will say in that day: "Give thanks to the LORD, call upon his name."
> The water that I shall give him will become in him a spring of water
> Welling up to eternal life.
> And you will say in that day: "Give thanks to the LORD, call upon his name."

St. Cecilia in Trastevere: Courtyard,
campanile, and portico

THE TRANQUIL SURROUNDINGS of the Basilica of St. Cecilia belie the brutal drama that took place here: fifteen feet below today's church, Cecilia, a Roman noblewoman and Christian convert in the mid-third century, was first suffocated, then beheaded, in her own home.

Cecilia's exemplary life, acts of generosity, and sheer joy helped to inspire the conversion of many who knew her, including her future husband, the aristocrat Valerianus. Emperor Alexander Severus, disturbed by the rapid spread of Christianity, decided to strike at the community's most influential members; under his orders, Cecilia's husband, his brother Tibertius, and Pope Urban I were martyred. Because she was well known and beloved by the Romans, Cecilia's murder required more discretion. After attempting to dispatch her quietly by leaving her locked in the steam baths of her house for three days, soldiers returned and tried, unsuccessfully, to decapitate her; they left her for dead, her head partially severed. With her dying breath, Cecilia forgave her persecutors. First buried in the catacomb of St. Callistus, her body was transferred here (along with the relics of Valerianus, Tibertius, and Popes Urban and Lucius) in the ninth century.

Although the basilica is mentioned as an important titular church in 499, it first flowered in the early Middle Ages. Pope Paschal I rebuilt the structure from 817 to 824, after the saint appeared to him in a dream, indicating the site of her tomb. Paschal found the grave and brought the martyr's body back to her home. The apse mosaic closely resembles that of St. Praxedes, its Esquiline sister-church, also restored by Paschal I: a golden-robed Christ on a blue ground is flanked by Peter, Valerianus, and Agatha on one side; on the other, Paul and Cecilia present Pope Paschal (the blue nimbus indicating that he was alive at the time of the portrait).

The high spires of Arnolfo di Cambio's 1283 marble *baldacchino* rest lightly on marble columns, an exquisite piece of medieval carving delicately framing the altar above St. Cecilia's tomb.

In 1599, just before the Jubilee of 1600, Cardinal Paolo Sfondrati, titular pastor of the church, found the sarcophagus of St. Cecilia, which was opened in the presence of prelates, scholars, and an artist. Cecilia was perfectly preserved, still wearing her bloodied robes, her hair caught up in a veil. Romans flocked to see her for the month she was left on view, and the sculptor Stefano Maderno immortalized her in marble. His image of Cecilia apparently sleeping peacefully—with only the odd angle of her head to indicate anything amiss—is beneath the altar.

Heavy modern restoration has ravaged the basilica. In the eighteenth century, Cardinal Francesco Acquaviva d'Aragona commissioned Ferdinando Fuga to rebuild the façade and porch and hired Sebastiano Conca for the ceiling fresco of *St. Cecilia in Glory*. The heavy interior piers are from the nineteenth century and support a ponderous gallery for the cloistered Benedictine sisters who have lived here since the sixteenth century.

In the crypt are the remains of a Roman house and the quiet, marble-encrusted chapel where Cecilia died. The convent contains fragments of the *Last Judgment* painted by Pietro Cavallini in 1293. [E.L.]

St. Mary in Trastevere: Stational Mass

THURSDAY OF THE SECOND WEEK OF LENT

Station at St. Mary in Trastevere

Holy Mass

Jeremiah 17.5–10

Psalm 1

Luke 16.19–31

Office of Readings

Exodus 18.13–27

St. Hilary: Treatise on the Psalms, 127

MAGNIFICENT TWELFTH-CENTURY MOSAIC depictions of the prophets Jeremiah and Isaiah frame the triumphal arch above the sanctuary in today's *statio* at St. Mary in Trastevere. In the first reading appointed for Holy Mass this day, Jeremiah's voice offers station church pilgrims a stark reminder that the Lenten journey of conversion, now well into its second full week, is one dedicated to radical healing—the healing of the fractured, tortuous human heart:

> The heart is deceitful above all things,
>> and desperately corrupt;
>> who can understand it?

I the LORD search the mind
   and try the heart,
to give to every man according to his ways,
   according to the fruit of his doings.

Only a thoroughly desiccated conscience would fail to recognize itself in this prophetic lament. As the American novelist Paul Horgan noted in his compassionate portrait of a boy growing up, *Things As They Are*, guilt—a painful recognition of the heart's deceits—is a burden that begins to weigh on us in childhood; for many, that burden increases over the course of a life. At the same time, along the same biographical trajectory, reflective men and women also recognize in themselves a longing to live with a whole and undivided heart.

This gap between that person I am and the person I ought to be defines the lifelong drama of the Christian moral life. And the Christian answer to life "in the gap" is ever closer configuration to the Lord: to the Christ who, on the Cross, took upon himself all our guilt and immolated it, with himself, in the fire of divine love. The scroll held by Jeremiah in today's station testifies to this fundamental truth of Christian faith, quoting the Vulgate rendition of Lamentations 4.20: *Christus dominus captus in peccatis nostris* [Christ the Lord, bound by our sins]. A similar reminder is found in the words of consecration at every Mass, every day, everywhere in the world: "This is the chalice of my Blood, the Blood of the new and eternal covenant, *which will be poured out for you and for many for the forgiveness of sins.*"

The price of the radical healing sought by the tortured human heart is nothing less than the blood of Christ, shed on the Cross.

The gospel reading of the day links the prophecy of Jeremiah, and indeed the entire witness of the Old Testament, to the New Covenant sealed in the blood of Christ. In preaching, this familiar story of Dives and Lazarus is usually presented as an admonition against greed and an exhortation to charity, both of which are obvious Lenten themes. There is another theme to ponder in this great parable, though; it can be found in the way Jesus crafts Abraham's rejection of Dives's plea that Lazarus be sent to his father's house to warn his decadent brothers against the fate that has befallen him in the afterlife: "If they do not hear Moses and the prophets, neither will they be convinced if someone should rise from the dead."

By ending the tale of Dives and Lazarus on this note, Jesus, the weaver of parables who will become the Risen One, is underscoring the essential unity of the Old and New Covenants in the divine plan of salvation—the project of God in history for the healing of the divided human heart. Moses and the prophets had pointed out the path of repentance and obedience; they were not heeded, and the corruptions of the human heart remained unhealed. The Son of Man, who will rise from the dead, began his public ministry with the same challenge that had been issued by Isaiah and Jeremiah: "Repent." The Good News of the Kingdom that Jesus offers in his preaching and in his healings does not contradict the path to righteous living contained in the Ten Commandments committed to Moses. Nor does that Gospel contradict the call to repentance issued by the prophets of Israel. The Kingdom breaking into history in the person of Jesus is the radical fulfillment of the Law and the Prophets, for his sacrifice is the fulfillment of the sacrifices of old, including the sacrifices of Abel, the just one, and of Abraham, whom the Roman Canon calls "our father in faith."

The tendency of contemporary biblical scholarship to dissect the Scriptures rather than unpack them and explicate them is an obstacle to grasping what is, for Christians, the essential continuity and unity between the Old and New Testaments. That continuity-and-unity comes into much clearer focus when the Bible is read theologically: that is, when Christians read the Bible through the prism of the faith called forth by God's self-disclosing revelation in these sacred books. As Pope Benedict XVI put it in his study of the New Testament Passion narratives, the analysis of the Bible by the tools of modern critical scholarship has "yielded its essential fruit." In the early twenty-first century, we know much more about the life and times of Jesus than was known, say, in the late eighteenth century. That knowledge now has to be combined with a faith-informed reading of the biblical texts. History and theology should work together, not at cross purposes, in bringing to light the richness of the biblical word of God and the continuity of the divine purpose as revealed from the Book of Genesis through the Book of Revelation: from the beginning of the created order to the end, which is a new and perfected eternal beginning.

Put another way, while there can be no return to a fundamentalist reading of Scripture that ignores the genuine insights of modern critical scholarship, there can be, and should be, a reading of the Bible that involves what French philosopher Paul Ricoeur called a "second naivete": a mature open-mindedness that lives comfortably on the far side of skepticism, because it has passed through the purification offered by the genuine fruits of modern biblical criticism. This means, among other things, learning to read the Bible once again as an integrated whole: and that means seeking out the continuities implied in Jesus's crafting of the story of Dives and Lazarus.

Today's stational church, one of the oldest and greatest of Marian shrines, offers the possibility of reflecting on Mary through a similar, second naivete. Isaiah and Jeremiah, who seem to stand guard over the great apse mosaic of Mary enthroned in heaven at the side of her divine Son, remind us that a daughter of Israel, Mary of Nazareth, is the human hinge between the law and prophets of the Old Covenant and the New Covenant in Jesus the Christ—just as John the Baptist is the prophetic hinge between the Old and New Testaments. Another great Marian shrine, the Dormition Abbey on Mt. Zion in Jerusalem, makes the same point in a different way. Within the abbey church is a cenotaph, a symbolic burial place, of Mary; inside the *baldacchino* surmounting a recumbent sculpture of the Virgin are representations of the women of valor of the Old Testament: Deborah, Judith, Ruth, and so on. Both today's *statio* and the Dormition Abbey embody the truth that Christianity affirmed when it condemned the heresy of Marcion (who rejected the Old Testament) in the second century: the same God speaks through the law, through the prophets, and through his Son, who is the son of Mary as well as the Son of God. Thus the witness of "Moses and the prophets"—the truths they spoke about the troubled human heart—remains of enduring value for those who would walk the way of the Lord Jesus.

St. Mary in Trastevere:
Cosmatesque pavement

ST. MARY IN TRASTEVERE is the jewel in the crown of churches of Trastevere, the bustling, populous quarter on the west bank of the Tiber. This neighborhood was once home to Rome's immigrants: merchants, sailors, and dockworkers lived in cosmopolitan proximity, and Christianity found fertile soil for its first Roman converts here. The locals' long-standing pride in their ancient Marian devotion spills into the streets every July, when the *Trasteverini* celebrate *Noantri* [Our Feast], carrying an enormous statue of the Virgin in procession.

The church's roots in antiquity stem from the story of a font of pure oil that sprang from the ground thirty-eight years before Christ was born. The oil flowed for a full year; later piety perceived it as heralding the imminent arrival of Christ, the Anointed One, and a shrine was constructed on the site. The *Taberna Meritoria*, as it was called, is englobed under the altar inside the church.

Pope St. Callistus I was martyred here in 222, thrown into a well from a window in his home next door. The basilica, one of the earliest Roman titular churches, first appears in official records under Pope Julian I (337–352), although little remains of the Julian edifice.

Today's church, rebuilt in 1140 by Pope Innocent II (a Trastevere native), closely resembles St. Mary Major, although it is one-third smaller. The brick bell towers and columned porches are familiar medieval additions, but the façade mosaics of the young women bearing oil lamps are unique.

The interior granite columns, capped with matching Ionic capitals from the Temple of Serapis on the Janiculum Hill, bear a richly carved cornice with a mosaic frieze. The interlocking circles on the Cosmatesque floor lead into the splendid apse, where dazzling mosaics proclaim the glory of Mary, Mother of God.

Over the triumphal arch, Isaiah is paired with Jeremiah. The symbols of the four evangelists hover above them, while below, an inventive image shows two *putti* holding a heavy cornucopia of fruit. These *putti*, along with the caged bird (a symbol of Christ imprisoned in an earthly body to redeem the world's sins), herald a Roman artistic revival by dipping into the visual vocabulary of antiquity.

The apse itself, with Mary swathed in a rich robe and seated next to Christ, is striking in its imagery and composition. That Mary shares the throne with her son attests to the remarkable Marian piety of the Middle Ages: the Mother of God appears as the regal spouse of Christ, and thus represents the Church. Peter, turned toward the Redeemer, breaks the frontal rhythm of the three figures.

(continues)

(continued)

The basilica's greatest aesthetic innovation dates from the thirteenth century and involves the panels under the apse. In these scenes from Mary's life, executed by Pietro Cavallini in 1290 as mosaic was being replaced by fresco, the antique medium reaches a brilliant apogee while trying to keep pace with the new naturalism of the age. In the *Nativity of Mary*, St. Anne, the Virgin's mother, reclines as two maidservants bring her food; as infant Mary is prepared for her bath, the midwife reaches out to test the water: everyday human gestures, glorified in shimmering stone.

The intricate shapes of the coffered ceiling frame Domenichino's *Assumption of Mary*, painted in 1617. The Blessed Virgin seems to soar through the heavy wooden panels as she rises toward the light, recalling Isaiah's promise that "the LORD will be your everlasting light, and the days of your mourning shall be ended" [Isaiah 60.20]. [E.L.]

St. Vitalis: Stational Mass

FRIDAY OF THE SECOND WEEK OF LENT

Station at St. Vitalis

Holy Mass

Genesis 37.3–4, 12–13a, 17b–28a

Psalm 105

Matthew 21.33–43, 45–46

Office of Readings

Exodus 19.1–19; 20.18–21

St. Irenaeus: Against Heresies

T HE MASS READINGS FOR this Friday deepen the examination of conscience that shapes the first weeks of Lent by focusing attention on jealousy, one of the seven capital sins—which, interestingly enough, were first defined by Gregory the Great, the pope who stabilized the order and fixed the liturgical texts of the Roman station church pilgrimage. Jealousy, or envy, is a hardy perennial among the weeds of the spiritual life, and it is the fulcrum on which both readings in today's Mass pivot: the story of Joseph and his brothers, and the confrontation between Jesus and his critics.

The Joseph cycle brings the first book of the Bible and the prehistory of Israel to a dramatic close even as it provides a bridge to the story of Israel-in-exile that begins the drama of the Exodus. There is something quite humanly fitting in the fact that Genesis, which begins with humanity's fall through the primordial capital sin—pride—concludes with a story-cycle that hinges on the capital sin of jealousy. Joseph's brothers are jealous for many reasons: their father, Jacob, imprudently, if understandably, shows him special favor "because he was the son of his old age"; Joseph is a dreamer, and his dreams hint that he will have authority over his brothers; he is also, the story hints, a bit of a shirker, for when his brothers go out to tend their father's flocks, he has to be given a special nudge by Jacob to get on with his work. Jealousy, in this instance, leads to thoughts of murder. But Joseph's life is spared when two of his brothers object to spilling a kinsman's blood; so they sell him into slavery, a fate from which his talents and wiles will extricate him so that he will ultimately become the savior of his father and his brothers in time of famine.

In the gospel reading of the day, Jesus confronts his opponents with the parable of the wicked tenants, who, jealous of the vineyard owner's son, commit the capital crime of homicide: they kill the heir so that they might seize his inheritance. In their turn, they lose everything when the owner of the vineyard wreaks a terrible vengeance and then hires tenants who will give the owner his due.

In both of these episodes, the ending that one might have expected is inverted. Joseph, sold into slavery, becomes the liberator. As for the lesson of the parable of the wicked tenants, Jesus, citing Psalm 118, reminds his opponents (who imagined themselves the builders of a new and reformed Israel) that he, the rejected Son, will be the One who redeems his people and the world: "The stone which the builders rejected has become the chief cornerstone. / This is the LORD's doing, and it is marvelous in our eyes."

Jealousy, it seems, can be woven into the fabric of divine providence and the divine project in history through the mysterious workings of grace. That was Dante's view, in the *Divine Comedy*.

Following his theological master, Thomas Aquinas, the Florentine poet treats jealousy, or envy, as the perversion of a virtue. The virtue in question is the satisfaction a good person takes in the accomplishments, the good luck, or the simple goodness of another. Inverted, that virtue becomes "sorrow for another's good" (according to Aquinas) or, in Dante's variant, "love of one's own good perverted to a desire to deprive other men of theirs." In the *Purgatorio*, the envious are purified on the Second Cornice of Lower Purgatory, which is halfway up Mount Purgatory. Sitting like paupers or beggars in rough cloth, they weep through eyes sewn shut with wire, a fit punishment for those who have enjoyed the sight of others in trouble or others cast down. Each group of sinners on Mount Purgatory recites a prayer appropriate to the purification it is undergoing; the particular prayer of the envious is the Litany of the Saints, as they invoke the aid of the men and women of all time who have rejoiced in the good, their own or others'; in this, they are guarded by the Angel of Generosity. Purged of their sin, the jealous will, when they are purified, be able to see things aright—which means being able, like the saints whose litany they chant, to take satisfaction from the good of others as well as being grateful for their own good.

Dorothy L. Sayers's summary of this tableau in her commentary on the *Divine Comedy* can help sharpen today's examination of conscience:

Envy (*Invidia*) differs from . . . Pride in that it contains always an element of fear. The proud man is self-sufficient, rejecting with contempt the notion that anybody can be his equal or superior. The envious man is afraid of losing something by the admission of superiority in others, and therefore looks with grudging hatred upon other men's gifts and good fortune, taking every opportunity to run them down or deprive them of their happiness. On the Second Cornice, therefore, the eyes which could not endure to look upon joy are sealed from the glad light of the sun, and from the sight of other men. Clad in the garments of poverty and reduced to the status of blind beggars who live on alms, the Envious sit amid the barren and stony wilderness imploring the charity of the saints, their fellow-men.

There is, however, another form of "jealousy" worth pondering today, and that is jealousy, or zeal, for the things of God. As the *Catechism of the Catholic Church* puts it, Jesus drove the money-changers and traders out of the Temple "because of his jealous love for his Father." Seeing him do this, the "disciples remembered that it was written [in Psalm 69], 'Zeal for your house will consume me'" [John 2.17]. "Jealousy" can be, and usually is, a matter of envy. But there is also zeal, and, as points for today's Lenten reflection, both meanings of the term deserve consideration.

Radical discipleship includes ridding ourselves of perverse pleasure in the troubles of others and of the fears that are at the root of that sin. Radical discipleship also calls the followers of the Lord Jesus to a zealous jealousy for the things of God, which may include, when necessary, a zealous defense of the rights of believers and the rights of the Church against those who would whittle away at religious freedom. This is an appropriate obligation on which to reflect in this stational church, as the Basilica of St. Vitalis was the titular church of St. John Fisher, who was martyred in 1535 for his zealous defense of Catholic truth against King Henry VIII.

St. Vitalis: Portico

THE ANCIENT PORTICO OF the Basilica of St. Vitalis, down a steep flight of steps from the Via Nazionale, has sheltered pilgrims since the time of Pope St. Leo the Great. The basilica was originally named for Sts. Gervasius and Protasius, two brother-martyrs from northern Italy, devotion to whom in Ravenna, Bologna, and Milan produced some of Italy's loveliest churches. The dedication to St. Vitalis, traditionally held to be the father of the two men, was added by 499.

In 400, Vestina, a Roman matron from this wealthy Esquiline neighborhood, bequeathed her possessions to pay for a church on this site, which had previously sheltered an oratory dedicated to martyrs. The design was conventional: an entrance porch, a wide nave, two side aisles, and a large apse. In the sixth century, Pope St. Gregory the Great fixed St. Vitalis into the urban fabric of Rome by appointing it a Lenten station church and selecting it as the departure point for the city's procession of widows, perhaps in honor of Vestina.

Although Pope St. Leo III (795–816) restored the church and gave it a bell tower, its position on the edge of the steep Esquiline Hill made the church susceptible to landslides; by the Renaissance, St. Vitalis was described as "ruined."

As part of his energetic preparations for the Jubilee of 1475, Pope Sixtus IV restored the church from the ground up, donating the main altar (which still bears his coat of arms) and closing off the side altars, thus forming a single-nave church with a wide expanse of wall space.

Today's church offers a panorama of martyrdoms through frescos executed by Andrea Comodo and Tarquini Ligustri in the early seventeenth century. The space is articulated with large trompe-l'oeil columns seemingly carved from exotic marbles: a series of stately frames for faux windows looking out into what seem, at first glance, peaceful, bucolic panoramas. Closer inspection, however, reveals early Christian martyrs sacrificing their lives amid lush valleys and craggy hills, their deaths occurring throughout the empire—St. Clement, an anchor around his neck, is thrown into the Black Sea; St. Ignatius falls under the lions as a crumbling Colosseum looms in the distance. As in gentle sylvan poetry, Ignatius prays quietly, while an angel accompanies St. Clement to an underwater chapel. Compared to the graphic, bloody scenes of the Basilica of St. Stephen, these martyrdoms seem like idyllic entries into paradise (a word derived from an ancient term for "garden").

The colors grow more vivid toward the sanctuary, where Agostino Ciampelli painted the martyrdoms of the dedicatory saints: Sts. Gervasius and Protasius are scourged and then beheaded, while St. Vitalis is stretched on a rack and then buried in a pit of rocks. The church's statues of the Doctors of the Church reflect on the Christian understanding of martyrdom; thus these words of St. Ambrose are inscribed above the statue: "Religion makes its prize from what unbelief thought a punishment."

All this heroic witness is crowned in the apse by Christ, who falls under the weight of the Cross. While some of the bystanders to the Passion wear the robes and tunics of first-century dress, others sport exotic turbans, a reminder of bitter Christian battles with the Turks during this age. [E.L.]

Sts. Marcellinus and Peter: Stational Mass

SATURDAY OF THE SECOND WEEK OF LENT

Station at Sts. Marcellinus and Peter

Holy Mass

Micah 7.14–15, 18–20

Psalm 103

Luke 15.1–3, 11–32

Office of Readings

Exodus 20.1–17

St. Ambrose: Flight from the World

FROM ASH WEDNESDAY THROUGH this Saturday of the Second Week of Lent, the liturgy asks Lenten pilgrims to undertake a thorough examination of conscience as an essential preparation for pondering, over the next three weeks, the imitation of Christ to which all are called in Baptism. Today's gospel reading, the parable of the prodigal son, prompts a reflection on the drama of conversion and purification through self-knowledge: an appropriate theme for this last day of the first phase of Lent.

Familiar parables like that of the prodigal son are always worth examining more closely in order to grasp precisely the lessons that Jesus the Divine Teacher is trying to get across. In today's parable, for example, we can only appreciate the magnitude of the father's mercy if we understand that, when the prodigal younger son said, "Give me the share of the property that falls to me," this demand was, in the culture of the day, the equivalent of saying, "I wish you were dead." The prodigal son is not simply a dissolute wastrel; he has, in his heart, committed a kind of patricide. Yet the father welcomes him home.

And what does the father do, in his act of mercy? As Blessed John Paul II used to put it, the merciful father restores to his wayward son the dignity of sonship that he had squandered. He restores to his son the dignity of his humanity. That moment of purification and conversion comes when the son, recognizing what he has become, confesses—"Father, I have sinned against heaven and before you; I am no longer worthy to be called your son"—and the father responds by embracing the penitent, kissing him, and clothing him. In doing so, the father accepts his son's confession and offers the absolution that makes the prodigal whole again.

This familiar story reminds us that the examination of conscience we are completing along the Lenten pilgrimage of conversion is one that should give us the humility and honesty to see ourselves for who we truly are. For in acknowledging what it is that requires repair in us, we are prepared to receive the grace of forgiveness that, as the Church will sing at the Easter Vigil, "restores lost innocence."

The end of the first phase of Lent is also an opportunity to continue the reflection on the purification of our lives after death that began yesterday with a brief visit to Dante's vision of Purgatory in the *Divine Comedy*.

The *Catechism of the Catholic Church* defines Purgatory as a condition: "A state of final purification after death and before entrance into heaven for those who die in God's friendship, but were only imperfectly purified; a final cleansing of human imperfection before one is able to enter the joy of heaven." Or, it might be added, before one is able to enjoy that joy. The saints, as noted before, are those who can live comfortably within the light and love of the Holy Trinity. Christians of other denominations usually find the Catholic doctrine of Purgatory peculiar, although many who reject the doctrine recognize in the *Purgatorio* the most humanly insightful and compelling section of Dante's great poem. Perhaps these dubieties about the doctrine of Purgatory would be eased if the bases of the Church's teaching were better understood (and by Catholics as well as by Christians of other communions).

The doctrine of Purgatory expresses the Catholic Church's conviction that the grace of God continues to work on us and in us, so that we are rid, finally, of the dross that has accumulated in even righteous lives: dross that impedes our full enjoyment of the joy of communion with the Trinity and the saints in glory. That is why Dante is so theologically insightful in his depiction of the punishments of Purgatory, which perfectly fit that-which-must-be-purified. These punishments are not a question of divine retribution or vengeance. Rather, the purification required of us "follows," as the *Catechism* puts it, "from the very nature of sin" and involves growth into the appropriate virtues: those who are gluttonous must learn temperance; those who are lazy must become zealous; the envious must learn to be generous; the proud must learn humility.

The selection in today's Office of Readings from St. Ambrose's treatise on spiritual detachment, *Flight from the World*, offers another insight into the process of purification that prepares us for the Beatific Vision of God. "No one is good but God alone," the great fourth-century bishop of Milan wrote. "What is good is therefore divine, what is divine is therefore good. . . . It is through God's goodness that all that is truly good is given to us, and in it there is no admixture of evil." The spiritual purification the Catholic Church calls Purgatory is thus intended to prepare us for what the Christian East calls *theosis*—divinization. In the seventh week of the Easter season, a Greek Father of the Church, St. Basil the Great, will put this remarkable conviction in its simplest, bluntest form, reflecting on the work of the Holy Spirit in the purification of our lives: "Through the Spirit we become citizens of heaven, we are admitted to the company of the angels, we enter into eternal happiness, and abide in God. Through the Spirit we attain a likeness to God; indeed, we attain what is beyond our most sublime aspirations—we become God."

Purgatory, in other words, is the purification that prepares us for the completion of our spiritual pilgrimage in the New Jerusalem, the eternal Wedding Feast of the Lamb.

Pope Benedict XVI's second encyclical, *Spe Salvi* [Saved in Hope], offers further insights into Purgatory, which the pope treated as an encounter with Christ who both judges and purifies, not unlike the merciful father in today's gospel reading:

For the great majority of people—we may suppose—there remains in the depth of their being an ultimate interior openness to truth, to love, to God. In the concrete choices of life, however, it is covered over by ever new compromises with evil. . . .

What happens to such individuals when they appear before the Judge? Will all the impurity they have amassed through life suddenly cease to matter? What else might occur?

. . . Some recent theologians are of the opinion that the fire which both burns and saves is Christ himself, the Judge and Savior. The encounter with him is the decisive act of judgment. Before his gaze, all falsehood melts away. This encounter with him, as it burns us, transforms and frees us, allowing us to become truly ourselves. . . . [In] the pain of this encounter, when the impurity and sickness of our lives become evident to us, there lies salvation. His gaze, the touch of his heart, heals us through an undeniably painful transformation as "through fire." But it is a blessed pain, in which the holy power of his love sears through us like a flame, enabling us to become totally ourselves and thus totally of God. . . .

In this way the interrelation between justice and grace also becomes clear: the way we live our lives is not immaterial, but our defilement does not stain us forever if we have at least continued to reach out towards Christ. . . . Indeed it has already been burned away through Christ's Passion. At the moment of judgment we experience and we absorb the overwhelming power of his love over all the evil in the world and in ourselves. The pain of love becomes our salvation and our joy.

**Sts. Marcellinus and Peter: Façade
(Girolamo Theodoli, 1751)**

I N A CITY OF LONGITUDINAL basilicas, the Greek cross plan of the Basilica of Sts. Marcellinus and Peter gives the church a distinctive character—appropriate enough, given the unlikely pair of martyr-companions honored here: Peter, a third-century exorcist whose rough personality was forged in combat with demons, and the Roman presbyter Marcellinus, who quietly assisted the pugnacious exorcist's work. Arrested under Diocletian, the two were martyred and buried in a dark forest outside Rome, where, officials hoped, their remains would not be discovered and venerated. Legend has it that their bodies glowed with such brilliance that the relics were quickly found and brought to the catacomb called the *ad duas lauros* on the Via Labicana, which bears their names today.

The basilica's strikingly modern design belies its ancient origins. Eighteenth-century excavations beneath the church found a tiny *confessio*. One fragmented inscription indicated that the church was founded by Pope St. Siricius (384–398) on the martyrs' feast day. Other inscriptions record donations and works during the eighth-century pontificate of Gregory III and under Alexander IV in the mid-thirteenth century.

The church was completely rebuilt in 1750 by Pope Benedict XIV, born Prospero Lambertini, whose unusual personality is reflected in the innovative design. Trained as a Church historian, Lambertini nurtured a love of the sciences and endowed chairs in chemistry and mathematics. As pope, he condemned several Enlightenment treatises; yet he was admired by Voltaire and many Protestant intellectuals. Thus it should come as no surprise that the pontiff who completed the Trevi fountain, rebuilt the façades of St. Mary Major and Holy Cross, and prepared the city to face the modern era should build such a distinctively modern church.

Benedict's architect was the Roman marquis Girolamo Theodoli, who, like Thomas Jefferson, was an academic and statesman with a deep interest in the architectural arts. Although the restrained spiral of the dome bears a faint echo of the Baroque architect Borromini, Theodoli's understated façade heralds the new tastes of the neoclassical era. The interior space is tightly contained by shallow side altars, which focus attention on the great loop of the apse. The altarpieces all reflect modern sensibilities. Gaetano Lapis, one of the busiest of eighteenth-century artists, painted the *Martyrdom of Sts. Peter and Marcellinus* for the high altar, while Filippo Evangelisti's *St. Gregory Frees a Soul from Purgatory* recounts a 1,500-year-old miracle on a 1750 canvas. The vault frescoes in the Chapel of Our Lady of Lourdes date from 1903.

These modern surfaces honor ancient witness: the relics of St. Marzia, another Diocletian-era martyr, repose under the main altar, along with other relics brought here from the catacombs. During the station Mass, golden reliquaries of the basilica's saints crowd the altar. [E.L.]

St. Mark: Apse mosaic (ninth century)

The
THIRD WEEK
of LENT

St. Lawrence Outside the Walls: High altar, *baldacchino*, and *confessio*

THE THIRD
SUNDAY IN LENT

Station at St. Lawrence Outside the Walls

Holy Mass

[A]	[B]	[C]
Exodus 17.3–7	*Exodus 20.1–7*	*Exodus 3.1–8a, 13–15*
Psalm 95	*Psalm 19*	*Psalm 103*
Romans 5.1–2, 5–8	*1 Corinthians 1.22–25*	*1 Corinthians 10.1–6, 10–12*
John 4.5–42	*John 2.13–25*	*Luke 13.1–19*

Office of Readings

Exodus 22.20–23.9

St. Augustine: Tractate 15 on John

T HE CHURCH BEGINS THE second phase of Lent—an extended meditation on Baptism—with one of the key gospel passages that were taught to the catechumens of the early Church as they prepared to receive the sacraments of initiation at the Easter Vigil: Baptism, Confirmation, and the Eucharist. Today's story of Jesus and the Samaritan woman, the longest dialogue in the four gospels, is such an important moment in the Forty Days that, although other gospel passages are appointed for this Sunday in years B and C of the Lectionary cycle, the Church asks that, in those years, this Gospel of "living water" be read on one weekday of the following week. Those who will be called to renew their baptismal promises at the Easter Vigil, as well as those being baptized or received into the full communion of the Catholic Church, are being addressed by the Lord in a special way today through his dialogue with the foreigner from whom he asks a drink of water: a conversation that teaches the entire Church something very important about prayer.

As the Old Testament readings in the Mass and the Liturgy of the Hours have reminded Lenten pilgrims for the past two and a half weeks, biblical religion is not the story of our search for God, although that instinct for communion with the Creator is built into the human heart. Rather, biblical religion is about God's coming into history in search of us, and our learning to take the path into the future that God is taking. If that is the truth of the entire Bible, then it should tell us something about prayer, our dialogue with the Lord. So the *Catechism of the Catholic Church* begins its discussion of prayer by pondering this gospel story of Jesus and the woman at the well, noting that the story begins with the divine thirst *for us*:

> "If you knew the gift of God!" [John 4.10]. The wonder of prayer is revealed at the well where we come seeking water: there, Christ comes to meet every human being. It is he who first seeks us and asks us for a drink. Jesus thirsts; his asking arises from the depths of God's desire for us. Whether we realize it or not, prayer is the encounter of God's thirst with ours. God thirsts that we may thirst for him.
>
> "You would have asked him, and he would have given you living water" [John 4.10]. Paradoxically, our prayer of petition is a response to the plea of the living God: "They have forsaken me, the fountain of living waters, and hewn out cisterns for themselves, broken cisterns that can hold no water!" [Jeremiah 2.13]. Prayer is the response of faith to the free promise of salvation and also a response of love to the thirst of the only Son of God.

The *Catechism* continues by noting that, while the Bible sometimes speaks of our soul or spirit as the source of prayer, it speaks of prayer arising from the *heart* more than a thousand times. What is this "heart"? In biblical terms, it is not the organ that circulates blood. It is *me*; it is that center of who-I-am that cannot be understood in merely rational categories; it is that place whose mysteries can only be fathomed by God himself. Or, as the *Catechism* puts it, "it is the place of truth, where we choose life or death. It is the place of encounter, because as image of God we live in relation: it is the place of covenant." The refrain to the American spiritual "Jesus Met the Woman at the Well" stresses that "he told her everything she'd ever done." From a deeper evangelical perspective, however, the key to this episode is not so much that Jesus unveiled the secrets of this woman's past life, but that his thirst for her faith initiated a genuine conversation, a dialogue—a prayer, if in a surprising form.

Prayer is a gift from God. In the first phase of the Lenten itinerary of conversion, pilgrims are reminded that the disciples had to ask Jesus how to pray. Now, on this Third Sunday in Lent, the Church reminds her sons and daughters that prayer is more than a matter of method. Prayer is a gift from God and has to be freely received as such. We long to pray, because the desire for communion with the Holy One is hard-wired into our "hearts"; we *can* pray because the Spirit is praying within us, enabling our prayer. Thus the *Catechism* concludes its introductory discussion of Christian prayer on a Trinitarian note:

> In the New Covenant, prayer is the living relationship of the children of God with their Father who is good beyond measure, with his Son Jesus Christ and with the Holy Spirit. The grace of the Kingdom is "the union of the entire holy and royal Trinity . . . with the whole human spirit" [St. Gregory Nazianzen]. Thus the life of prayer is the habit of being in the presence of the thrice-holy God and in communion with him. This communion of life is always possible because, through Baptism, we have already been united with Christ. Prayer is *Christian* insofar as it is communion with Christ and extends throughout the Church, which is his Body. Its dimensions are those of Christ's love.

Today's *statio*, St. Lawrence Outside the Walls, is the second Lenten station dedicated to the great deacon-martyr and patron of Rome. One of

St. Lawrence's seventeenth-century namesakes, the Carmelite mystic known as Brother Lawrence, provided another insight into the nature of prayer when he wrote that prayer is "practicing the presence of God." In prayer, Christians respond to God's thirst for us by opening our hearts and minds to God, thereby entering his sanctifying presence. In the Catholic tradition, active prayer—"saying our prayers," as it's often put—is just the beginning of prayer, something analogous to the Samaritan woman's dialogue with Jesus. The highest form of personal prayer is contemplative prayer: prayer in silence, prayer as "practicing the presence." This form of prayer is not for gifted mystics only; it's a way of praying available to all, if space is cleared in our lives for it.

Catholics who have rediscovered Eucharistic adoration are practicing a form of contemplative prayer, the beauty and simplicity of which are captured in a story about St. John Vianney, patron saint of parish priests. The Curé of Ars noticed that an elderly peasant in his parish spent hours before the Blessed Sacrament. Unable to restrain his curiosity one day, John Vianney approached the old man as he was leaving church after a lengthy spell in front of the tabernacle. "What are you doing?" the curé asked his parishioner. "I look at him and he looks at me," came the reply.

That is the essence of contemplative prayer and it is available to everyone. More than fourteen centuries before John Vianney, St. Ambrose, unpacking Jesus's command to "go to your room and pray" [Matthew 6.6], explained why: "By 'room,' you must understand, not a room enclosed by walls . . . but the room that is within you, the room where you hide your thoughts, where you keep your affections. This room of prayer is always with you, wherever you are, and it is always a secret room, where only God can see you."

God thirsts for us always. Pilgrims can meet God anywhere, at any time.

St. Lawrence Outside the Walls:
Capital detail

ST. LAWRENCE OUTSIDE THE WALLS is the greatest of Rome's Laurentian churches.

After Lawrence's martyrdom in 258, the Roman deacon's remains were collected by St. Cyriaca and brought to her family land on the *Ager Veranus*, from which an adjoining cemetery, Campo Verano, takes its name. As Lawrence's simple tomb drew huge numbers of pilgrims, Constantine built a small oratory for the martyr-deacon and a large, covered cemetery around the tomb so that people might be buried near one of Rome's favorite saints.

The basilica's simple porch, supported by six Ionic columns and decorated with thirteenth-century frescos of the lives of Sts. Lawrence and Stephen, shelters ancient and modern witnesses to the church's history and importance. *Putti* frolic on a sarcophagus used for Pope Damasus II in 1048, while the tomb of Alcide de Gasperi, a post–World War II leader of Italy's Christian Democratic Party, testifies to contemporary devotion to St. Lawrence.

Across the threshold, the basilica narrows dramatically into a long, slender nave. The double arcade extending along the sides closely envelops the space, which is the same length as the nave of St. Mary Major. This curious interior was born from a distinctive history: two basilicas, six hundred years apart, fused into one.

Although Constantine's cemetery had been augmented by chapels and a portico that covered pilgrims all the way from the Tiburtine Gate, damp conditions and damage led Pope Pelagius (579–590) to build a new church flanking the older building: facing the opposite direction, it was praised for its spaciousness and luminosity. Pelagius also transferred the relics of St. Stephen the Protomartyr, who shares Lawrence's sarcophagus, to his church. A set of walls grew up around the basilica and the buildings huddled by it; this improvised medieval village was named Laurentipolis.

In 1220, Pope Honorius III demolished the apse of Pelagius's church and added a new basilica to its length, so that the sixth-century church became the new structure's chancel. A notable artistic family, the Vassalletti (also responsible for the cloisters of St Paul's Outside the Walls), did the opulent stonework, its colorful inlay carpeting the floor with intricate patterns that extend into the pulpits, ambos, paschal candlestick, and *cathedra*.

Illumination from the fretwork windows makes the church glow rather than shine, as light plays elusively in the upper gallery. Honorius's nave culminates in Pelagius's basilica, where the presbytery rises up a series of steps. The older structure is slightly angled to the nave, but the splendid decoration distracts from the asymmetry.

The columns, taken from an earlier pagan structure, boast beautiful carved capitals. The mosaic spanning the former apse of Pelagius's church shows Christ with Sts. Peter, Paul, Lawrence, Stephen, and Hippolytus as well as Pope Pelagius (presented to the sacred conversation by Lawrence).

Golden light draws the eye down to the *confessio*, where marble sheathes the walls of a chapel containing the relics of Sts. Stephen and Lawrence. Just beyond is the tomb of Blessed Pius IX, the longest-serving pope in recorded history, who rests beneath the altar in a glittering chapel decorated with the mosaic coats of arms of religious orders, cathedral chapters, and dioceses: a quiet place of repose for the pontiff whose body anticlerical Romans once tried to throw into the Tiber. [E.L.]

St. Mark: Stational Mass

MONDAY OF THE THIRD WEEK OF LENT

Station at St. Mark

Holy Mass
2 Kings 5.1–15b
Psalm 42.2–3; 43.3–4
Luke 4.24–30

Office of Readings
Exodus 24.1–18
St. Basil the Great: On Humility

THROUGHOUT THE NEXT THREE weeks of Lent, Christians already baptized are invited to join in the intensified preparation for Baptism of "the elect," the Church's catechumens. If the entire Forty Days are an "annual catechumenate" for those who are already members of the Body of Christ, the days between the Third Sunday of Lent and Saturday of the Fifth Week of Lent ask Lenten pilgrims to "put on Christ" in a deeper, more thorough way. Today's readings at Mass and in the Liturgy of the Hours offer numerous reminders that the imitation of Christ is, most fundamentally, a matter of self-abandonment to divine providence—that is, of imitating the profound humility of the Son before the will of the Father.

The first of today's lessons in this school of humility is taught by one of the foremost Eastern Doctors of the Church, St. Basil the Great. In the Office of Readings, Basil reflects on the question of human greatness: In what does this consist? "Here is man's greatness," Basil writes. "Here is man's glory and majesty: to know in truth what is great, to hold fast to it, and to seek glory from the Lord of glory." For, as St. Paul taught the Church, "Let him who boasts, boast in the Lord" [1 Corinthians 1.31]. This is, clearly, a special kind of pride; Basil defines it in challenging terms that anticipate one of the key themes in Reformation theology: "Boasting of God is perfect and complete when we take no pride in our own righteousness but acknowledge that we are utterly lacking in true righteousness and have been made righteous only by faith in Christ."

Yesterday's gospel reading of Jesus and the Samaritan woman will resonate throughout the Third Week of Lent, beginning today. If true prayer begins with God's thirst for us—if prayer is a gift to be received before it is a practice to be perfected—then pride is a major obstacle to growth in the life of prayer. Pride, the *Catechism of the Catholic Church* teaches, is a form of competition with God. And it is difficult, if not impossible, to sense God's thirst for us when we are self-absorbed or when we cling to our autonomy (to use the vocabulary of postmodernity). The autonomous, self-absorbed self is not receptive; the autonomous, self-absorbed self cannot recognize gifts when they are offered, because it cannot acknowledge its need to be given utterly gratuitous and unmerited graces. The autonomous, self-absorbed self is competing with God.

Pride in this form is not, the gospels remind us, a problem for heathens and pagans only. In the familiar parable of the Pharisee and the publican (with which the Church will complete this Third Week of Lent on Saturday), the Pharisee is certainly a believer; but he is a believer comfortable with his own righteousness, which he identifies with his indisputably good works. Believers are as vulnerable to the temptation to compete with God as nonbelievers—a point further emphasized in today's liturgy by the Old Testament reading at Mass, the story of the Syrian leper Naaman and his cure by the prophet Elisha.

Naaman is, in principle, prepared to believe that there is a God in Israel: he takes his servant-girl's advice that he seek out the prophet Elisha; he secures his king's cooperation in the project; he undertakes a not-insignificant journey in search of healing; he is willing to offer compensation for what he is given. But when Elisha wounds his national vanity by instructing him to bathe seven times in the Jordan, Naaman balks: Why should he, commander of armies that are superior to Israel's, bathe in an Israelite river? Aren't the great rivers of Aram (today's Syria) mightier than this piddling Israelite stream? It takes another intervention from Naaman's servants to convince him to obey Elisha's instructions. And when, after bathing in the Jordan, he is healed, Naaman has the humility to recognize that his pride might have been an obstacle to the cure he so desperately sought. Out of that humility—that confession that he is not an autonomous self—he can say, "Behold, I know that there is no God in all the earth but in Israel."

The story of Naaman, the man from the East whose healing is recounted in the *statio* dedicated to the evangelist whom tradition holds to have been the first patriarch of the great Eastern see of Alexandria, teaches a baptismal lesson for Lenten pilgrims today: we, too, must return to our Jordan, the Jordan of our baptism, in order to know the living God. By imaginatively reentering the catechumenate, by reaffirming our baptismal promises at the Easter Vigil, and by being blessed with the same waters of regeneration in which the elect are baptized, we, too, can be healed of the various leprous scabs that distort out own lives and, as in the days of Naaman, strain our capacity for fellowship with others.

The gospel reading of the day, in which St. Luke recounts the rejection of Jesus by his fellow-townsmen, speaks of another form of pride and a different type of competition with God: the temptation to get ourselves the kind of redeemer we would like, rather than receiving gratefully the kind of redeemer God has appointed.

As Luke renders the scene, it is precisely their familiarity with Jesus that is an obstacle keeping his fellow-townsmen from receiving him as the gift from God that he is. Just prior to the passage read today, Jesus goes to the synagogue of Nazareth, takes the scroll of the prophet Isaiah, and reads aloud the messianic proclamation: "The Spirit of the Lord is upon me, because he has anointed me . . . to proclaim the acceptable year of the Lord"; he then tells those with whom he had grown up, "Today this scripture has been fulfilled in your hearing." The Nazarenes' first reaction is a positive one: "All spoke well of him, and wondered at the gracious words that proceeded from his mouth." Then pride asserts itself: "Is not this Joseph's son?" How could one who grew up among us be God's anointed? A mere carpenter? Please. We had something else in mind. So they try to throw him from the brow of the hill on which Nazareth was built, "but passing through the midst of them he went away" [Luke 4.18a, 21, 22, 30].

Like men and women throughout human history, the Nazarenes are far more comfortable with the kind of God, the kind of redeemer, they can imagine—or fashion—for themselves. (A prototype of this temptation will be on display tomorrow in the Office of Readings, in the story of the Israelites and the golden calf in the Book of Exodus.) The imitation of Christ to which this phase of the itinerary of conversion calls us requires stripping ourselves of the pride that imagines that we have a better idea of what a redeemer would look like than God does. That lesson will continue to be driven home as the pilgrimage of Lent leads up to Jerusalem and, inexorably, to the Cross.

St. Mark: *Adoration of the Shepherds*
(eighteenth century)

O N THE CAPITOLINE, the steepest of Rome's seven hills, the earliest Romans built an imposing temple to Jupiter Optimus Maximus, the greatest of their gods. Other sacred sites sprang up around it, and by the first century B.C., the Capitoline was filled with manifestations of Roman polytheism. Yet, according to ancient tradition, St. Mark began work on his gospel, while living in Rome as an aide to St. Peter, at the marshy base of this lofty hill. In a hovel dwarfed by grandiose pagan temples Mark wrote the succinct, sixteen-chapter account of the events that would eventually sweep away the ancient divinities. And in 336, during the reign of Constantine, Pope St. Mark built a church to his namesake on this site.

As the low-lying area was subject to flooding, the Basilica of St. Mark required several restorations. The first church was replaced in the ninth century by Pope Gregory IV, who raised the basilica to its present level and turned it 180 degrees, to face the Capitoline. The apse mosaic, with its luminous jewel tones and regal assembly, is the most striking remnant of this period. Standing at the center on a platform bearing the symbols Alpha and Omega, Christ, in purple and gold, holds an open book reading, "I am the Resurrection." Pope St. Mark, in ruby red, stands next to the Lord, with Sts. Agapitus and Agnes; on the left, St. Felicissimus (who was martyred with Agapitus) stands next to St. Mark the Evangelist, who in turn presents his friend, the still-living Gregory IV.

Gregory IV also brought the relics of the Persian martyrs Abdon and Sennen to the basilica and built an annular crypt, still accessible, where pilgrims could venerate their remains. Above them, in the high altar, Pope St. Mark reposes in an urn of imperial porphyry.

St. Mark the Evangelist's relics are reportedly kept in Venice; two Venetian merchants are famously said to have smuggled the body out of Alexandria (covered in pork to thwart Muslim inspectors), bringing it to the "Queen of the Adriatic." The Roman basilica honoring the second evangelist has enjoyed a long connection to the capital of the Veneto, as Cardinal Pietro Barbo, the cardinal-titular who became Pope Paul II in 1464, lived here as both cardinal and pontiff and gave the basilica to the Venetians as their national church in Rome.

Paul II commissioned the elegant portico. Designed by Leon Battista Alberti and shaped like a triumphal arch, it looks across the piazza toward the few extant ruins of Jupiter's temple. Paul II also gave the basilica the portal sculpture by Isaia da Pisa, although the two lions (the symbol of St. Mark) that flank the door are medieval. An odd marble basin sits on the right; once used as a holy-water font, it bears a medieval inscription anathematizing anyone who sold water drawn from it. The dignified wooden coffers of the interior Renaissance ceiling, the oldest in Rome, are another gift of Paul II.

The baroque paintings and stucco reliefs in the nave date from a major eighteenth-century restoration. Neoclassicism was kind to the church, as Antonio Canova produced the funerary monument to Leonardo Pesaro at the height of his fame. In the early twentieth century, St. Mark's was challenged by fascism: Benito Mussolini lived in the Palazzo Venezia next door and planted trees in front of the basilica to hide it from view. [E.L.]

St. Pudenziana: Stational Mass

TUESDAY OF THE THIRD WEEK OF LENT

Station at St. Pudenziana

Holy Mass

Daniel 3.25, 34–43

Psalm 25

Matthew 18.21–35

Office of Readings

Exodus 32.1–20

St. Peter Chrysologus: Sermon 43

THE IMITATION OF CHRIST to which this second phase of the itinerary of conversion calls Lenten pilgrims demands more than strict justice: that message is crisply conveyed by today's gospel reading. Peter asks the Lord how many times he must forgive his erring brother; Jesus answers, in effect, "As often as forgiveness is sought; as often as forgiveness is required; as often as forgiveness is necessary." The brethren of the Lord are to conform themselves to the superabundance of mercy manifest in the world through the Son, who reveals the Father of mercies.

Revisiting the theme of the divine mercy is especially appropriate at this *statio*, which tradition identifies as the site where Peter lived during his time in Rome: Peter, who was always getting things wrong and having to ask the Lord's forgiveness; Peter, who was called to a greater abandonment of self in the service of the brethren; Peter, whom we can imagine imitating his Lord's words of forgiveness from the cross, as he himself was crucified upside down in Nero's Circus for the amusement of the Roman mob. In the station at St. Pudenziana, whom tradition holds to have been the daughter of Peter's Roman host, we are close to the foundations of the Church of Rome—and to the Gospel imperative of mercy.

Peter's example reminds the Lenten pilgrim that mercy and contrition go together. So does the first reading of today's Mass, in which Azariah, one of the Israelite exiles in Babylon cast into the fiery furnace for refusing to worship a golden idol, prays in mourning, not over his own fate, but over his people's: "For we, O Lord, have become fewer than any nation, and are brought low this day in all the world because of our sins. And at this time there is no prince, or prophet, or leader, no burnt offering, or sacrifice, or oblation, or incense, no place to make an offering before thee or to find mercy." Yet mercy will be found, Azariah proclaims, because Israel will come before God with the highest form of sacrifice: "With a contrite heart and a humble spirit may we be accepted, as though it were with burnt offerings or rams and bulls, and with tens of thousands of fat lambs. . . . And now with all our heart we follow thee, we fear thee and seek thy face." Mercy, sought, is obtained: Azariah and his companions, Hananiah and Mishael, are miraculously saved from the flames, and the tyrant Nebuchadnezzar is compelled to acknowledge that "there is no other god who is able to deliver in this way."

In today's Office of Readings, St. Peter Chrysologus further deepens the Church's Lenten reflection on the divine mercy by linking it to fasting and prayer, the two other traditional disciplines of the Forty Days. "Fasting," the fifth-century bishop of Ravenna and Doctor of the Church wrote, "is the soul of prayer, mercy is the lifeblood of fasting. Let no one try to separate them; they cannot be separated. If you have only one of them or not all together, you have nothing. So if you pray, fast; if you fast, show mercy; if you want your petition to be heard, hear the petition of others. If you do not close your ear to others, you open God's ear to yourself." Fifteen hundred years before the Lenten fast became transformed, in some minds, into a weight-loss program, Peter Chrysologus was counseling his people against any such confusions, which mistake righteousness-through-works for true conversion: "Fasting bears no fruit unless it is watered by mercy. Fasting dries up when mercy dries up. Mercy is to fasting as rain is to the earth. However much you may cultivate your heart, clear the soil of your nature, root out vices, sow virtues, if you do not release the springs of mercy, your fasting will bear no fruit." In sum: "Prayer knocks at the door, fasting obtains, mercy receives."

This strong emphasis on the imperative of mercy suggests that a Christian society and culture will have distinctive characteristics that exceed the moral norm of justice. The different forms of justice—legal justice, or sound constitutional and legal definitions of civic obligations; commutative justice, which honors obligations to others; distributive justice, which requires that the civil community abandon no one to destitution—can be known by reason. A Christian culture and society will be more than just; thanks to the effects of supernatural grace, it will be merciful. Indeed, contemporary scholars of religious history argue that, from a purely sociological point of view, what gave early Christianity its comparative advantage in the late classical world was its ability to create a counterculture of compassion and mutual support in a brutal social environment. Thus, from the outset, Christianity was not only culture-forming: Christianity was a culture-in-itself, a culture that had the power to reform other cultures and to create more humane ways of living. At the root of that form of Christian power is the divine mercy, embodied in the lives of Christians who take today's gospel injunction to heart: the Father will not forgive, "if you do not forgive your brother from your heart."

Blessed John Paul II's encyclical *Dives in Misericordia* [Rich in Mercy] is another fruitful source of reflection on the imitation of Christ through living out his commandment to be merciful. Published in November 1980, *Dives in Misericordia* was the second panel in John Paul's Trinitarian triptych of encyclicals that began with his inaugural encyclical on Christian humanism, *Redemptor Hominis* [The Redeemer of Man, 1979] and was completed by his reflection on the Holy Spirit, *Dominum et Vivificantem* [Lord and Giver of Life, 1986]. In *Dives in Misericordia*, the Pope was particularly interested in stressing the linkage between mercy and fatherhood: the kind of fatherhood exemplified by the merciful father of the prodigal son, whose ability to restore to his wayward child the squandered dignity of his sonship has already been a theme for Lenten reflection. In his commentary on this parable in the encyclical, John Paul insisted that true mercy does not weaken or humiliate those who receive it. Rather, true mercy strengthens the recipient by relieving a burden of guilt and by deepening a sense of one's capacity to live a righteous life: if I am worthy of forgiveness because I have had the humility to seek out mercy, then there must be more to me than the sum total of the dross in my soul.

Mercy is not only stronger than sin, though. At the dramatic climax of the Lenten journey, at Easter, mercy will be shown to be stronger than death itself. To be merciful along the lifetime pilgrimage of conversion, therefore, is to prepare oneself to be capable of receiving the divine mercy at the moment of death and judgment. Mercy prepares us for redemption, and for the Wedding Feast of the Lamb.

St. Pudenziana: Reliquary altar, *Delivery of the Keys* (Giacomo della Porta, 1596)

B Y EVOKING MEMORIES OF the earliest layers of Rome's Christian tradition, the Basilica of St. Pudenziana embodies three important themes: Peter's presence in Rome and his personal care of the Christian community; the universality of Christ's salvific sacrifice; and the cult of the martyrs.

According to an inscription, the basilica sits atop the house of Senator Pudens, "the first to give hospitality to St. Peter" (who is also thought to be the "Pudens" mentioned in 2 Timothy 4.21). Tradition has it that Peter began his evangelizing mission in Rome here, with the assistance of the senator's daughters, Praxedes and Pudenziana. Pudens's elaborate home and the neighboring Baths of Novatius were transformed by Pope St. Pius I in 145, when the bath complex was fused into a single worship space, the Oratory of the Holy Pastor.

In 384, Pope St. Siricius rededicated the oratory to St. Peter and rebuilt the church with the assistance of the presbyters Massimo, Leopardo, and Illicio (as recorded in a marble engraving made during their lifetimes). The orientation was shifted ninety degrees, granite columns from the old hall were used to line the nave, and the apse was placed into the curved exedra of the earlier building. To extend the structure into a Latin cross, the other curving side of the hall was demolished and the nave elongated.

The apse was then decorated with the city's oldest extant Christian mosaic—one of the first attempts to render artistically the glory and mystery of the Incarnation: Christ, framed by a cityscape, appears enthroned under a jeweled cross, and is flanked by seated apostles. Above him float the four evangelists, who appear for the first time as a winged man (Matthew), a winged lion (Mark), a winged ox (Luke), and an eagle (John). The apostles sit within the enclosure of the exedra (although two are missing because of the resizing necessary to construct the dome overhead). Sts. Peter and Paul sit closest to Christ, Paul in the robe of a Roman senator and Peter in the philosopher's *chiton*. Two women lift wreaths over their heads; often described as Praxedes and Pudenziana, the two women more likely represent the Church of the Gentiles and the Church of the Jews—a theme repeated in the basilicas of St. Sabina and St. Mary Major.

Several chapels are tucked away behind the apse in the remains of the bath complex's ambulatory. The first, on the left, is ancient and has always been dedicated to St. Peter. The marble sculpture of the delivery of the keys is by G. B. della Porta from 1596, but faint traces of fresco remain from the time of the church's construction. The altar contains fragments of wood said to be from the table where St. Peter first celebrated the Eucharist in Rome.

The original Oratory of the Holy Pastor was rebuilt by Pope St. Gregory VII (1073–1085) into what may have been the baptistery; an inscription on the right wall dates from that era and lists the relics contained in the church. In 1588, Cardinal Enrico Caetani rebuilt another chapel into a fine example of Counter-Reformation art, its inlaid marble and mosaics providing a splendid cornice for the altar. [E.L.]

St. Sixtus: High altar and apse

WEDNESDAY OF THE THIRD WEEK OF LENT

Station at St. Sixtus

Holy Mass

Deuteronomy 4.1, 5–9

Psalm 147

Matthew 5.17–19

Office of Readings

Exodus 33.7–11, 18–23; 34.5–9, 29–35

St. Theophilus of Antioch: To Autolycus

THE BIBLICAL TEXTS PRESCRIBED for Holy Mass and the Liturgy of the Hours yesterday and today are closely linked thematically: they deepen the Church's Lenten reflection on the intertwined relationships among law, worship, and way-of-life under the Mosaic covenant. These truths, which God taught the people of Israel at Sinai, remain true under the New Covenant, as Jesus emphasizes in the gospel reading appointed for this midpoint of the Third Week of Lent.

God intended Israel's experience at Sinai to be one of purification and conversion, aimed at forging a new kind of human community: an elect people who live in covenant relationship with the one, true God, so that they might be a light to the nations. The Sinai experience was one in which those who had acquired the community-dissipating habits of slaves during their long captivity in Egypt were given the materials and precepts by which they were to be formed into a true community, a people God would call his own. As Cardinal Joseph Ratzinger put it in *The Spirit of the Liturgy*, "on Sinai, the people receive not only instructions about worship, but an all-embracing rule of law and life. Only thus can it become a people. A people without a common rule of law cannot live. It destroys itself in anarchy, which is a parody of freedom, its exaltation to the point of abolition. When every man lives without law, every man lives without freedom."

The struggle to live this comprehensive way of life, first proclaimed at Sinai, provides the dramatic context for virtually the entire history of Israel, for from the outset these former slaves had a hard time accepting the character of the God who had liberated them. Forging the golden calf—an early and in many ways paradigmatic failure—was not a matter of abandoning the God of Abraham, Isaac, and Jacob, the God of the Passover; the people do not take up the worship of other gods. But they do try to fashion for themselves an object of worship of their own design, a deity they can control. As Ratzinger wrote, "The people cannot cope with the invisible, remote, and mysterious God. They want to bring him down into their own world, into what they can see and understand." This leads, immediately, to a distortion of worship, in the revelry around the golden calf: "Worship is no longer going up to God, but drawing God down into one's own world. . . . [Thus] worship becomes a feast that the community gives itself, a festival of self-worship. Instead of being worship of God, it becomes a circle closed in on itself . . . a kind of banal self-gratification."

Even Moses, in today's Liturgy of the Hours, must struggle with this unexpected kind of God. As the passage from Exodus in the Office of Readings for today explains, "the LORD used to speak to Moses face to face, as a man speaks to his friend." But this, it seems, was not enough. Having spoken to God, Moses longed for more: "I pray thee, show me thy glory." But this cannot be: "I will make my goodness pass before you and will proclaim before you my name . . . and while my glory passes by I will put you in a cleft of the rock, and I will cover you with my hand until I have passed by; then I will take away my hand and you shall see my back." In this world, the glory of the Lord can only be seen by discerning with the eyes of faith what God has done in history—by seeing God's "back" (or perhaps the divine footprints) after God has blazed the trail that his people are to follow.

Then there is the law. Like human beings throughout the ages, Israel confuses freedom with license. Israel imagines that the freedom for which it has yearned during its Egyptian captivity is a matter of doing whatever one likes. But that is an immature and ultimately inhuman kind of freedom, for freedom-as-willfulness can neither satisfy the hungers of the human heart nor build true human community. The freedom God offers in the covenant, whose fundamental moral tenets are expressed in the Ten Commandments, is a different kind of freedom. The Dominican theologian Servais Pinckaers called it *freedom for excellence*: the freedom to choose, freely, the things that are truly good and that make for genuine human flourishing. Genuine freedom consists in developing the moral habit—the virtue—of making good decisions. And the template for those decisions (and for the moral life) can be found in the Commandments. Here, God offers Israel—and through Israel, all the nations of the world—the gift of liberating obedience.

Blessed John Paul II spoke of this surprising, challenging gift at Mt. Sinai in 2000:

> The Ten Commandments are not an arbitrary imposition of a tyrannical Lord. They were written in stone; but before that, they were written on the human heart as the universal moral law, valid in every time and place. . . . They point out all the false gods that draw [humanity] into slavery: the love of self to the exclusion of God, the greed for power and pleasure that overturns the order of justice and degrades our human dignity and that of our neighbor. If we turn from these false idols and follow the God who sets his people free and remains always with them, then we shall emerge, like Moses, after forty days on the mountain . . . ablaze with the light of God.

That the sons and daughters of the New Covenant are to be formed into a true people through this gift of liberating obedience is underscored in today's gospel reading: "Think not," Jesus says, "that I have come to abolish the law and the prophets; I have come not to abolish them but to fulfill them." That fulfillment will take the form of perfect obedience, for the perfect obedience of the Son to the Father is the most radical and complete fulfillment of the law, as it is the vindication of the prophets. This perfect obedience will lead Jesus, and his Church, into another mystery: the mystery of liberating suffering. On the Cross, Jesus fulfills the will of the Father in perfect obedience. In the grace poured out from the Cross of Christ, the Lord makes it possible for us to live the mysteries of liberating obedience and liberating suffering (as did the patron of today's station, Pope St. Sixtus II, martyred in 258 during the Valerian persecution). For, as St. Paul wrote, it was for our sake that Christ "became obedient unto death, even death on a cross" [Philippians 2.8].

The Lenten pilgrimage, which inexorably leads to Calvary, is thus a preparation for a lifelong journey on an itinerary of conversion in which we not infrequently encounter our inability to act on our best intentions. The frustrations of spiritual and moral failure can, and must, be brought to the Cross. "For our sake," Christ became "obedient unto death." For our sake, the Lord invites us to bring our incapacities to the Cross, and to lay them on him. In the Paschal Mystery of the Cross and Resurrection, the victory has already been won, in him. It remains to be won in us. The grace of the Cross, and the willingness of the Son of God to take upon himself the sins of the world, offers a vision of final victory for his companions, whose imperfect obedience is transformed by the grace of his perfect obedience—vindicated by the Father on Easter morning.

St. Sixtus: Memorial inscription and image of Pope St. Sixtus II

THE BASILICA OF ST. SIXTUS is located near the Porta Capena, the gate in the Severan walls leading to the Via Appia where, in 258 A.D., Roman soldiers killed Pope Sixtus II and six of his deacons while they were celebrating Mass in the catacombs. Four centuries later, Sixtus's relics were taken from the catacombs and brought here, along with those of other popes and martyrs.

The first church on the site dates from the pontificate of St. Anastasius I (399–401) and was known as the *Titulus Crescentiana*. At the dawn of the seventh century, Gregory the Great conferred the martyr-pope's name on the church. The entire complex rests upon the remains of a third-century Roman building; the cloister contains a dainty mosaic from that era.

Anastasius's church was typically paleo-Christian—a large nave and two side aisles, an apse illuminated by three large windows, an external porch attached to a courtyard; here, catechumens received their final instructions before walking to St. John Lateran for Baptism. When the Iconoclast Controversy rocked Eastern Christianity in the eighth century, the church offered shelter to exiled Greek monks, who settled here in the Convent of St. Mary *in Templo*.

Pope Innocent III rebuilt the basilica during his reform of women's religious orders. There were few religious sisters in medieval Rome, and no organized convents or rules; the Basilica of St. Sixtus became home to sixty of these women in a monumental new structure. As the church was subject to floods, the floor was raised ten feet and the side aisles were closed off, creating a single nave. Left incomplete at Innocent's death in 1216, the project was continued by the Order of Preachers, as Innocent's successor, Honorius III, entrusted the church to Dominic Guzman and his new community when they arrived in Rome. Construction accelerated, and a bell tower and cloister were added. Tradition ascribes a miracle to the site: A worker fell to his death during the building project, and St. Dominic restored him to life. The story was recorded in fresco by Paul Besson on the chapter house wall. When Dominic and his companions moved to St. Sabina on the Aventine, they left the convent in the hands of Dominican sisters, the first order of cloistered nuns.

To honor his namesake, Pope Sixtus IV restored the church for the Jubilee of 1475, although little remains of his work beyond an inscription over the door.

The church's antiquity is hard to discern today. Pope Benedict XIII, a Dominican, commissioned Filippo Raguzzini, Rococo architect extraordinaire, to renovate the church in the 1720s. The floors gleam with polished marble, and the bright interior radiates golden light. The delicate decoration of white stucco moldings on a yellow ground is interspersed with eighteenth-century images of Dominican saints. The decoration intensifies in the apse, with plaster effects and *putti* surrounding a medallion of the Trinity. The stained-glass window replicates the *Madonna of St. Sixtus*, a ninth-century Byzantine icon the Dominican sisters took to a new convent on Monte Mario when malaria broke out in the area.

Behind the glossy modern surface, traces of ancient history remain. Small lateral doors lead behind the new apse into Innocent III's church, where fresco fragments are visible: ghostly traces of New Testament stories and images of St. Dominic and St. Peter of Verona, painted less than a century after their deaths. [E.L.]

Sts. Cosmas and Damian: Stational Mass

THURSDAY OF THE THIRD WEEK OF LENT

Station at Sts. Cosmas and Damian

Holy Mass

Jeremiah 7.23–28

Psalm 95

Luke 11.14–23

Office of Readings

Exodus 34.10–28

Tertullian: On Prayer, 28–29

A S JESUS DRAWS CLOSER to Jerusalem and the destiny that awaits him there, resistance to his mission and his message will stiffen. So will the challenge to the imitation of Christ to which this phase of the Lenten pilgrimage is dedicated. This Thursday of the Third Week of Lent is the twentieth day of the forty. Half the journey has been completed; the pilgrim path will get rockier and steeper as the climax of the drama of redemption draws nearer—an apt preparation for the life of faith and the moment of death. Today's gospel reading identifies two of the major challenges that will recur time and again along the itinerary of conversion. Both call for intensified reflection during the second chronological portion of the path to Calvary.

The first challenge is similar to that posed this past Monday: the challenge to let God be God, which means to abandon the logic of the world and its power and thus be quit of our own notions of how-God-should-redeem-us. On Monday in the station at St. Mark (the *collecta* from which today's stational pilgrimage set out during the first millennium), the Nazarenes demanded a messiah more to their liking. In today's *statio* (dedicated to two more saints from the East, the martyred physicians Cosmas and Damian), stational pilgrims hear crowds demanding a miracle more to their taste than the exorcism that Jesus performs. God's project in history rarely follows the path we imagine it should take: that was the experience of Israel; that is the experience of the disciples as they follow Jesus up to Jerusalem; that will be the experience of disciples today as we ponder injustice, the deaths of innocents, unpunished cruelties, the unexpected ways in which prayers are or are not (according to our lights) answered. The path of salvation history, whether viewed in temporal macrocosm or in personal microcosm, is always a journey in learning to say, with the Lord, "Father, into thy hands I commit my spirit!" [Luke 23.46].

The second challenge posed by today's gospel reading is perhaps a distinctively modern one. In Jesus's debate with the crowd over his exorcism of the mute man, it's obvious to everyone involved that Satan is real; the question at issue is whether it is by Satan's power that Jesus drives out demons. Twenty-first-century listeners doubtless hear this text somewhat differently than Christians of the past. For many today, "Satan" is either what historian Jeffrey Burton Russell called "an ironic personification of the corruption and foolishness of humanity," or a kind of rhetorical intensifier: Hitler, Stalin, and other mass murders are often described as "satanic," but the reality of the Evil One is not easy for late-moderns or postmoderns to grasp.

Overcoming this skepticism about the reality of the Evil One is an important moment along the itinerary of conversion. The challenge is posed daily by the recitation of the Lord's Prayer. For as the *Catechism of the Catholic Church* teaches, the petition that we be delivered from evil is not generic, and it is most certainly not ironic: "In this petition, evil is not an abstraction, but refers to a person, Satan, the Evil One, the angel who opposes God. The devil (*dia-bolos*), is the one who 'throws himself across' God's plan and his work of salvation in

Christ." The *Catechism* also reminds Lenten pilgrims that our constant petition to be delivered from evil involves the world as well as our individual lives: "When we ask to be delivered from the Evil One, we pray as well to be freed from all evils, present, past, and future, on which he is the author or instigator. In this final petition, the Church brings before the Father all the distress of the world."

In working through the challenges to let God be God and (as it were) to let Satan be Satan, prayer is an indispensable aid and tool. Prayer is the fuel of the imitation of Christ; it is also a privilege conferred by Baptism, by which the Christian is empowered to offer true worship to God. There is, of course, an ordained ministry in the Church for the celebration of the sacraments, but the Church has also long taught that a priestly character is conferred upon every baptized person. That character enables us to receive the gift of prayer, and thus to pray. And prayer is more than speaking; prayer involves listening, too.

Thus the prophet Jeremiah, in the first reading of today's Mass, insists that hearing the voice of the Lord, rather than listening to our "own counsels," is essential to conversion, both personal and corporate. Hearing the voice of the Lord is a key to living as an elect human being, as someone in a covenant relationship with the one, true God; hearing the voice of the Lord is also what forms Israel (and, by extension, the Church) into a true People of God. The mere physical reality of "hearing" is not enough, though, as today's Responsorial Psalm and its antiphon remind us: "If today you hear his voice, harden not your hearts." "Hearing" ought to lead to conversion. "Hearing" ought to lead to a deeper imitation of Christ. The Church takes this injunction so seriously that the Liturgy of the Hours begins, each day, with Psalm 95: "O that today you would hearken to his voice! Harden not your hearts."

The second-century North African theologian and controversialist Tertullian offers a charming portrait of an entire creation at prayer in today's Office of Readings—an encouraging reminder that, when we pray, we do not pray alone: "All the angels pray. Every creature prays. Cattle and wild beasts pray and bend the knee. As they come from their barns and caves they look up to heaven and call out, lifting up their spirit in their own fashion. The birds too rise and lift themselves up to heaven: they open out their wings, instead of hands, in the form of a cross, and give voice to what seems to be a prayer."

The passage from Exodus that precedes Tertullian's reflection on prayer continues the instruction of the Israelites in what makes for righteous living as a covenanted people: instructions that bear as well on Lenten pilgrims. The injunction to keep, annually, the "feast of unleavened bread" is more than a divinely mandated national holiday: each year, Israel is to relive the Exodus experience of liberation through the celebration of Passover so as to deepen its understanding and appreciation of what true liberation means. The injunction to keep the Sabbath as a day of rest is also aimed at deepening the conversion of the people whom God is forming into his own: the God of liberation enjoins his people to do what the same God, as Creator, did on the seventh day—rest. From a Christian perspective, the sabbath rest is another means of preparing to be able to celebrate the Wedding Feast of the Lamb in the Kingdom come in its fullness. Through sabbath rest now, we are made, by grace, into the kind of people who can freely accept the gift of eternal rest that the Church begs for the deceased.

Keeping Sunday as something special, all day long, is a countercultural challenge in the twenty-first century. It is also an essential witness the Church gives to the world.

Sts. Cosmas and Damian:
Triumphal arch detail

ROME LOVES TWINS: it worshipped twin gods; it was founded by twin brothers; the seeds of its Christian rebirth were planted by twin martyrs. In the Basilica of Sts. Cosmas and Damian, the ancient Roman fascination with twinning was assimilated into the worship and art of Christian Rome.

The basilica was built along the Via Sacra, the principal street of ancient Rome and an avenue flanked by some of antiquity's most prestigious buildings, including the Temple to Peace and a medical library built by Vespasian. A Christian church on this site was a statement.

Slightly to the left of the Palatine Hill, in the heart of the Forum, stood one of Rome's oldest temples, dedicated in 484 B.C. to Castor and Pollux, twin deities who personified the pagan conviction that men could become gods. When the Ostrogoth king Theodoric gave the vestibule of the temple and one of its halls to Pope Felix IV in 526, Christian Rome dedicated the space to another set of twins: the brother-martyrs Cosmas and Damian, killed by Diocletian for refusing to believe in men-turned-gods while proclaiming their belief in God-made-man. A small, round, and dark vestibule led into a basilica flooded with light by clerestory windows, the contrast aptly expressing the enlightenment of Christian conversion. The relics of the two martyrs were kept in the altar that still stands in the old church's apse.

Owing to flooding, the church's floor had become a marsh by the seventeenth century. In 1632, Pope Urban VIII undertook a massive restoration that lifted the floor level twenty feet higher than the original. Side chapels and the elegant wooden roof, painted by Marco Tullio Montagna and depicting *Sts. Cosmas and Damian in Glory*, were added. The side chapels were decorated by major figures: Giovanni Baglione, archrival of Caravaggio, painted the Chapel of the Madonna; Il Spadarino did the remarkably modern-looking canvas of St. Anthony of Padua; and Cavaliere D'Arpino painted the delicate Chapel of St. Barbara.

The remarkable apse mosaic is the basilica's oldest extant decoration. Jesus glows in the center against a lapis night sky surrounded by stripes of red and blue that soon evolve into cherubim and seraphim. A phoenix, symbol of the Resurrection, is at Christ's right as he floats between heaven and earth. Peter and Paul, once imprisoned nearby, appear as heavenly senators in their Roman togas as they greet Cosmas and Damian, who are wearing the cloaks and tunics of travelers, symbolic of the origin of devotion to the physician-martyrs in the East. Pope Felix offers a model of the basilica, while St. Theodore offers his martyr's crown. This striking composition was the last great expression of artistic naturalism until the eleventh century: the grass and stones have volume; the feet of the saints cast shadows.

The exquisite inlaid wooden choir was given to the Franciscan Friars of the Third Order Regular, who have cared for the church since 1512, and is decorated with images of holy members of the Third Order, including St. Elizabeth of Hungary and St. Louis of France. [E.L.]

St. Lawrence in Lucina: Nave and high altar

FRIDAY OF THE THIRD WEEK OF LENT

Station at St. Lawrence in Lucina

Holy Mass

Hosea 14.2–10

Psalm 81

Mark 12.28–34

Office of Readings

Exodus 35.30–36.1; 37.1–9

St. Gregory the Great: Moral Reflections on Job, 13

THE CONFLICT BETWEEN JESUS and the religious leaders of his time continues to intensify as the Third Week of Lent draws to an end. In today's gospel reading, one of the Temple scribes gives Jesus an orthodoxy check, asking him to name the greatest of the Commandments. The answer given (love of God and love of neighbor) suffices to end that line of theological attack on the unexpected Galilean preacher and miracle-worker: "And after that, no one dared to ask him any questions." But the conflict will grow sharper in the weeks ahead. Understanding the background to these gospel texts, which means understanding the theological tensions within Judaism at the time, is crucial in grasping the originality and challenge of Jesus's person and message.

The religious life of the Sadducees was centered on the Temple and the Temple cult of sacrifice: the Temple, sheltering the Ark of the Covenant, was the place where God dwelt among his people, and where the chosen people could approach God through daily sacrifices and seasonal pilgrimages. In the early first century A.D., the Sadducees were the religious establishment, the "conservative" party within Judaism. The Pharisees, by contrast, were reformers. For them, the Law was God's greatest gift to his chosen people, and a painstaking observance of the Mosaic Law was the divinely appointed pathway by which to approach the God of Israel.

Jesus revered the Temple and, at certain points in the gospels, praises the Pharisees' devotion to the Law. Yet Jesus's understanding of his vocation posed a sharp challenge to both Sadducees and Pharisees—which is why they could temporarily overcome their opposition to each other in their opposition to his claims. The opposition to Jesus comes into focus when we grasp just how radical Jesus's claims were. As biblical scholar N. T. Wright explained in *The Challenge of Jesus* (occasionally using the tetragrammaton YHWH for the God of Israel), Jesus understood himself in these dramatic terms:

> Jesus . . . believed himself called [by God] to evoke the traditions which promised YHWH's return to Zion. [Thus] in Jesus himself . . . we see the biblical portrait of [Israel's God] come to life: the loving God, rolling up his sleeves [Isaiah 52.10] to do in person the job that no one else could do; the creator God, giving new life; the God who works *through* his created world, and supremely through his human creatures; the faithful God, dwelling in the midst of his people; the stern and tender God, relentlessly opposed to all that destroys or distorts the good creation, and especially human beings, but recklessly loving all those in need and distress. "He shall feed his flock like a shepherd; he shall carry the lambs in his arms, and gently lead those that are with young" [Isaiah 40.11]. It is the Old Testament portrait of YHWH; but it fits Jesus like a glove.

And how did Jesus "know" this of himself? N. T. Wright again:

> It was not a mathematical knowledge, like knowing that two and two make four. . . . It was more like the knowledge I have that I am loved by those

St. Mary in Trastevere: *The Enthroned Madonna Nursing the Child Jesus,*
Flanked by Ten Lamp-Bearing Women

St. Mary in Trastevere: *Jeremiah*

St. Mary in Trastevere: *The Life of the Virgin*

St. Vitalis: *Horsemen of the Apocalypse*

St. Lawrence Outside the Walls: Cosmatesque Floor

St. Lawrence Outside the Walls: Gallery

St. Mark: Interior

St. Sixtus:
Fresco Fragment

St. Sixtus:
Fresco Fragment

Sts. Cosmas and Damian: Apse Mosaic

closest to me; like the knowledge I have that sunrise over the sea is beautiful; like the knowledge of the musician not only of what the composer intended but of precisely how to perform the piece in exactly that way—a knowledge most securely possessed, of course, when the performer is also the composer. It was, in short, the knowledge that characterizes *vocation*. . . . [As] part of his human vocation, grasped in faith, sustained in prayer, tested in confrontation, agonized over in further prayer and doubt, and implemented in action, [Jesus] believed he had to do, and be, for Israel and the world, that which according to scripture only YHWH himself could do and be.

Writing on the New Testament Passion narratives in the second volume of *Jesus of Nazareth*, Joseph Ratzinger, Pope Benedict XVI, made a similar point through an analysis centered on the Ark of the Covenant, the building of which is described by the Book of Exodus in today's Office of Readings. Brought to Jerusalem by King David, the Ark was kept within the Holy of Holies of the Temple, the inner sanctum that the high priest could enter but once a year, on the Day of Atonement. Pope Benedict suggested that the Ark and its place in the ritual of the Day of Atonement could shed light on the question of who Jesus understood himself to be—and how the early Church came to understand this unexpected kind of messiah.

When St. Paul wrote to the Romans about the blood of Christ as an "expiation" for the sins of all [Romans 3.25], Benedict noted, the Apostle to the Gentiles used the Greek equivalent of a Hebrew word for "the covering of the Ark of the Covenant." This, the Pope continued, "is the place over which YHWH appears in a cloud, the place of the mysterious presence of God." And it is here that the blood of the sacrifice was sprinkled on Yom Kippur, the Day of Atonement, for the expiation of sins. Thus when St. Paul used the equivalent word to describe what has happened through the Cross of Christ, he was proposing that the God of Israel is present in Jesus in a new and radical way—and that Jesus understood himself to be the presence of the God of Israel among the people of Israel and in the world. As Pope Benedict wrote, "God and man, God and the world, touch one another in him."

In the Christian experience, neither Law nor Temple is the exclusive place of God's dwelling among his creatures. Law and Temple have both been fulfilled and completed in God's final revelation of himself, through his Son. Jesus, the new Ark of the New Covenant, holds within himself all that is precious of the Law ("Think not that I have come to abolish the law and the prophets; I have come not to abolish them but to fulfill them" [Matthew 5.17]), and all that was worthy in the Temple's cult of sacrifice (its recognition of humanity's dependence on the divine mercy for the forgiveness of sins). The blood of the New Covenant, "which is poured out for many for the forgiveness of sins" [Matthew 26.29], brings both Law and Temple to fulfillment in the expiation of sins that opens the pathway to life in the Kingdom of God, present among us. Those who embrace the Cross, becoming friends of Jesus, thereby enter a new world of "transformation and expiation."

To be a friend of Jesus, then, is to live *vocationally*, which means to live in constant attention to the question, "What is God asking me to do *now?*" Living vocationally is not a matter of career or job or status. It is a matter of disposition, of attentiveness, of the kind of openness enjoined by Psalm 95, which has become a familiar companion on this Lenten journey: "If today you hear his voice, harden not your hearts." Today's station, the third of the Laurentian *stationes*, is replete with reminders of vocational living, from the painting of the crucifixion behind the high altar to the Chapel of St. Lawrence himself (which claims another portion of the gridiron on which the deacon-martyr gave his life) and the Chapel of St. John Nepomuk, the Bohemian priest who, tradition claims, was drowned for refusing to reveal a confessional secret. Vocational living has its costs. The reward for the price paid is a place at the table at the Wedding Feast of the Lamb.

St. Lawrence in Lucina: Ceiling coffers with arms of Pope Pius IX

T HE AREA SURROUNDING the Basilica of St. Lawrence in Lucina is no stranger to the sacred: Augustus's *Ara Pacis*, the Altar of Peace, was discovered under its stone floor. An exquisitely carved marble enclosure commemorating Augustus's successful campaigns, which led to an era of peace after three hundred years of war, the Ara Pacis celebrated the Pax Romana and its prosperity.

Time and urban development—first, a *domus*, then an apartment building—eventually overwhelmed Augustus's monuments. Lucina, owner of the apartment, is believed to have donated the property for Christian use, thereby associating her name with this site. In 435, Valentinian authorized Pope Sixtus III to erect here a basilica dedicated to St. Lawrence; modern excavations discovered parts of this church and its paleo-Christian baptistery.

Pope Paschal II rebuilt St. Lawrence almost entirely in the twelfth century, adding a portico, a bell tower, a Cosmatesque pavement, and an apse decoration of Christ with Sts. Peter, Paul, Lawrence, and Stephen. Consecrated on May 26, 1196, by Pope Celestine III, the new church became one of Rome's busiest parishes. Pope Paul V then gave the church in 1606 to the Clerics Regular Minor; this transfer sparked more seventeenth-century renovations.

The church today largely reflects nineteenth-century tastes, yet flashes from its baroque facelift add some flair. The portico's ancient columns recall the antique glory of this area. The medieval tomb reliefs on the porch were unearthed nearby; one differs from the others—an elegant neoclassical relief carved in 1825 by Pietro Tenerani for the tomb of Clelia Severini, a work that inspired the poet Giacomo Leopardi.

A broad nave stretches down to the 1676 high altar and a haunting altarpiece by Guido Reni. Painted shortly before Reni's death in 1642, the crucified Christ emanates light against the churning, smoky clouds gathering behind him. From a distance he appears suspended in midair, looking up to the Father as he offers his own sacrifice.

The coffered ceiling and restrained frescoes were gifts of Blessed Pius IX; the seventeenth-century side chapels recount stories of the people of this church and their devotions. The first chapel on the right was built by the Montana family to house the relic of Lawrence's grill, or *craticola*, which was venerated here. The paintings, from 1716, recount tales of the patron; the altarpiece displays *Lucina Presenting a Design of the Church to St. Lawrence*. Between the second and third chapels is a monument to Nicholas Poussin, the most famous French painter of the seventeenth century, commissioned by René Chateaubriand in 1830. The third chapel is dedicated to St. Francis Caracciolo, founder of the Clerics Regular Minor; its altar contains the skull of Pope St. Alexander I, martyred in 116.

The fourth is the celebrated Fonseca Chapel, built in 1664 for Pope Innocent X's wealthy Portuguese physician. Gabriele Fonseca hired sixty-six-year-old Gian Lorenzo Bernini, who designed the cupola, commissioned the altarpiece of *The Annunciation* in its black marble frame, and carved the doctor's bust, recognizable by its energetic thrust toward the altar.

The baptismal chapel on the left, directly above the old baptistery, is a rare example of Roman Rococo, its delicate stucco completely integrated into the architecture and fresco. Like the Augustan decoration that inspired it, the teeming mass of leaves, flowers, and *putti* represent abundance and prosperity, now spiritual rather than material. [E.L.]

St. Susanna: Stational Mass

SATURDAY OF THE THIRD WEEK OF LENT

Station at St. Susanna

Holy Mass
Hosea 6.1–6

Psalm 51

Luke 18.9–14

Office of Readings
Exodus 40.16–38

St. Gregory Nazianzen: Sermon on Love of the Poor

O N THIS EVE OF Laetare Sunday, which offers a momentary pause in the penitential rhythms of the season, the Office of Readings begins with Psalm 107. Its opening verses capture poetically both the starker aspects of the Forty Days and the anticipation of Easter exultation embodied in the Fourth Sunday of Lent:

> Some wandered in desert wastes
>> finding no way to a city to dwell in;
> hungry and thirsty,
>> their soul fainted within them.
> Then they cried to the LORD in their trouble,
>> and he delivered them from their distress;
> he led them by a straight way,
>> till they reached a city to dwell in.

Let them thank the LORD for his steadfast love,
>   for his wonderful works to the sons of men!
For he satisfies him who is thirsty,
>   And the hungry he fills with good things.

The Exodus passage in the Office of Readings today describes the Dwelling, built by Moses to house the Ark of the Covenant. In its essential features, the Dwelling and its surrounding meeting tent anticipate the design of the Temple in Jerusalem: here, in the desert, Moses builds a primitive Holy of Holies that is surrounded by pavilions in which specific kinds of sacrifices and prayers are offered. As commanded by God, Moses also builds a laver so that he, his brother Aaron, and Aaron's sons (the first of Israel's priests) can wash themselves before approaching the altar of sacrifice or entering the Lord's dwelling. Moses was the man to whom God talked familiarly, with complete freedom; yet even Moses must be cleansed before he approaches the glory of the Lord.

That image—the man to whom God was closest nonetheless being cleansed before he meets the Lord—offers Lenten pilgrims an opportunity to reflect on the sacrament of Penance, also known as the sacrament of Reconciliation, on this Saturday midpoint along the itinerary of conversion.

Fifty years ago, Saturday was the day when many Catholics "went to confession," which meant acknowledging the sins and failures of the past week, accepting a penance (usually in the form of a brief series of prayers), and then receiving sacramental absolution. The practice of "going to confession" has decreased dramatically throughout the Catholic world over the past half-century, despite the Church's efforts to make it more accessible and less threatening (which it rarely was, the mythology surrounding the dark confessional notwithstanding). At precisely the time in Western culture when various forms of psychotherapy are flourishing, Catholics have increasingly abandoned the ancient form of cleansing guilt to which they once came readily. A diminished sense of sin surely has something to do with this anomaly. So, perhaps, does a too-easy sense of familiarity with holy things, such that twenty-first-century postmoderns do not feel any need to be cleansed before approaching the Lord. Both attitudes deserve reexamination during the pilgrimage of Lent.

In his 1984 postsynodal apostolic exhortation, *Reconciliatio et Paenitentia*, Pope John Paul II characteristically tried to reframe the Church's thinking about "going to confession" and receiving the Sacrament of Penance: what sometimes seemed a strange or arcane Catholic practice, John Paul proposed, should in fact be understood in terms of the personal drama of every human life, which is the drama of freedom. Taking freedom seriously means taking the abuse of freedom, which is sin, seriously. And to take sin seriously requires us to name the wounds in our lives as the first step toward their being healed. Thus, John Paul taught, the very fact of someone kneeling to name the wounds he or she bears adds to that man's or woman's human dignity. Confession of sins, far from being demeaning or dehumanizing, is liberating and ennobling.

Regular confession of sins is also, the pope suggested, an essential part of configuring oneself to Christ, for the Cross of Christ is the fountainhead from which all reconciliation between God and humanity flows. Indeed, the very geometry of the Cross expresses the two dimensions of the reconciliation that every sensitive soul seeks: the vertical beam symbolizes our need for reconciliation with God, while the horizontal crossbeam represents the imperative of being reconciled with our neighbors. As individuals we crave forgiveness from God for the guilt we carry along the journey of life; the human family craves reconciliation within itself. Both aspirations are embodied in the Cross.

In an interview with a local newspaper in 2011, Cardinal Francis E. George, OMI, the archbishop of Chicago, said that he intended to devote more of his priestly life to the ministry of the confessional as he entered his meridian seventies. "The most important conversations on the planet take place in the confessional," the cardinal said. "It's where you have a soul who bares who they are before God and you're witness to that. It's God who forgives, but you're witness to that and you try to assist. If [I] can do that well for just a few people, I'll be able to tell the Lord . . . I did a few things right anyway." And those penitents will be able to approach the glory of the Lord cleansed, like Moses, Aaron, and the priests of the Old Covenant.

The gospel reading appointed for today's Mass, the familiar parable of the Pharisee and the publican, sheds further light on the drama of human freedom as embodied in the reception of the sacrament of Penance: the drama of naming sins, repenting of them, accepting a penance, and receiving absolution. The humble publican, a traitor to his people because he collected taxes for the pagan occupying power, is analogous to the Samaritan woman at the well, whose story this past Sunday set the spiritual context for this entire Third Week of Lent. As she could ask Jesus for living water because of his thirst for her faith, so the publican could ask for God's mercy because of God's thirst for his repentance and confession of sinfulness. To receive the gift of repentance is another virtue to be learned along the itinerary of conversion. By receiving this gift precisely *as* a gift, the pilgrim learns that confession of sins is not a duty imposed from without, but a baptismal privilege, the desire for which wells up from within.

Confessed and forgiven sins should lead to changed lives—to lives like those of the martyrs Susanna, Gabinus, Felicity, and Vitalis, whose relics are venerated in the *confessio* beneath the high altar at today's station. In the patristic selection in today's Office of Readings, the great Eastern father Gregory of Nazianzus reflects on a less dramatic, but nonetheless important, expression of genuine conversion. Those who receive mercy through conversion or sacramental absolution must then turn and serve the Lord present in the least of his brethren:

> [Let] us visit Christ wherever we may; let us care for him, feed him, clothe him, welcome him, honor him, not only at a meal, as some have done, or by anointing him, as Mary did, or by lending him a tomb, like Joseph of Arimathea, or by arranging for his burial, like Nicodemus, who loved him half-heartedly, or by giving him gold, frankincense, and myrrh, like the Magi before all these others. The Lord of all asks for mercy, not sacrifice. . . . Let us then show him mercy in the persons of the poor and those who today are lying on the ground, so that when we come to leave this world they may receive us into everlasting dwelling places, in Christ our Lord himself, to whom be glory for ever and ever. Amen.

St. Susanna: Crypt chapel
(sixteenth century)

SIXTEEN HUNDRED YEARS AGO, the Basilica of St. Susanna would have been dwarfed by a neighboring behemoth: Diocletian's baths. Built in 303, the largest thermal complex in Rome could accommodate 3,000 bathers simultaneously; tradition holds that it was constructed by Christians enslaved by the early Church's worst persecutor. Only the nucleus of the baths remains, transformed by Michelangelo into the Basilica of St. Mary of the Angels and Martyrs; another remnant became the dainty church of St. Bernard, across the street from St. Susanna.

In 1603, Carlo Maderno gave St. Susanna its monumental façade, the prototype for the front of St. Peter's, which he completed a decade later. The protruding columns and pilasters accelerate rhythmically toward the central portal, focusing all attention on the church entrance. The façade's grandeur recalls the elegant *domus* that once stood here outside the great baths, home to a family that defied the rising tide of persecution.

St. Susanna was born into the highest Roman aristocracy: a cousin of Diocletian, she was also the daughter of the Roman presbyter Gabinus and the niece of Pope Gaius. Converted to Christianity at an early age, she made a vow of perpetual virginity. The emperor, however, wanted her to marry into the imperial family and chose Maximian as her future spouse. Susanna refused. The family was divided; her cousins Claudius and Maximus wanted to stay in the emperor's good graces, while her uncle and father remained true to Christ. Susanna converted her cousins, but Diocletian eventually had her decapitated in her house.

That site is believed to have grown into this church in the fifth century. After the area had deteriorated into a desolate rural outback, Pope Sixtus V (1585–1590) tried to repopulate the neighborhood, building the road that led from the Porta Pia and adding the Moses fountain across the street. His sister, Camilla Peretti, endowed the chapel to the left of the altar, dedicated to St. Lawrence; the large image of the Roman deacon's martyrdom is by Cesare Nebbia, Sixtus's favorite painter. The chapel also celebrates the martyr St. Genesius, patron saint of actors, and Pope St. Eleuterius.

Maderno trimmed the original church's nave and two side aisles into a single apsed hall, leaving vast expanses of wall to decorate. Baldassare Croce swathed the nave with stories of the Old Testament heroine Susanna, who, like her Christian namesake, risked all to preserve her chastity and was vindicated by the prophet Daniel [Daniel 13]. The scenes are rich with landscapes or elegant courtyards, their serene beauty offering a sharp contrast to the lurid intentions and murderous calumny of the Susanna story. Above, Old Testament prophets molded in stucco look down, promising a future savior. Twisting columns framing the faux tapestries proclaim loyalty to St. Peter, whose tomb is defined by similar decoration.

The broad apse rises above a crypt containing the relics of Susanna and Gabinus (as well as St. Felicity and her sons) and is festooned with stucco garlands and cherubs framing stories of St. Susanna. A luminous rainbow of saints and angels welcome Susanna to heaven, where Christ gives her the crown of martyrdom as a princess of his Kingdom.

The many angels throughout the basilica, emerging from the gilt stucco surfaces, give the walls a sense of movement, as these flying or music-making cherubs bring messages of comfort from heaven to earth. [E.L.]

St. Lawrence in
Damaso: Tomb of
Prince Massimo and
Christina of Saxony
(Filippo Gnaccarini,
1840)

The
FOURTH WEEK
of LENT

Holy Cross in Jerusalem: Nave and apse

THE FOURTH
SUNDAY IN LENT

Station at Holy Cross in Jerusalem

Holy Mass

[A]	**[B]**	**[C]**
1 Samuel 16.1b,	*2 Chronicles*	*Joshua 5.9a, 10–12*
6–7, 10–13a	*36.14–16, 19–23*	*Psalm 34*
Psalm 23	*Psalm 137*	*2 Corinthians 5.17–21*
Ephesians 5.8–14	*Ephesians 2.4–10*	*Luke 15.1–3, 11–32*
John 9.1–41	*John 3.14–21*	

Office of Readings

Leviticus 8.1–17; 9.22–24

St. Augustine: Tractate 34 on John

THE PARADIGMATIC GOSPEL STORY for Laetare Sunday, Jesus's cure of the man born blind [John 9.1–41], was one of the three principal New Testament texts taught to the catechumens of the early Church as they drew closer to their baptism at the Easter Vigil. It begins with Jesus's startling act of making mud by spitting on the ground and anointing the blind man's eyes, then instructing him to wash in the pool of Siloam; the man regains his sight, stirring a controversy among the Pharisees, who object to the act of healing taking place on the Sabbath. Finally, the man who has been healed proclaims his belief in the Lord and worships him. Like the two other gospel anchors of these middle Sundays of Lent—last Sunday's conversation about "living water" between Jesus and the Samaritan woman, and next Sunday's story of Jesus raising his friend Lazarus from the dead—the episode of the man born blind holds important lessons for those undergoing the annual catechumenate of the Forty Days: those who, while not being rebaptized at the Vigil, will be blessed with paschal water and asked to reaffirm their baptismal promises.

I n the early Church, the sacrament of Baptism was often referred to as "Illumination." To be converted to Christ and washed free of sin was to pass from darkness to light, from confusion to truth, from distorted vision to clear vision—and, ultimately, from death to life. To be converted and conformed to Christ means recognizing in Jesus of Nazareth the Light of the world, who not only restores or gives sight (as in today's gospel reading), but who also gives insight. Through the light of Christ, symbolized at Baptism by the baptismal candle lit from the paschal candle, disciples are empowered to see, and to see not only *out*, but *in*.

This double illumination is clear in the healing of the man born blind. He sees *out*, in that he can now see and appreciate the beauties of creation and the splendor of the Temple, the dwelling place of God among his elect people of the Mosaic Covenant. Just as importantly, though, the miraculous touch of the Lord enables the man born blind to see *in*: to see in Jesus the promised Messiah, the Anointed One of God, who is the new dwelling place of God in history. This new power to see *in* ought not end with the act of faith: "Lord, I believe." That is the first step in the interior illumination offered by friendship with Jesus and commitment to his cause. Over the course of a lifetime, that illumination also permits disciples to see whatever remains dark inside their own hearts and to remedy that through repentance, so that, through the Light, they can become ever more brilliant sons and daughters of light, for the conversion of the world.

The gospel reading underscores that "Siloam" (the name of the pool in the southeast corner of the City of David, just beyond the walls of the Old City of today's Jerusalem, where the blind man of the gospel account gains his sight) means "Sent." Illumination and conversion imply mission. Those who can now see are sent into the world for its illumination. Conforming themselves to the Light of the world, they are empowered to be light in the world's darkness—

which can mean shedding light on the world's disbelief. That is why the gospel story read to the catechumens and to twenty-first-century pilgrims, which might have ended with the happy resolution of the blind man's disability, continues with a sad story of disbelief among the Pharisees in which even the cured man's parents get caught up. To be light for the world is not something the world always appreciates. That is one of the reasons why the design of salvation history—the "project" that God wishes to accomplish in history through his Son—involves the Church.

The eye cannot see itself, even when it is functioning perfectly. The only way that disciples can "see" themselves truly is through the eyes of the community of faith—the community of solidarity and forgiveness that is the Body of Christ, the Light of the world. The Church is not an adjunct to salvation history. The Church is essential to the continuing conversion-into-Christ to which all are called in the sacrament of Baptism, in which all are empowered in the sacrament of Confirmation, and from which all are nourished in the sacrament of the Holy Eucharist—the three sacraments of initiation that the catechumens will receive at the Easter Vigil.

The Church is also the community from which those who have been illuminated are sent: in that sense, the Church is the Siloam of the New Covenant in Jesus Christ. This characteristic of the Church as a community of "sending," like the "illumination" of Baptism, has two dimensions. First, it is within the Church that disciples come to see Jesus as the Anointed One sent from God for the salvation of the world. Second, it is from the Church that the Lord's disciples are sent out to ask the world to consider the possibility of its redemption. Thus the adventure of Baptism has both inner and outer aspects: the ongoing discovery of the depths of the Truth who is the God revealed in Christ by the power of the Spirit, and the proposing of Christ to the world as the answer to the question that is every human life.

The Second Vatican Council retrieved and renewed the Church's understanding that the sacrament of Baptism confers three offices on all those who are illuminated by it: all the baptized share in the three "offices" of Christ as priest, prophet, and king (offices anticipated in David's royal anointing by Samuel in the Old Testament reading appointed for today in Lectionary Cycle A). Being conformed to Christ, all the baptized can worship in truth (the priestly office); all the baptized can proclaim the truth (the prophetic office); all the baptized can serve the brethren and the world in truth (the kingly office). These are ecclesial offices. They are conferred by the Church in Baptism, and they are exercised from the Church as the baptized go forth in mission.

Today' station, the Basilica of the Holy Cross in Jerusalem, evokes the memory of St. Helena, mother of Constantine and one of the most important of the early Holy Land pilgrims. In 325, Helena went to the places where Jesus had walked. Her journey, according to tradition, led to the discovery of the True Cross on which the Light of the world had offered up his life, and many other relics of the Passion; today's *statio*, which was once Helena's Roman residence, houses some of those relics. Helena's life and vocation caught the imagination of Evelyn Waugh, who wrote his most spare novel about the Dowager Empress and her particular itinerary of conversion. In a letter, Waugh described his fondness for his subject in these striking terms: "I liked Helena's sanctity because it is in contrast to all that moderns think of as sanctity. She wasn't thrown to the lions, she wasn't a contemplative, she wasn't poor and hungry, she didn't look like an El Greco. She just discovered what it was God had chosen for her to do and did it . . . by going straight to the essential physical historical fact of the redemption."

Baptismal illumination; discipleship; vocational discernment in and from the Church: all are made possible by the Cross, which is ever closer on the horizon of the Forty Days' journey.

Holy Cross in Jerusalem: *Our Lady Presenting St. Helena and Constantine to the Trinity* (Corrado Giaquinto, 1742)

Tꜰ BASILICA OF THE HOLY CROSS in Jerusalem is Rome's spiritual gateway to Calvary: here, 1,700 years ago, the Dowager Empress Helena placed the earth she had gathered from the Holy Land and laid to rest her relic of the True Cross.

The basilica's walls date from the last century of pagan Rome, when the Sessorian Palace was built for the Severan emperors. This magnificent structure became Helena's residence when she moved to Rome after Constantine's conquest of the city; under the apse are the chamber and Chapel of St. Helena, with remnants of the splendid mosaic decoration commissioned by Valentinian in the fifth century. Heavily restored by Francesco Zucchi in 1593, the shimmering golden skin of the vault is nonetheless dazzling. A marble statue of Helena—a surprising mélange of a pagan statue of Juno, with head, arms, and cross added to transform the goddess into a Christian saint—dominates the chapel entrance.

The church itself was built into the imposing atrium of the palace; immense granite columns underscore the building's grandeur. Pope Lucius II restructured the church in the twelfth century, adding the bell tower, cloister, and Cosmatesque floor. During another restoration, in 1492, a walled-in cavity was discovered in the basilica's triumphal arch; it contained a casket of the relics of Christ's Passion, undoubtedly hidden because of constant pillaging during the Middle Ages. This rediscovery galvanized another major decorative program. Scholars still debate whether Melozzo da Forlì or Antoniazzo Romano was commissioned to decorate the apse with jewel-toned fresco of the epic legend of the True Cross, but the result is a delightful merging of medieval color and Renaissance narrative.

The relic chapel was built in 1929–1931. Recalling the design of Helena's original chapel, a ramp leads to the shrine through the Stations of the Cross. After every three steps there is a pause at a small landing, recalling the three times Christ is traditionally said to have fallen beneath the cross. The chapel, lined with marble, feels several degrees cooler than the rest of the church and is reminiscent of a stone tomb. In the back, a glass case contains objects said to be from the Passion: the fragment of the Cross, a nail, two thorns from the crown of thorns, stones from the column of the flagellation, and the headboard of Christ's cross (scrawled with the title "Jesus of Nazareth King of the Jews" in three languages), as well as a bone reputed to be from the index finger of doubting Thomas. The Passion relics' power to inspire contemporary sanctity is embodied in a tomb situated at the foot of the relic chapel: it is the resting place of Antonietta Meo (1930–1937), a child who, stricken with cancer, offered her suffering to the Lord, writing many letters to Jesus in her last days. Her beatification cause is under way.

The basilica's flamboyant exterior belies its solemnity. The Baroque façade was commissioned by Benedict XIV and executed in 1743 by Pietro Passalacqua and Domenico Gregorini, who also fashioned the nave's barrel vault. At the same time, Corrado Giaquinto painted the vault fresco of St. Helena in glory and the altarpieces, which display episodes of the lives of Cistercian saints. [E.L.]

Four Holy Crowned Martyrs: *Ecce Homo* (fourteenth century)

MONDAY OF THE FOURTH WEEK OF LENT

Station at the Four Holy Crowned Martyrs

Holy Mass
Isaiah 65.17–21

Psalm 30

John 4.43–54

Office of Readings
Leviticus 16.2–28

Origen: Homily on Leviticus

T HE THIRD-CENTURY ALEXANDRIAN THEOLOGIAN Origen was a master at reading the Hebrew Bible typologically: that is, finding in the history of Israel deep and perhaps unexpected meanings for the people of the New Israel, the Church. In today's Office of Readings, Origen extends the motif of light and illumination from yesterday's liturgy into the fourth week of the Forty Days by reflecting on the ritual instructions given to Moses (and recorded in today's reading from Leviticus) for the offering of Israel's sacrifice of atonement:

There is a deeper meaning in the fact that the high priest sprinkles the blood toward the east. Atonement comes to you from the east. From the east comes the one whose name is Dayspring, he who is mediator between God and men.

You are invited then to look always toward the east: it is there that the sun of righteousness rises for you, it is there that the light is always being born for you. You are never to walk in darkness; the great and final day is not to enfold you in darkness. Do not let the night and mist of ignorance steal upon you. So that you may always enjoy the light of knowledge, keep always in the daylight of faith, hold fast always to the light of love and peace.

Origen's homily and its emphasis on Jesus Christ as the Light of the world complements the liturgy of today's Mass, in which the Church begins reading John's gospel day by day, until Wednesday of Holy Week. The fourth gospel has any number of interesting features. It is the most richly theological telling of the story of Jesus: "In the beginning was the Word, and the Word was with God, and the Word was God" [John 1.1.]. It describes multiple visits of Jesus to Jerusalem during his public ministry, whereas in Matthew, Mark, and Luke, Jesus goes "up to Jerusalem" but once. It is the gospel of sharply drawn contrasts: light and darkness; Jesus and the Evil One; God and "the world." It is the gospel in which Jesus is fully in control, the protagonist who shapes events with sovereign indifference to what others find appropriate and royal disregard for how others read the situation: "You would have no power over me unless it had been given you from above" [John 19.11].

And it is the gospel in which the conflict between Jesus and "the Jews" is a dominant motif. Because these portions of the Johannine gospel will be read throughout the balance of the Lenten pilgrimage, and because they have caused so much misunderstanding, pain, and grief over two millennia, it is important, at the outset of this serial reading of the gospel of St. John, to remember what the *Catechism* of the Council of Trent said more than four hundred years ago about responsibility for the death of the Messiah—the death that the Johannine Jesus embraces:

> Should anyone inquire why the Son of God underwent his most bitter Passion, he will find that besides the guilt inherited from our first parents, the principal causes were the vices and crimes that have been perpetrated from the begin-

ning of the world to the present day, and those which will be committed to the end of time. In his Passion and Death the Son of God, the Savior, intended to atone for and blot out the sins of all ages, to offer for them to his Father a full and abundant satisfaction.

Besides, to increase the dignity of this mystery, Christ suffered not only for sinners, but even for those who were the very authors and ministers of all the torments he endured. Of this the Apostle reminds us in these words addressed to the Hebrews: "Consider him who endured from sinners such hostility against himself, so that you may not grow weary or faint-hearted" [Hebrews 12.3]. In this guilt are involved all those who fall frequently into sin; for, as our sins consigned Christ the Lord to the death of the cross, most certainly those who wallow in sin and iniquity crucify to themselves again the Son of God . . . and make a mockery of him. This guilt seems more enormous in us than in the Jews, since according to the testimony of the same Apostle: If they had known it, "they would never have crucified the Lord of glory" [1 Corinthians 2.8]; while we, on the contrary, professing to know him, yet denying him by our actions, seem in some sort to lay violent hands on him.

The language may be a bit baroque, but the truth being taught is unmistakable: if you want to find the party or parties responsible for the suffering and death of Jesus, look in the mirror.

In the first reading of today's Mass, the prophet Isaiah offers a vision of the Messianic Age, which Jesus proclaimed to have begun in himself and by his ministry. The Easter "surprise" toward which the Forty Days leads pilgrims is that this Messianic Age, the Kingdom or Reign of God, will break into history in a wholly unexpected, even counterintuitive, way: it will be established through a new Passover marked by the Cross, the Resurrection, the Ascension, and the sending of the Holy Spirit at Pentecost. And as a result, a new People of God that embraces both Jews and Gentiles will be born into history. For now, Jesus gives another sign of the inbreaking of the Kingdom in today's gospel reading, the cure of the royal official's son. The official, like all disciples, must abandon himself to the divine will: as Father Benedict Bro, a Dominican, put it, "God is God only when I accept the fact that I need him."

Another Dominican, Bede Jarrett, developed the same theme in a way that sheds more light on the imitation of Christ, the obedient Son, to which this phase of the Forty Days calls us:

> This life of ours . . . is a gift from God. It is not of our choosing. It comes to us by his choice. Since it is of his choosing, it is of his designing. We neither made ourselves nor can we manage ourselves as we like, nor manage the life that comes to us. For that reason we can take a most hopeful view of life. . . . [For] the thought that it is his gift and after his design gives us courage. If to this remembrance of God's creatorship we add the mystery of the Resurrection, we shall take even larger draughts of hope; for not only life but life's triumph lies entirely in the hands of God.

The last petition in today's Morning Prayer reminds Lenten pilgrims of another facet of the imitation of Christ that is made possible by the illumination of Baptism: the "imitation" of the Lord's capacity to "see" the divine imprint within the hearts of everyone he meets. The petition at Morning Prayer asks that we be forgiven "for failing to see Christ in the poor, the distressed, and the troublesome, and for our failure to reverence your Son in their persons." It is the same insight, the same capacity to see *in*, that prompted Blessed Teresa of Calcutta to describe the poor whom she picked up off the hard streets of Calcutta as "Jesus in disguise." It is the same baptismal illumination that inspires the Little Sisters of the Lamb, the Dominican mendicants who live near today's station church, to spend their lives in prayer and beg their food from door to door. The insight and the illumination are both born from the same grace that allows us to see the Light of the world in a man crucified on Calvary: an insight and an illumination that come to us through the experience of Easter.

Four Holy Crowned Martyrs: Cloister

DESPITE ITS SOMEWHAT AWKWARD first impression, the stational church of the Four Holy Crowned Martyrs deftly unites art with witness.

The *Santi Quattro Coronati* [Four Holy Crowned Ones] were in fact two groups of martyrs, nine in all, killed during the Diocletian persecution of 303–306. The first group counted four soldiers—Secundus, Severianus, Carpoforus, and Victorius—who refused to offer pagan sacrifice and were executed. The second group involved five stonemasons—Claudius, Nicostratus, Simpronianus, Castorius, and Simplicitus—who would not carve an idol of Asclepius; they were placed in lead caskets and drowned in a river, later to be declared the patron saints of sculptors—exemplars of heroic witness from the world of art.

The basilica is located on the Caelian Hill. Its stocky tower, rising over a low archway, served as lookout post and belfry and is the oldest of its kind in Rome: a sentinel, watching the road descending from the Appian Gate into the city. Although the *Titulus Santi Quattro Coronati* is mentioned in 595, the first construction of a basilica-plan church here took place in 630. It was a large building with a bell tower leading into an atrium; today's second archway was this first church's façade. Remains of its nave can still be seen in the walls of the second courtyard.

The church was burnt to the ground in the Norman Sack of Rome of 1084. After this, Pope Paschal II reconstructed the basilica, giving it a smaller and more elegant Romanesque plane. The svelte new building, consecrated on January 20, 1116, boasts a narrow nave articulated with two stories of springing arches. The arcade propels the eye toward the broad embrace of the apse, which was retained from the original church.

The importance of the church's relics ensured that the new structure would be generously embellished. The ninth-century crypt remains intact and includes three sarcophagi containing the relics of the martyred soldiers and sculptors as well as those of Sts. Barbara, Sixtus, and Nicholas. Above these tombs, the Cosmatesque apse pavement gives way to frescoes of the patron saints that were painted in 1630, the same year that Giovanni Baglione (the famous rival and biographer of Caravaggio) added the left nave altarpiece, *St. Sebastian Healed by Lucina and Irene.*

The greatest artistic treasures of this church-and-monastery complex are outside the church itself. The first gem is an exquisite medieval monastic cloister, complete with garden and fountain, entered through a small door to the left of the nave. The St. Sylvester Chapel, accessible from the second courtyard outside the church, is a small room covered with remarkably well-preserved thirteenth-century frescoes of the *Conversion of Constantine*, inspired by the *Golden Legend*, the enormously popular hagiography published in 1260 by Jacobus de Voragine. Another hall of the monastery displays recently discovered calendrical frescoes from the same period. [E.L.]

St. Lawrence in Damaso: Stational Mass

TUESDAY OF THE FOURTH WEEK OF LENT

Station at St. Lawrence in Damaso

Holy Mass
Ezekiel 47.1–9, 12

Psalm 46

John 5.1–16

Office of Readings
Leviticus 19.1–18, 31–37

St. Leo the Great: Sermon 10 on Lent

THE ENTRANCE ANTIPHON OF today's Mass, inspired by Isaiah 55.1, invites all who thirst to "Come to the waters." In the reading from Ezekiel in the Liturgy of the Word, the prophet describes the life-giving waters that will flow from the postexilic, restored Temple, the dwelling place of the Holy One of Israel. The responsorial, Psalm 46, extols the "river whose streams make glad the city of God." The setting for today's gospel story is the pool of Bethesda in Jerusalem, thought to have curative powers; but Jesus, the One who promised the Samaritan woman "living water," extends healing to the sick by his word, healing a man who has been an invalid for thirty-eight years who cannot get to the pool. Baptismal imagery thoroughly infuses the Church's celebration of the Eucharist at the fourth stational church honoring the martyr-deacon Lawrence.

That imagery, and the baptismal motif that dominates this phase of the Forty Days, poses an interesting question as the liturgy continues to prompt pilgrims to reflect on how well we are imitating Christ—which means living out the implications of our baptismal promises.

Different cultures have different ways of lifting up and celebrating individual lives. Birthdays are the norm in Anglophone cultures. In Poland, birthdays are far less important than "name-days," the feast of one's patron saint. Some cultures celebrate both birthdays and name-days. But the day of one's baptism? Surely that is a day to be remembered and celebrated every year: the day of one's salvation, made possible by the living waters of sacramental rebirth.

A baptismal certificate is often filed among other important papers, as it is necessary documentation for other aspects of a Catholic life: making one's first Holy Communion; receiving the sacrament of Confirmation; entering a Christian marriage or religious life; receiving Holy Orders. The stational pilgrimage of Lent might well be a moment to take that baptismal certificate out of the file drawer and note the date on one's calendar—and on future calendars. On his first return home to Poland as pope, Blessed John Paul II visited the parish church in which he had been baptized, knelt, and kissed the font. It is a gesture well worth remembering on the major anniversaries of one's baptism: the day one entered into the abundant life enlivened by the living waters flowing from the new Temple, Christ the Lord.

The Office of Readings continues the day's reflection on the miraculous power of Baptism by confronting Lenten pilgrims with the brief command in which God tells his elect people, Israel, what their covenant relationship with him requires: "You shall be holy; for I the LORD your God am holy." In the priestly vocabulary of the Hebrew Bible, to be holy—which is often rendered as being "sanctified" or "purified"—is to be able to enter the divine presence in order to worship the true God. In the New Testament, to be washed clean is to be enabled to enter into friendship with Jesus, to become a member of the Body of Christ, who makes such fellowship possible by the truth he speaks and the blood he sheds.

In both the Old and New Testaments, this covenant relationship of the chosen people of God with the Holy One himself is not something added on to creation, as if it were an afterthought or a mere remedy for something gone awry; it is, rather, the very reason for creation. In *Jesus of Nazareth—Holy Week*, Pope Benedict XVI explained this concept by reference to ancient Jewish thought: "According to rabbinic theology, the idea of the covenant—the idea of establishing a holy people to be an interlocutor for God in union with him—is prior to the idea of the creation of the world and supplies its inner motive. The cosmos was created, not that there be manifold things in heaven and earth, but that there might be space for the 'covenant,' for the loving 'yes' between God and his human respondent."

God creates the world, and God redeems the world through his Son, so that God's holiness may be shared. God thirsts for the holiness of his people, as Jesus thirsted for the Samaritan woman's faith.

Thus when Jesus sanctifies his brethren so that they may share his intimacy with the Father, he also sanctifies them for mission. When he prays to the Father at the Last Supper, that those whom the Father has given him may be consecrated in the truth, it is so they may know the Father and make the Father known in the world. To be holy, then, is to be in mission. A failure to share the gifts that God has bestowed on his people suggests the possibility that those gifts have not been fully received, or fully appreciated. Thus the imitation of Christ, the Son of the Holy One, requires an effort, of all Christ's brothers and sisters—an effort to make the possibility of that "loving 'yes' between God and his human respondent" available to all.

Another important measure of holiness is generosity, as Pope St. Leo the Great teaches in today's Office of Readings. There, Leo suggests that our ability to receive God's gifts is contingent on our willingness to offer similar gifts to others. And this, he proposes, is a good point for self-examination during Lent:

> The faithful should therefore enter into themselves and make a true judgment
> on their attitudes of mind and heart. If they find some store of love's fruit in

their hearts, they must not doubt God's presence within them. If they would increase their capacity to receive so great a guest, they should practice greater generosity in doing good, with persevering charity.

If God is love, charity should know no limit, for God cannot be confined. . . .

As we prepare to celebrate that greatest of all mysteries, by which the blood of Jesus Christ did away with our sins, let us first of all make ready the sacrificial offering of works of mercy. In this way we shall give to those who have sinned against us what God in his goodness has already given us.

Today's gospel story offers a final point for reflection on the imitation of Christ. The healing of the sick man at the pool of Bethesda brings about another conflict between Jesus and those who have different ideas of holiness and mercy: the Pharisees, who believe that healing is work, and work should not be done on the Sabbath; carrying a sleeping mat is also work, and Jesus should not have told the cured man to pick up his mat and walk. While Jesus offers no response to this criticism in today's reading, the response implicit in his cure is not difficult to discern: the Law and the Sabbath are means to holiness, not ends in themselves. When they become ends in themselves, such that they impede the holiness that expresses itself in mercy, they have been misunderstood to the point that they are no longer means of sanctification. This "response" is not a divine mandate for willfulness or autonomy. It is a divine call to a sense of proportion—the sense of true proportion that grows from understanding the superabundance of love that the God of the Law and the Sabbath pours into the world for its healing and sanctification, which make possible the intimacy of creation and Creator.

St. Lawrence in Damaso:
St. Hippolytus of Rome
(seventeenth-century copy)

THE BASILICA OF ST. LAWRENCE IN Damaso is the cradle of the Roman cult of martyrs: here, in his home, Pope St. Damasus I (366–384) compiled the stories of the martyrs and organized devotions to them, assisted by his secretary, St. Jerome. Damasus also rebuilt martyr-shrines, funded new churches in honor of the martyrs, and wrote many of their histories himself; these *passiones*, in poetic meter, were inscribed in the elegant, distinctive Damascene script.

Damasus had a special devotion to St. Lawrence and established a shrine to the deacon-saint in his home, located in a busy neighborhood: the stables of the green chariot team of the Circus Maximus were nearby; shops were crowded between Pompey's theater district and Domitian's Odeon; there was even a Mithraic shrine next door. Amid it all, Damasus administered the Church from his ancestral residence and established the first Vatican archives here.

After Rome's fall from world power, this neighborhood became the heart of the city, and today's stational church lumbered along through the centuries, undergoing the occasional repair. During Rome's late fifteenth-century urban rebirth, orchestrated by Pope Sixtus IV, Cardinal Raffaele Riario, Camerlengo of the Holy Roman Church and the pope's nephew, chose this site to build his palace—with funds rumored to have come from an overnight card game. The stone was quarried from Pompey's long-abandoned theater, and the palace became the first in Rome with an entirely travertine façade.

With Bramante as his architect, Cardinal Riario rebuilt the church of St. Lawrence in Damaso within the palace walls, moving it slightly north of its original position but maintaining the same orientation. A large, airy space featuring Renaissance vaults, much of the basilica's decoration was completed a century later. Close to the entrance are statues of Sts. Francis Xavier (who ministered here) and Charles Borromeo by Stefano Maderno, who sculpted the arresting *St. Cecilia* in Trastevere. The apse fresco of the *Coronation of the Virgin* by Maderno's contemporary Federico Zucchari was commissioned by Cardinal Alessandro Farnese, who lived in the palace. His secretary, the celebrated Italian poet Annibale Caro, is buried in the church. The high altar contains the remains of two canonized popes, Damasus and Eutychianus.

Gian Lorenzo Bernini left his mark here with the *Tomb of Alessandro Valtrini*; another Baroque genius, Pietro da Cortona, painted the Chapel of the Immaculate Conception. The ceiling includes a rare Roman Rococo work, Corrado Giaquinto's *Eternity Appears to St. Nicholas*.

The flamboyant Baroque gave way to the more restrained neoclassical with Pietro Tenerani's funerary monument to Gabriella di Savoia Massimo. The panel of *The Virgin with Sts. Philip Neri and Nicholas* by Sebastiano Conca also reflects this period's quiet elegance.

The basilica houses an interesting curiosity: the ancient statue of St. Hippolytus, the second-century theologian and martyr. The original, found in 1551, was restored and is now in the Vatican museums. The base of the seventeenth-century copy includes an inscribed paschal calendar for the Greek and Latin Churches as well as writings by St. Hippolytus. [E.L.]

St. Paul Outside the Walls: Nave

WEDNESDAY OF THE FOURTH WEEK OF LENT

Station at St. Paul Outside the Walls

Holy Mass
Isaiah 49.8–15
Psalm 145
John 5.17–30

Office of Readings
Numbers 11.4–6, 10–30
St. Maximus the Confessor: Letter 11

A S THE PATHWAYS OF Lent draw ever closer to Calvary, the liturgy multiplies its images of the Messianic Age—the Kingdom of God—that is being inaugurated in the person of Jesus: in his preaching, in his healings and other "signs," and, ultimately, in his atoning death, vindicated in the Resurrection. Thus Isaiah in the Old Testament reading for today's Mass speaks of the "time of favor," the "day of salvation" that will extend God's covenant with Israel to those who will "come from afar" to enjoy the mercy and bounty of the Lord. Jesus, in his ongoing confrontation with those who object to him calling God his "Father," prophesies in today's gospel reading that "the hour is coming" when anyone who hears his word and "believes him who sent me" will have "eternal life"—and not as something that happens after death, but here and now, in the world and in history.

The Messianic Age is erupting into history in the person of Jesus, who seeks not his "own will but the will of him who sent me." Those who have entered into friendship with Jesus the Lord are thus empowered by their imitation of him to live, now, the eternal life he has shared with the Father from all ages. Disciples can live "in the Kingdom" now. They can, as St. Maximus the Confessor teaches in today's Office of Readings, "imitate him by [their] kindness and genuine love for one another," living "like our heavenly Father, holy, merciful, and just."

Kingdom-living is life lived through the virtues. Thus today's liturgical readings, and the great *statio* at the tomb of the apostle who taught the Church the "more excellent way" by which love completes faith and hope [see 1 Corinthians 12.32b–13.13], afford Lenten pilgrims an opportunity to reflect on the theological and cardinal virtues as the spiritual and moral framework of the New Life promised by Jesus and won by his Cross and Resurrection.

The theological virtues of faith, hope, and love are gifts that God gives us in Baptism. As the Catholic Church understands them, faith, hope, and love are not natural capacities that can, like muscles, be trained and tuned to a certain pitch. Rather, through Baptism, it is God's justifying grace that enables us to believe in him and in the One whom he sent (faith), to trust in him and in his promises (hope), and to cherish him above all else while treating our neighbors as we would wish to be treated by them (love). That same grace of justification enables the baptized, as the *Catechism of the Catholic Church* puts it, to "live and act under the promptings of the Holy Spirit through the gifts of the Holy Spirit," which tradition lists as "wisdom, understanding, knowledge, counsel, piety, fortitude, and fear of the Lord." Finally, the justifying grace conferred in the sacrament of Baptism empowers disciples to live the New Life by growing "in goodness through the moral virtues."

Chief among these moral virtues are the cardinal virtues, which are human capacities to be developed and strengthened by the work of the New Life within the disciple's mind, heart, and soul. Their name comes from the Latin *cardo* [hinge], because these virtues are the pivot of the moral life, around which other virtues are clustered. The *Catechism* defines the cardinal virtues in these terms:

Prudence, or right judgment, is the cardinal virtue by which we learn to see what is truly good in every circumstance in which there is a menu of possibilities before us, and to "choose the right means of achieving it."

Justice is the cardinal virtue by which we desire "to give [what is] their due to God and neighbor," and do so as a matter of habit.

Courage (Fortitude) is the cardinal virtue of standing fast for the good in times of difficulty and holding firm to a steady course over a lifetime of some- times wrenching choices. Through courage, and the grace of the New Life that develops this virtue within us, disciples are enabled to conquer fear through the power of the One who took the world's fear upon the Cross and immolated it there. Through courage, disciples can stand against the world when necessary, convinced by the Lord that he has "overcome the world" [John 16.33].

Moderation, sometimes called "temperance," is the cardinal virtue that "pro- vides balance in the use of created goods" and "keeps desires within the limits of what is honorable."

As the Dominican theologian Servais Pinckaers taught in his masterwork, *Sources of Christian Ethics*, growth in these virtues can be compared to learning a language or mastering a musical instrument.

Start with language. As everyone who has tried to learn a second language knows, hearing and speaking are the best way to make progress; that, after all, is the way everyone learned his or her primary language. At a certain point in the process, however, whether it's a question of a primary language or another language, one has to learn the rules of grammar and master a vocabulary (which is another set of "rules"). These rules—or habits, or virtues (for "virtue" is the English equivalent of the Latin *habitus*)—make speech possible, and real speech makes communication possible. And when there is communication, language becomes a way of encountering and engaging another. To be sure, in speaking grammatically and by choosing our words properly, we have learned a disci- pline of living within certain rules. But those rules empower us to live what Father Pinckaers called "a new kind of freedom": the freedom to communicate, to choose the words by which we communicate—the freedom to avoid mistakes without thinking about it, which is the habit, or "virtue," of speaking intelligibly, even eloquently.

A similar process takes place when mastering a musical instrument. Anyone can bang on a piano, but banging on a piano is making noise, not music. Repeating what can seem to be boring exercises trains the mind and the fingers to play the piano well, so that we can, eventually, play what we like, and even create new compositions of our own. What had once seemed to be constraint now seems, with mastery, a new liberation—another "new kind of freedom."

Father Pinckaers called this genuine freedom, which the cardinal virtues make possible, "freedom for excellence." True freedom is not a matter of "doing it my way." True freedom is a matter of doing the right thing, in the right way, at the right time (if there are choices of moment involved)—and doing so as a matter of habit.

The contemporary demand for freedom resonates in the Christian soul, because it was "for freedom [that] Christ has set us free" [Galatians 5.1]. Christian freedom is not the rudimentary freedom of willfulness, however. If that were the case, every two-year-old ever born, every one of whom is a beautiful bundle of willfulness, would embody true freedom. A mature freedom, a Christian freedom, is found in a life of virtue, lived through those moral habits that the grace of Christ enables us to develop over the course of a lifetime.

The imitation of Christ to which Lent calls us is an imitation of his virtues, which are summarized by his obedience:

Christ also suffered for you, leaving you an example, that you should follow in his steps. He committed no sin; no guile was found on his lips. When he was reviled, he did not revile in return; when he suffered, he did not threaten; but he trusted himself to him who judges justly. He himself bore our sins in his body on the tree, that we might die to sin and live in righteousness. By his wounds you have been healed [1 Peter 2.21–24].

St. Paul Outside the Walls (*confessio*): Paul's Chains

ST. PAUL'S CHRISTIAN LIFE, which began on the road to Damascus and encompassed thousands of miles of evangelical travel, ended on the road to Ostia, where he was beheaded at the Aque Salvie, a district about 2 miles south of Rome; his body was carried a mile to this site, where a small *celle memoriae*, a monument to his memory, was erected. That humble marker on the Via Ostiense was a pilgrimage site even during the fiercest persecutions. Ultimately, Constantine erected a modest basilica here: situated between the Tiber and the main road to Rome's seaport, it was a fitting resting place for the man who traversed the empire preaching the Gospel.

The emperors Theodosius, Valentinian, and Arcadius rebuilt the original Constantinian church, reorienting it toward Old St. Peter's and decorating it with the lavish murals described by the Christian poet Pudentius in his *Dittochaeon*. The massive structure "outside the walls" included a mile-long covered portico, which stretched back to the city to shelter pilgrims visiting St. Paul's tomb.

The Middle Ages were generous to the basilica, as its care by the Benedictines led to many aesthetic wonders. Hildebrand of Soana (elected Pope Gregory VII in 1073) added monumental bronze doors to the basilica. Crafted in Constantinople, their fifty-four incised panels, inlaid with silver, were the gift of an Amalfi merchant, Pantaleone, and can still be seen today in the church's counter-façade; the donor included a portrait of himself kneeling before Christ and St. Paul, praying that Christ would "open the doors of life" to him.

In the twelfth century, the Vassalletti stoneworkers added a tranquil cloister, brightened by a variety of twisting, inlaid columns, and carved the basilica's eighteen-foot paschal candlestick with its scenes of Christ's Passion.

In preparation for the first jubilee in 1300, other artistic masters were summoned to the basilica. Skilled Venetian mosaicists decorated the apse with the image of Christ enthroned among Sts. Peter, Paul, Andrew, and Luke; the donor, Pope Honorius, pays homage to the Savior. Pietro Cavallini lined the side walls with mosaics of St. Paul's life and decorated the façade, while Arnolfo di Cambio built the Gothicizing *baldacchino* above the altar. While its high spires and angels (flying upside-down to incense the altar) evoke imaginative northern sculpture, the representation of Adam and Eve, surprisingly naturalistic, is drawn from Roman classical models.

(continues)

(continued)

The basilica received many illustrious pilgrims. St. Bridget of Sweden prayed before the Blessed Sacrament Chapel crucifix in the fourteenth century, and, in 1541, Ignatius Loyola and his companions professed their vows in front of the little mosaic icon of *Our Lady, the Guide*, forming the Society of Jesus.

Much of this history and beauty was destroyed on July 15, 1823, when embers left on the roof by workmen caused a conflagration that burned the structure to the ground. Although the Church had been left impoverished and marginalized by the revolutionary politics of the era, the entire world responded to Pope Gregory XVI's appeal to contribute to the church's reconstruction: the four alabaster columns framing the inside entrance and the alabaster window panes were gifts from Egyptian rulers, while the malachite altars were donated by the Russian emperor. The reconstruction resulted in what is, today, Rome's closest approximation of a Constantinian basilica, its vast interior evoking the spaciousness of paleo-Christian design.

The simplicity of St. Paul's tomb is in contrast to the surrounding grandeur. The opened section of wall under the altar allows a view of the side of the apostle's marble sarcophagus; the lid, covered by the altar, reads "Paul Apostle and Martyr," but a small stretch of the apostle's Roman chains are visible. During the 2008-2009 Pauline Year, Vatican archaeologists found here first-century bone fragments and scraps of purple cloth shot with gold, fabric similar to that which may have been used to bind the bones of St. Peter, a finding that came to light when archaeologists examined bones excavated from beneath St. Peter's Basilica in the mid-twentieth century. [E.L.]

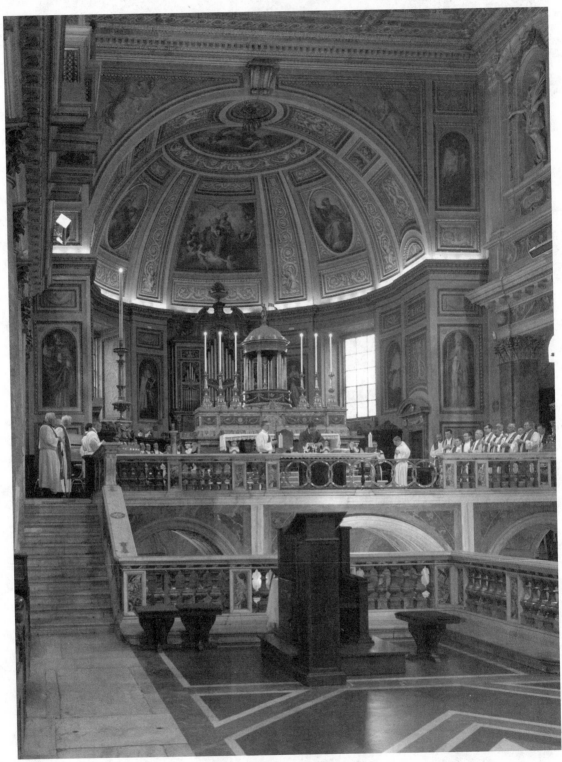

Sts. Sylvester and Martin: Stational Mass

THURSDAY OF THE FOURTH WEEK OF LENT

Station at Sts. Sylvester and Martin

Holy Mass

Exodus 32.7–14

Psalm 106

John 5.31–47

Office of Readings

Numbers 12.16–13.3, 17–33

St. Leo the Great: Sermon 15 on the Lord's Passion

I N THIS SECOND HALF of the Fourth Week of Lent, Jesus continues to heighten the crisis created by his person and his mission. Thus in today's gospel reading, he proclaims that, as the Kingdom breaks into history here and now, it is not enough to obey the Law—or even to search the Scriptures—in order to know the God of Abraham, Isaac, Jacob, and Moses. To know this God, whom Jesus dares call "Father," everyone must now come through the One the Father has sent. Obedience to the Son, which is neither slavish nor coerced, but freely given, is the new form of faith. Friendship with the Son is the path to the Father; friendship with the Son is the bond of the New Covenant; friendship with the Son is the path to worshipping God in spirit and in truth; friendship with the Son is the guide to righteous living.

This confrontation underscores Jesus's insistence that his witness is not of his own making: "If I bear witness to myself, my testimony is not true [but] there is another witness to me, and I know that the testimony which he bears to me is true. . . . For the works which the Father has granted me to accomplish, these very works which I am doing, bear me witness that the Father has sent me." That witness is consistent with, even as it fulfills, the Mosaic covenant and the design of salvation history that was first revealed in the events of the Exodus: "Do not think that I shall accuse you before the Father; it is Moses that accuses you, on whom you set your hope. If you believed Moses, you would believe me, for he wrote of me. But if you do not believe his writings, how will you believe my words?"

These challenges are addressed to twenty-first-century pilgrims just as forcefully as they were addressed to Jesus's own people, in his own time and place. Five centuries after Christ, Pope St. Leo the Great issued a similar challenge to his Roman congregation: to put aside their own conceptions of the kind of redeemer that made sense and to fix their attention on the redeemer, and the means of redemption, the Father had already chosen. In today's Office of Readings, Leo teaches twenty-first-century pilgrims, as he taught fifth-century Romans, that Jesus the Christ had to take on our infirmities, "the nature of a slave," in order to heal that nature and render us capable of intimacy with the Holy One:

For that reason the only-begotten Son of God became also the son of man. He was to have both the reality of a human nature and the fullness of the godhead.

The body that lay lifeless in the tomb is ours. The body that rose again on the third day is ours. The body that ascended above all the heights of heaven to the right hand of the Father's glory is ours. If we then walk in the way of his commandments, and are not ashamed to acknowledge the price he paid for our salvation in a lowly body, we too are to rise to share in his glory. The promise he made will be fulfilled in us: "So every one who acknowledges me before men, I also will acknowledge before my Father who is in heaven" [Matthew 10.32].

The challenge, then, involves not being "ashamed of the price." The issue in meeting that challenge is pride: that was the issue in the Garden of

Eden; that was the issue in the incident of the golden calf at Mt. Sinai; that was the issue during the public ministry of Jesus; and that is the issue today. Will humanity fashion for itself a God in its own image and likeness? Will we fashion a redeemer who will fix everything as we imagine things should be fixed, and in the way we think they should be fixed? Or will we submit, in reverence and obedience, to the "form" of redemption designed by a God who is *not* within our control, a redemption that compels us to confront the salvific character of what often strikes us as absurd: suffering and death?

In his 1981 apostolic letter *Salvifici Doloris* [Redemptive Suffering], Pope John Paul II reflected on the fact that only human beings *suffer*. Animals experience pain, but only men and women suffer. This suggests that suffering, including the most physically painful suffering, has an essentially spiritual character; suffering touches the soul, not merely the nervous system. The Bible, which John Paul described as a "great book about suffering," teaches that "love is . . . the fullest source of the answer to the question of the meaning of suffering." To learn that truth fully, however, humanity required a demonstration, not an argument. That demonstration is what the Father has "given . . . in the cross of Jesus Christ."

To embrace the Cross, then, is to embrace the logic of salvation as the Father defined that logic. This is perhaps the hardest challenge of Lent. Yet, as the remaining two weeks of the Lenten pilgrimage will make unmistakably clear, the life of Christ, and thus the imitation of Christ, lead inexorably toward Calvary. The "works" that Jesus does, and that bear witness that his testimony is true, involve the physical and psychological healing of suffering—signs that the Kingdom is breaking into history in the lives of real men and women. Yet even as he heals, Jesus suffers. He suffers misunderstanding (How can the carpenter's son do these things?). He suffers from being anathematized by his fellow-believers (for he has dared to identify himself with the Father). He will ultimately suffer ridicule while he is dying ("He saved others; let him save himself, if he is the Christ of God, his Chosen One!" [Luke 23.35]).

Thus Christ experienced "an incomparable depth and intensity of suffering," because his suffering was "capable of embracing the measure of evil" stored up in the entirety of human history. So wrote John Paul II in *Salvifici Doloris*. Swiss theologian Hans Urs von Balthasar made a similar point even more starkly in his brief meditations on the Creed and the Sorrowful Mysteries of the Rosary: What would it be like, Balthasar asked, to "bear the burden of the world's guilt, to experience in oneself the inner perversion of a humankind that refuses any sort of service, any sort of respect, to God?" We cannot, literally, imagine this: we cannot imagine what it would be like to suffer as the Son suffered when he took upon himself "all that the Father finds loathsome."

Yet here, on the Cross, we meet what Balthasar described as the eternal, Trinitarian project in history: "to clear out all the refuse of the world's sins by burning it in the fire of suffering love." At Calvary, the burning passion of God, which is both the divine wrath at the world's evil and the divine mercy determined to heal what sin has broken, coincide. In the power of the Spirit, the Son offers the perfect act of atonement to the Father, and by that act of obedience, the burning fire of divine love reaches into history and immolates everything in the world that cannot bring forth love, including suffering and death.

The redemption is a Trinitarian drama: an action of the thrice-holy God who is Father, Son, and Holy Spirit. The Church drives that point home today and tomorrow, both in the liturgy and in the station churches. Today's *statio* at Sts. Sylvester and Martin honors the pope who, according to tradition, received on this spot the decrees of the Council of Nicaea, confirming the Church's faith in the Triune God, while at the same time despoiling the works of Arius, whose anti-Trinitarian teaching had divided Christianity for decades. Tomorrow's station honors a Roman priest and martyr who died in defense of the divinity of Christ and thus the doctrine of the Trinity.

Redemptive suffering, God as a Trinity of Persons who effect humanity's salvation through burning, purifying love: the embrace of these challenging truths is central to the imitation of Christ. For that embrace leads from the Son to the Father and the Spirit, and into the embrace of Trinitarian love and divine glory.

Sts. Sylvester and Martin: Pope St.
Sylvester kneeling before the
Virgin Mary (eleventh century)

T HE SITE OF THE HOME of the Roman presbyter Equitus, today's station became a house church in the third century. It was first used for clandestine worship; decades later, it became closely associated with the defense of Christ's divinity. The orthodox party met here in 324 before the Council of Nicaea, and the first public refutation of Arianism took place when the writings of Arius and Sabellius were burned at this site. The remains of the ancient house are remarkably well preserved beneath today's basilica.

An antique "Hall of Six Rooms" was unearthed in the seventeenth century when Baroque artist Pietro da Cortona was designing the crypt; several spaces opened off the hall and a staircase led to an upper story. While some archaeologists concluded that this indicated a commercial site, frescoes amid the labyrinth of brick and plaster testify to pre-Constantinian Christian communities meeting here. The finely wrought stucco decoration of palm leaves and garlands was a seventeenth-century addition, and around one altar faint traces of an elaborate, faux-architectural painting (a Baroque specialty) are still visible, framing an eleventh-century mosaic of Pope St. Sylvester I kneeling before the Madonna.

This crypt area is associated with an oratory to the martyrs that Sylvester built in the fourth century; a church dedicated to St. Martin of Tours is also mentioned as being in this area. In 500, Pope Symmachus seems to have built a church on top of the oratory (which then became the crypt), dedicating the structure to the two saints. The crypt contains a remarkable number of relics, including those of Pope St. Martin I (who died in defense of orthodoxy in the seventh century). The list of saints' remains translated here from the catacombs is inscribed on plaques leading up to the nave.

The Baroque stairway from the crypt to the church is a passageway from paleo-Christianity to the time of Charlemagne, as Pope Sergius II replaced the sixth-century church with a basilica in 845; the tufa blocks along the base are typical of Carolingian constructions, as is the reuse of ancient columns from the old basilica. Today's gleaming church is the result of an elaborate seventeenth-century restoration by Filippo Gagliardi, who oversaw the decoration and designed the *confessio*, the high altar, and the access to the crypt; the high altar contains relics of Sts. Artemis, Paolina, and Sisinnius, brought from the catacombs of Priscilla.

Three cardinals-titular of the church have become popes: Boniface VIII, Pius XI, and Paul VI. Two other cardinals-titular, St. Charles Borromeo and his friend, Cardinal Gabriele Paleotti, were responsible for the basilica's avant-garde decoration, as both men were actively involved with the aesthetic reform that led to the Baroque era. Paleotti wrote a treatise for painters on art suitable for sacred spaces, and the church's exceptional decoration seems to have been inspired by this great patron.

Landscape paintings, an innovation in seventeenth-century religious commissions, cover the walls. Gaspard Dughet's Old Testament stories and images of the prophet Elijah lead to the Chapel of Our Lady of Mt. Carmel, where the Virgin's icon is framed by souls in purgatory imploring her assistance. The two architectural interiors painted by Filippo Gherardi are also unique in church décor; the fresco of St. John Lateran depicts the first Christian basilica prior to its 1650 remodeling by Francesco Borromini. Girolamo Muziano, a leading Counter-Reformation artist, painted the altarpiece of *St. Albert*, while the elusive-yet-brilliant Pietro Testa left one of his rare altarpieces in the *Vision of St. Angelo the Carmelite*. [E.L.]

St. Eusebius: *Glory of St. Eusebius* (Anton Raphael Mengs, c. 1757)

FRIDAY OF THE FOURTH WEEK OF LENT

Station at St. Eusebius

Holy Mass

Wisdom 2.1a, 12–22

Psalm 34

John 7.1–2, 10, 25–30

Office of Readings

Numbers 14.1–25

St. Athanasius: Easter Letter

S T. ATHANASIUS WAS THE great defender of the full divinity of Christ, the Word of God, during the Arian controversy, which roiled Christianity throughout the fourth century. In today's Office of Readings, Athanasius reminds his Alexandrian congregation that Easter, which defines the entire liturgical year, is celebrated annually because Easter "guides us through the trials that meet us in this world." "[In] the wonder of his love," Athanasius writes, the Lord "gathers to this feast those who are far apart, and brings together in unity of faith those who may be physically separated from each other," in order to experience in the liturgy the truth that "the grace of [Easter] is not restricted to one occasion. Its rays of glory never set."

The same point is made by the liturgical proclamation of the date of Easter, which ought to be (but rarely is) made in every parish shortly after Christmas, on the Solemnity of the Epiphany. On the day the Church marks the public inbreaking, the "epiphany," of the Kingdom, that proclamation describes the entire year of grace as a pilgrimage to and from Easter, and rightly describes Sunday as the re-embodiment of Easter every week:

Dear brethren: The glory of the Lord has been made manifest to us and will always be visible in our midst until his return. Amidst the rhythms and turnings of time, we remember and live the mysteries of salvation. The center of the entire liturgical year is the Triduum of the crucified, buried, and risen Lord, which culminates on Easter Sunday, _____. On every Sunday, which is the Easter of each week, the holy Church makes present this great event in which Christ conquered sin and death. From Easter stem all the other holy days: Ash Wednesday, the beginning of Lent, which is _____; the Ascension of the Lord, which is _____; Pentecost, which is _____; and the First Sunday of Advent, which will be celebrated on _____. In the feasts of the holy Mother of God, the apostles, and the saints, as well as in the commemoration of the faithful departed, the pilgrim Church on earth proclaims the Easter Passover of the Lord. To Christ who was, who is, and who will come again, the Lord of time and of history, be endless praise for ever and ever. Amen.

"Spirituality" of the sort found in most twenty-first-century bookstores tends toward the gnostic: religion detached from the stuff of the world and floating in an ethereal world-without-time; faith presented as a personal lifestyle choice; worship misconstrued as self-therapy. The Church's proclamation of dates, and Athanasius's emphasis on the centrality of Easter, are both important reminders that Christian faith is grounded in history, not in "myth" or "narrative." And history, as philosopher Peter Kreeft has taught, is "His-story." Because of the divine passion to save, certain things happened in the eastern borderlands of the Roman Empire two millennia ago. Those events forced men and women not so different from us to make decisions. And those decisions, which are themselves historical facts, changed the history of the world—a change that is another historical fact. Certain things happened in history; men and women were transformed; the human story, which is ultimately His-story, changed as a result.

Salvation history is the history of the world, read at its proper depth and against an appropriately ample horizon. That is why there is no such thing as "Ordinary Time," the conventions of twenty-first-century liturgical translations notwithstanding. Because history is His-story, all time is his time and there is nothing "ordinary" about that. Living that reality—living in *that* time—is the challenge of the imitation of Christ.

The Arian controversy did not end in 325 A.D. when the First Council of Nicaea affirmed three Persons in one Godhead, as we are reminded by the life of St. Eusebius, the martyr whose defense of the doctrine of the Trinity, through his defense of the divinity of Jesus Christ, is commemorated in today's *statio*.

The Christology of Arius—that the Word, the *Logos*, "had a beginning of existence," such that there was a time when "the Son was not" (as Arius put it)—was also anti-Trinitarian, implying as it did that God was not Father from before-the-ages. While these notions were rejected by the first ecumenical council, they were revived decades later and given imperial support by Emperor Constantius II, who was an Arian. The station "at St. Eusebius" is reckoned by tradition to be the site of the house of the martyr-priest for whom the basilica is named, who died in the persecution of orthodox Christians launched by Constantius II.

Trinitarian doctrine has always posed a challenge for preachers, at least as judged by the frequency with which one hears the complaint from the pulpit on Trinity Sunday that "this is the hardest Sunday of the year on which to preach." In our decidedly pragmatic and antimetaphysical culture, so different from the culture that produced a creed that identified the Son as "God from God, Light from Light, true God from true God, consubstantial with the Father," perhaps the difficulty comes from trying to dumb down the high-altitude theology of the Trinity proposed by such giants as Augustine and Aquinas. And perhaps the resolution to that problem comes from thinking in terms of relationships in history, rather than in terms of "substances," "spirations," and the rest of the technical vocabulary of classic Trinitarian theology.

As the Lenten pilgrimage of conversion has reminded us, the God of the Bible is the Holy One who comes into history in search of humanity, and who asks humanity to take the same path into the future that he is taking. This God is a God of relationships: he makes covenants with Abraham and with the chosen people, Israel; he makes a new and universal covenant with Jews and Gentiles alike in his Son, who draws disciples to himself in relationships of fidelity and friendship. The Father and the Son pour out the Holy Spirit, from which the Church, a communion of disciples in relationship to the Triune God and to one another, is born. These disciples are then sent into the world in mission, to bring others into the New Life of Trinitarian love through baptism "in the name of the Father, and of the Son, and of the Holy Spirit."

The God of Israel, who is the God of the Church, is a God of relationships. And God could not "be with" us, intimately and personally, unless "being with," personally, were somehow part of the character or nature of God in himself, as Hans Urs von Balthasar taught. The God whom Christians are called to worship is, in his Godhead, a vibrant eternal event, a communion of self-giving and receptivity. The truths we discern about God-in-history, God-for-us, give us a glimpse (which we express in the Creed) into God-in-himself, whom we shall know, even as we are known, at the Wedding Feast of the Lamb. There, the faith of the Church teaches, those who have been saved by the blood of the Lamb and sealed with the gift of the Holy Spirit live forever within the light and love, the giving-and-receiving, of the Trinity itself.

That is the truth for which St. Eusebius gave his life. That is the truth into which Lenten pilgrims are called to grow during the Forty Days.

St. Eusebius: Choir stalls (Celestine monks, 1600)

T HE BASILICA OF ST. EUSEBIUS rests upon an ancient Roman necropolis, a slight plateau of graves dating to the ninth century B.C. In republican times, this was one of Rome's most unsavory areas, a desolate home to mass burials. The neighborhood's status improved after the Roman art patron Maecenas built his celebrated gardens nearby and when, in 226, the grand fountain of the Aque Alexandrina brought water to the Esquiline Hill.

The remains of an ancient house with traces of heavy third- or fourth-century rebuilding have been excavated here, suggesting that the house church associated with the Basilica of St. Eusebius is one of the oldest in Rome. After Christianity was legalized, this *domus* was replaced by a new structure, perhaps erected by Pope Liberius in 360, in testimony to Christian veneration for the site. From its first written attestation in 494, the church has been dedicated to St. Eusebius, whose story is a reminder that martyrdom continued after the Edict of Milan.

According to the *Golden Legend*, Eusebius was born just before Constantine legalized Christianity. Chosen by Pope Julian as bishop of Vercelli, near Milan, Eusebius took up his duties when the Arian heresy had been embraced by much of northern Italy and by Constantine's son, Constantius. Summoned to Milan, Eusebius was ordered to sign an imperial document endorsing the heresy. Eusebius refused, withstanding imprisonment, beatings, and torture before eventually dying from his wounds.

Today's church seems rather distant from those tumultuous times, its elegant eighteenth-century façade suggesting tranquility; only the brick-and-mortar crypt evokes the site's ancient history. A small bell tower is the last remnant of Gregory XI's thirteenth-century rebuilding.

The basilica's complete refurbishment by Carlo Stefano Fontana and Niccolò Piccinini between 1711 and 1750 gave Rome one of its first examples of the pared-down, neoclassical style. Cream-colored walls with subdued stucco decoration open onto a vault frescoed by Rome's favorite neoclassical painter, Anton Raphael Mengs. Mengs produced few works for churches, but his *Glory of St. Eusebius*, a rare and wonderful exception, offers an alternative meaning of "enlightenment": swathed in white and lifted by lithe angels toward pure light, St. Eusebius points toward a tablet inscribed (in Greek) with the words "consubstantial with the Father"—the creed he died to uphold.

The altar, with its high marble backdrop, contains the relics of Sts. Eusebius, Orosius, and Paulinus. The magnificently carved choir stalls date from the late sixteenth century. The small chapel on the left is dedicated to Pope St. Celestine V, who abdicated in 1296, thinking himself unsuited for the papacy: this *Great Renunciation* is depicted above the altar.

The piazza includes an image of the Immaculate Conception, erected in 1954 for the centenary of that Marian dogma. Every January 17, on the feast of St. Anthony the Abbot, Romans gather here with their pets for the blessing of animals. The Chapel of the Crucifix contains the names of parishioners who died in World War I; the painted sculpture of the Madonna and Child inside a lapis blue niche is a remnant of the nineteenth-century neo-Gothic revival. [E.L.]

St. Nicholas in Prison: High altar and apse

SATURDAY OF THE FOURTH WEEK OF LENT

Station at St. Nicholas in Prison

Holy Mass
Jeremiah 11.18–20
Psalm 7
John 7.40–53

Office of Readings
Number 20.1–13; 21.4–9
Vatican II: Pastoral Constitution on the Church in the Modern World, 37–38

IMAGES OF THE PASSION from the Old Testament will multiply as the Church draws closer to Calvary on its Lenten pilgrimage. The liturgical readings of the next several weeks illustrate the unity of the Scriptures as the Church reads them through the lens of her faith in the Lord Jesus.

Thus Jeremiah, in today's Mass, speaks of the "gentle lamb led to the slaughter" and of the prophet who is like a "tree with its fruit," the just one whom the sinful will try to "cut off from the land of the living." In today's Office of Readings, the Church's Lenten reflection on the Exodus cycle concludes with the chosen people being healed of their affliction when God lifts up before their gaze the bronze serpent. Jesus will identify himself with this image, saying: "As Moses lifted up the serpent in the wilderness, so must the Son of Man be lifted up, that whoever believes in him may have eternal life" [John 3.14–15].

This imagery brings us to a transition in the Forty Days. For the remainder of Lent, the Office of Readings will draw pilgrims deeply into the Letter to the Hebrews through a sequence of reflections that strengthen the link between the covenant at Sinai and the covenant sealed in the blood of Christ: the "high priest who is seated at the right hand of the throne of the Majesty in heaven, a minister in the sanctuary and the true tent which is set up not by man but by the Lord" [Hebrews 8.1–2].

As the pace to Calvary quickens, the Church also reminds pilgrims that, as the Christ who loved his brethren will abandon himself to the Father's will in a perfect act of priestly self-giving, so, as friends of Jesus, we must both cherish the gifts God has given us in creation and learn a certain spiritual detachment from them. The Fathers of the Second Vatican Council taught this important lesson in the selection today from the Pastoral Constitution on the Church in the Modern World:

[Redeemed] by Christ and made a new creature in the Holy Spirit, man is able to love the things themselves created by God, and ought to do so. He can receive them from God and respect and reverence them as flowing constantly from the hand of God. Grateful to his Benefactor for these creatures, using and enjoying them in detachment and liberty of spirit, man is led forward to a true possession of them, as having nothing yet possessing all things. "All are yours, and you are Christ's, and Christ is God's." [1 Corinthians 3.22–23]

The debate over Jesus in the Johannine gospel reading of today's Mass is yet another Lenten reminder that the Redeemer whom God has sent is not necessarily the redeemer humanity would have sought. Some in the crowd believe Jesus is, indeed, the promised Holy One, or at the very least a prophet to whom attention should be paid. But then come the skeptics: A prophet from Galilee? "Galilee of the Gentiles," the outback, the sticks, the backwater: Why would God bring forth the promised redeemer of Israel from *there*? As the argument continues, the authorities get involved. They, too, think the very idea of a Galilean messiah is risible. Then, after the debate dies out, "each went to his own house"—that is, each went off to his own concept of "the Prophet," his own auto-constructed "Christ." Hardened hearts have not yet been converted, despite prophetic signs.

Nicodemus is here, too: the paradigm of the tentative disciple who is drawn into Jesus's orbit but who cannot, yet, bring himself to make an unreserved commitment to Jesus's cause. He makes an appeal to legal rationality and tradition—"Does our Law judge a man without first giving him a hearing and learning what he does?"—without realizing that the inbreaking of the Kingdom, in the person of Jesus, has changed the standards by which prophecy and "signs" are judged. Nicodemus tries, in his tentative way, to get Jesus off this particular hook, forged of snobbery. Yet he still cannot embrace the New Life, because he has not been radically converted. And in his tentativeness, he cannot bear fruit; he has not begun to engage in that unreserved imitation of Christ to which this phase of the Lenten itinerary of conversion summons us.

And so, as the fourth full week of Lent draws to a close and the Church prepares to enter what was once called "Passiontide," Lenten pilgrims are taught that, while compelling prophetic speech and miraculous signs can point to the Anointed One of God, only faith can grasp who the Christ is—no matter where he may seem to come from. And if it challenges our pride to imagine the Messiah coming from a boondocks like Galilee, how much more does it challenge that pride to recognize a Messiah who comes from God, who is God among us—and whose mission appears to end in the seeming catastrophe of the Cross?

Today's *statio* honors St. Nicholas, bishop of Myra in Asia Minor. Nicholas was persecuted under Diocletian, survived to become one of the defenders of the full divinity of Christ at the Council of Nicaea, and is remembered today as the man whose charity inspired the idea of Santa Claus. One tradition has it that Bishop Nicholas took a punch at Arius during the Council of Nicaea, which does not, perhaps, fit the "jolly old elf" imagery of "The Night Before

Christmas." It does, however, remind us, on this third consecutive day of stations whose names or relics evoke memories of the first ecumenical council, that, for the Church of the fourth century, getting the truth about Christ and the truth about the Trinity right were not trivial matters; they were matters of spiritual life and death.

Nicholas was not imprisoned here; the station's name refers to the possibility that the building that was transformed into today's basilica may have been a jail near the ancient Roman vegetable market. Nicholas was, however, imprisoned for his faith during one of the great persecutions of antiquity, and a *statio* at what may once have been a prison is no bad way to end this phase of Lent and enter Passiontide.

Twenty-first-century pilgrims along the Lenten itinerary of conversion are living in the greatest era of persecution in the history of the Church—a fact that registers on the Christian imagination too infrequently, at least in the relatively secure Christian communities of the Western world, where "martyrdom" is often regarded as something that happened to mythic figures from the distant past. Yet the truth of the matter is that more Christians died for the faith in the twentieth century than in the previous nineteen centuries of Christian history combined.

Martyrdom is an ever-present possibility for those who are not tentative disciples. Suffering for the faith, even if that suffering takes the form of enduring ridicule—the twenty-first-century equivalents of "*Galilee?*"—is one facet of the imitation of Christ.

St. Nicholas in Prison: *Christ in Glory* (Vincenzo Pasqualoni, 1860)

Two MILLENNIA AGO, three pagan temples, honoring Juno, Janus, and Spes [Hope], were wedged here between Rome's produce market and the Tiber. A few blocks of travertine are all that remain of the market; the Tiber was tamed by a high embankment. Hope, in Christian form, lives on in the Basilica of St. Nicholas in Prison.

This area was already home to a thriving Greco-Syrian population when the eighth-century Iconoclast Controversy drove other Greek-speaking, image-loving Christians to Rome and the adjacent neighborhoods, although Christian graves beneath the building suggest that the site already housed a church in the fifth century. St. Nicholas is first mentioned in connection with the church in the eleventh century, while the "surname" likely derives from a nearby medieval prison, mentioned in an eighth-century document of Pope Adrian I.

From the east, an ancient temple skeleton is visible in the Doric columns supporting the church's entablature. The medieval church was richly decorated with twelfth-century frescos; several were found in the crypt during a nineteenth-century restoration. Rodrigo Borgia, later Pope Alexander VI, whitewashed the walls and removed inscriptions and furnishings to give the church the clean lines preferred by the Renaissance.

A few works hint at the church's *Quattrocento* (fifteenth-century) prominence. The right nave includes a detached *Madonna and Child* fresco by Antoniazzo Romano, while Lorenzo Costa, a prestigious painter from Ferrara who would be brought into the court of Isabella D'Este, executed the crisp linear panel painting of the *Ascension*.

In the spirit of the sixteenth-century Catholic restoration, Cardinal Federico Borromeo underscored the site's antiquity by reopening the crypt and bringing relics of Sts. Mark, Marcellino, Simplicius, and Faustinus to the high altar; the remains of the ancient temples can be seen in the crypt today. Pietro Aldobrandini, Borromeo's successor as cardinal-titular, continued the church's decoration: Orazio Gentileschi and Giovanni Baglione, respectively the best friend and direst enemy of Caravaggio, worked here, and while Gentileschi's works are gone, the Rosary Chapel, formerly the Blessed Sacrament Chapel, contains Baglione's Eucharistic frescoes. Cardinal Aldobrandini was also responsible for the façade, with its smooth travertine blocks carved in a low relief.

Blessed Pius IX added a coffered ceiling in the nineteenth century; his coat of arms is visible amid the gilded tracery. Pius also commissioned Guido Guidi to decorate the nave with stories of St. Nicholas, while Vincenzo Pasqualoni was given charge of the apse. His surprisingly monumental

(continues)

(*continued*)

fresco begins with a flow of figures at the Council of Nicaea, where Nicholas of Myra anathematizes the Arians for denying Christ's divinity. Above, Christ sits in majesty, flanked by Mary and St. Nicholas between the Church Militant and the Church Triumphant. In addition, Pius had copies of some of Rome's best seventeenth-century paintings made for the otherwise barren walls: Guercino's *Trinity* with its mesmerizing blue and Annibale Carracci's powerful *Assumption* add a splash of color. In that period, the church also became a center of devotion to Our Lady of Guadalupe, Patroness of the Americas, in whose honor a Mass is celebrated here on the twelfth of every month.

One moving inscription among the dozens in the church commands attention: "Here lies the great sinner who was canon of this venerable church. Pray for his salvation, you, my friends." [E.L.]

St. John Before the
Latin Gate: Crucifix
with Mary and St. John
(twentieth century,
from the Val Gardena)

The
FIFTH WEEK
of LENT

St. Peter: Altar of the Chair (Gian Lorenzo Bernini, 1653)

THE FIFTH
SUNDAY IN LENT

Station at St. Peter

Holy Mass

[A]	[B]	[C]
Ezekiel 37.12–14	*Jeremiah 31.31–34*	*Isaiah 43.16–21*
Psalm 130	*Psalm 51*	*Psalm 126*
Romans 8.8–11	*Hebrews 5.7–9*	*Philippians 3.8–14*
John 11.1–45	*John 12.20–33*	*John 8.1–11*

Office of Readings

Hebrews 1.1–2.4

St. Athanasius: Easter Letter

THE JOHANNINE ACCOUNT OF the raising of Lazarus is the last of the three great catechetical gospel stories taught to the catechumens of the early Church as they prepared to receive Baptism at the Easter Vigil. As with the Johannine accounts of Jesus and the woman at the well and the cure of the man born blind, the Lazarus account is so important to the spiritual and liturgical rhythm of the Forty Days that it can be substituted for the gospel reading assigned to this Sunday in Lectionary Cycles B and C, and, if not proclaimed on Sunday, should be read at a Mass during the Fifth Week of Lent. Here we are coming close to the central dynamic of the Lenten itinerary of conversion.

The Lazarus episode unfolds in two dramatic moments linked by an inner spiritual unity. After some initial scene-setting—Lazarus is ill; Jesus delays his departure for Bethany, where his sick friend is being attended by his sisters, Martha and Mary, also friends of Jesus; the disciples, as is often the case, don't get the significance of what Jesus has in mind—we come to the first dramatic moment: a conversation between Jesus and Martha that ends with Martha's confession of faith in him as the Anointed One of God. A second drama then unfolds: Lazarus is called out from the grave by the power of God at work in Jesus.

In restoring Lazarus to his sisters and his friends after he has been in the grave for four days, Jesus creates another "sign" that the New Covenant in him is breaking into the world and into history, perfecting and completing the Mosaic covenant. The fourth day after burial (which occurred on the day of death) was reckoned in many rabbinic traditions as the day on which the body definitively "returns to the dust" from which it came and the breath of life is called back by the God who first breathed it into man. Thus Jesus reveals that, in him, humanity is being introduced to the deepest truth about the trajectory of life, which is the reality of life-after-death: the eternal life that is available here and now through friendship with Jesus; the life-after-death through which, as St. Ignatius of Antioch wrote, "I shall be a man."

As Pope Benedict XVI pointed out in his Lenten Message for 2011, this demonstration of the availability of eternal life through Jesus has more than individual meaning, important as that was for Lazarus and important as it is for every Christian disciple. The fullness of life that God wills to bring into the world through the person and mission of Jesus gives history its final and definitive meaning. History is not just one thing after another. History is His-story, and in His-story, his saving will and redeeming love have the final word.

The catechetical explication of the Lazarus story that twenty-first-century pilgrims can imagine being offered to third-century catechumens invites everyone making the Lenten pilgrimage to Calvary and the Empty Tomb to identify with the characters in the biblical drama that will unfold during these next two weeks of Passiontide: a drama that is the axial point of human history. In our failure to embrace fully the imitation of Christ, we are like the uncomprehending disciples and the unconverted crowd in Bethany, whose lack of belief causes Jesus to weep in frustration (for Jesus's tears were not only for his dead friend, Lazarus, but for those who cannot see that he tarried in order to manifest the power of God). Like Martha in today's paradigmatic gospel account, we, too, are called to a confession of faith in Jesus as Lord. And, at the climax of the story, we are all Lazarus because of our baptismal resurrection: through the waters of Baptism and the cleansing of sins in the name of Father, Son, and Holy Spirit, we, too, are raised; we, too, are unbound and our eyes opened; we, too, are set free to live the New Life that cannot be taken away, even by death.

And we, too, are Mary, "who anointed the Lord with ointment and wiped his feet with her hair." When Jesus finally arrives in Bethany on the fourth day after the death of her brother, Mary remains at home while Martha goes to meet the Master. After Martha's confession of faith—"Yes, Lord, I believe that you are the Christ, the Son of God, he who is coming into the world"—she goes to call her sister, presumably distraught, with a quiet invitation: "The Teacher is here and he is calling for you." During the second conclave of 1978, Cardinal Maximilien de Fürstenberg (who had been the rector of Rome's Belgian College in 1946–1948, when a young Polish priest named Karol Wojtyła lived there while completing his doctoral studies in theology) paraphrased those very words of Martha to Mary in a query to Cardinal Karol Wojtyła (who was shaken by the way the voting was going, as it indicated that he might be elected pope)— although the Belgian prelate now put it as a question in Latin: *Deus adest et vocat te?* [God is here and calling you?]. Wojtyła had a special affection for the gospel of St. John and used to read it aloud to himself in Polish when he lived at the Belgian College. He could not have missed the subtle challenge being posed by his old rector: Can you, like Mary, who could not understand why Jesus had not come earlier and saved her brother, conform yourself to the Lord's will, no matter how puzzling it may seem?

The same question is posed to every Christian, of every time and every place, along the itinerary of conversion.

The distinctive Johannine rendering of this dramatic story underscores that Jesus is in sovereign control of events. He knows what is happening and he bends the vagaries of history (such as Lazarus's unexpected death, which might have called his messianic mission and person into question) to his own ends: Lazarus dies so that the glory of God may be revealed in his being called out from the tomb, unbound, and set free. This same sovereign assurance will be displayed throughout the Johannine gospel readings of the remaining days of Lent. What the Letter to the Hebrews in today's Office of Readings calls the "final age" is breaking into history in Jesus, shattering expectations while bringing the drama of salvation history—the true history of the world—to its climax. And throughout this inbreaking, Jesus is exercising the sovereign will of the Son, conformed in obedience to the Father.

Yet as the drama unfolds according to the design of the Father as executed by the Son in the power of the Holy Spirit, resistance to that Trinitarian project in history intensifies. The Entrance Antiphon today offers a quiet warning that the contest between Jesus and the Ancient Foe will become ever stronger, as the Church prays, with the psalmist and the Son, "Give me justice, O God, and plead my cause." As the sovereign authority of Jesus drives events forward to the climax the Father has ordained, Satan's fury increases. It will reach a fever pitch of loathing and hatred in the Garden of Gethsemane and on the Cross, when the Evil One himself, and those whose minds and hearts he warps, make one last, desperate attempt to have their way.

For now, the raising of Lazarus, an act of life-giving mercy, accelerates the sequence of events that will lead to Jesus's rejection and death. Yet here, too, obedience to the design of the Father will conquer the "oppression of the enemy" [Psalm 42.2b]. For through the redeeming death of the Son, all the faithful, not just Lazarus, are saved into a life that will not end, even in death.

Thus St. Athanasius taught his Alexandrian congregation in the fourth century, and thus he teaches us today: "If we follow Christ closely we shall be allowed, even on this earth, to stand as it were on the threshold of the heavenly Jerusalem, and enjoy the contemplation of that everlasting feast, like the blessed apostles, who in following the Savior as their leader, showed, and still show, the way to obtain the same gift from God."

St. Peter, *St. Veronica* (Francesco Mochi, 1629)

WITH ITS COMBINATION of Baroque and Renaissance architecture, the sprawling space of New St. Peter's Basilica was the seventeenth century's most daunting decorative project. Gian Lorenzo Bernini, the genius who proved worthy of the task, worked at it under four popes from 1623 to 1680, taming the basilica's vast interior and giving it the stunning appearance the world admires today.

Red marble veneers give the space warmth, while a symmetrical decorative scheme imposes order. Statues of the founders of reforming religious orders, carved by Bernini's disciples and increasing in size as they approach the altar, punctuate the nave: St. Ignatius of Loyola, St. Teresa of Avila, St. Philip Neri, and others. Each bay is framed by a triumphal arch, with two virtues perched at the keystone. Above, Christ's words to Peter form the cornice for a gilt vault flooded with light: an arrangement that draws the eye upward from the saints, and their virtuous example, to heaven. Saints and relics grace every altar: Pope St. Leo the Great is buried below an unusual marble relief of his confrontation with Attila, carved by Alessandro Algardi, while Blessed John XXIII rests under a mosaic copy of Domenichino's *Communion of St. Jerome*.

As Maderno's extension of the nave had made Michelangelo's dome invisible from the entrance, Bernini's first task was to refocus attention on Peter's tomb—a challenge solved by Bernini's extraordinary bronze *baldacchino*, ninety-five feet tall, which "connects" the dome and the tomb while covering the high altar. Stressing the continuity between the old and new basilicas, Bernini fashioned for this colossal canopy bronze columns that replicate the marble columns placed around Peter's grave by Constantine: Eastern features amid Greco-Roman architecture, they mirror Peter's journey from Jerusalem to Rome.

Constantine's original columns frame the chapels high up in the four great dome-supporting piers; each chapel contains a relic of Christ's Passion (thus linking the paschal drama in Jerusalem to Rome), and each pier displays a statue of the saint appropriate to the chapel's relic. Windswept *Veronica*, by Francesco Mochi, seems to rush toward the visitor, while Duquesnoy's *St. Andrew* looks lovingly at his cross. Bernini's *Longinus* is especially arresting: kinetic energy streams through the figure, capturing the moment the Roman soldier realizes that the crucified one is "the Son of God."

Bernini's art aims to reveal the physical world and the divine milieu in collision: thus in the basilica's apse he created an experience of Pentecost. The oval window puncturing the masonry is filled with yellow glass, and as the sun sets, golden light pours in, just as the Holy Spirit penetrated the upper room. Its rays play off the gilt angels that cascade from the opening and billow into clouds around Peter's throne: this enormous bronze chair, which seems to float unsupported in midair, contains the wooden shards of Peter's Roman *cathedra*. Standing alongside the bronze throne, their robes seemingly rustled by the winds of the Holy Spirit, are Sts. Ambrose, Augustine, Athanasius, and John Chrysostom, who set the early Church ablaze with missionary zeal.

Bernini's last work is in the left transept: a striking funerary monument to Pope Alexander VII that explores the theme of a "good death." The pope is neither standing nor sitting; he kneels humbly in prayer, bareheaded, his tiara put aside, the gold and white stucco décor around him representing the state of grace. The pope kneels above a massive undulating curtain in red marble: This curtain, often used in Baroque art, alludes to the stage, and suggests that every person plays a starring role in his or her own drama. A skeleton holding an hourglass interrupts Alexander's contemplative prayer: it is rising from beneath the curtain, indicating that the pope's time is up. Yet, despite death's surprise attack, the pontiff is spiritually prepared for heaven. [E.L.]

St. Chrysogonus: Stational Mass

St. Lawrence in Lucina: Fonseca Chapel

Four Holy Crowned Martyrs: St. Sylvester Chapel

Four Holy Crowned Martyrs: Fresco Fragment

St. Lawrence in Damaso: Apse Dome

St. Paul Outside the Walls: *Paul the Apostle*

Sts. Sylvester and Martin:
St. John Lateran

St. Chrysogonus:
Apse Detail

St. Mary in Via Lata: Transept Ceiling

St. Apollinaris: Apse

St. Apollinaris:
St. Francis Xavier

St. Stephen on the Caelian Hill: *Scenes of Martyrdom*

MONDAY OF THE FIFTH WEEK OF LENT

Station at St. Chrysogonus

Holy Mass
Daniel 13.1–9, 15–17, 19–30, 33–62
Psalm 23
John 8.1–11

Office of Readings
Hebrews 2.5–18
St. John Fisher: Commentary on Psalm 129

A T FIRST GLANCE, THE readings for Mass today seem to lead us back into a Lenten examination of conscience, with the capital sin of lust being the object of our self-scrutiny. And certainly, unruly passions (coupled with dishonesty) set the dramatic context for the Susanna story from the Book of Daniel as well as today's gospel episode of the woman caught in adultery. On closer examination, however, these two readings lead us deeper into the imitation of Christ and offer further insights into the Kingdom that is breaking into history in the person and mission of Jesus.

The Church will open the Book of Daniel once more during Lent, when, at Mass this coming Wednesday, the familiar miracle-story of the three young men who survive Nebuchadnezzar's fiery furnace is read. The Book of Daniel, redolent of Israel's experience during the Babylonian exile, is an intriguing composite of prophetic and apocalyptic writing. Daniel's prophetic gift for the interpretation of dreams and visions make clear to the powers of the world that the God of Israel is no tribal deity to be sneered at. The miraculous rescue of Hananiah, Azariah, and Mishael from the white-hot fury of the king, whose god they refused to worship, like Daniel's rescue of the innocent Susanna in today's Mass reading, demonstrates the power of the true God to save his servants from death-dealing predicaments. The deeper insights of the Book of Daniel may, however, be found in its apocalyptic chapters, which anticipate the New Testament's Book of Revelation in their vision of a cosmic contest between the powers of good and evil, with Michael the archangel delivering those whose names "shall be found written in the book" [Daniel 12.1].

It is this apocalyptic aspect of the Book of Daniel that provides a link to the heightening tensions reflected in today's gospel reading, where Jesus is once more put to the test by those who try to trap him into rejecting the Law: this time, in judging the case of the woman caught in adultery. Jesus's seeming insouciance during the drama in which his teaching and authority are challenged—he bends down and doodles in the sand, twice—is not indifference. Rather, it is a reiteration in action of his claim that, in him, the Kingdom of God is breaking into the world and into history, forcing men and women to rethink their relationship to the Law and the Temple, where this confrontation is played out. In Jesus, and by his authority as Son, mercy trumps the strict demands of legal justice as understood at the time—just as the divine mercy rescued Susanna from death at the hands of false accusers, and just as the divine mercy vindicated the fidelity of Hananiah, Azariah, and Mishael in the fiery furnace.

Today's gospel reading also reinforces the image of the sovereign Christ, who, throughout his public ministry, is in full control of events, turning the unexpected and dangerous (and, ultimately, the seemingly catastrophic) to the accomplishment of the salvific task for which "the Word became flesh and dwelt among us, full of grace and truth" [John 1.14]. As Dame Maria Boulding, the Benedictine biblical scholar, pointed out in an insightful reflection on this passage, the story presents a sharp contrast between Jesus and his opponents: "The Pharisees are tense, but he is calm and relaxed throughout; he accepts the woman openly and lovingly, as an adult and as a person. He has a sureness of touch; he can handle the situation and the relationship with her because he has nothing to be afraid of in himself." At the end, this sovereign Jesus, who has been given full authority by the Father, exercises the divine mercy, offers the woman new life, and yet admonishes her that she must not "fall back into the way that leads to death," as Australian exegete Francis Moloney wrote in his commentary on John's gospel.

In *Jesus of Nazareth—Holy Week*, Pope Benedict XVI also reflected on the linkage between the apocalyptic vision of Daniel and the revelation of God in the person of Jesus. Daniel, Benedict noted, mentions a "Son of Man" who is given everlasting "dominion and glory and kingdom" [Daniel 7.13–14]; but the exilic prophet is unable to fill in the picture of who this Son of Man might be. Jesus completes the picture by making clear to those with the eyes of faith that he, who so often described himself as the Son of Man, is the fulfillment of this prophetic vision of the final age. What Daniel's vision perceived as an event is now a person: in Jesus, "the future is already here," and no "future" will be different from the future Kingdom whose initiation in history is his mission. What could have seemed apocalyptically destructive, in Daniel, is now revealed in Jesus to be the foundation of the promised Reign of God:

> "Heaven and earth will pass away, but my words will not pass away" [Matthew 13.31]. The word—which seems almost nothing in comparison to the mighty power of the immeasurable material cosmos, like a fleeting breath against the silent grandeur of the universe—the word is more real and more lasting than the entire material world. The word is the true, dependable reality: the solid ground on which we can stand, which holds firm even when the sun goes dark and the firmament disintegrates. . . . [The] word of Jesus is the true firmament beneath which we can stand and remain.

The Letter to the Hebrews reminds us today that this sovereign Christ is also a fully human Christ. High Priest of the New Covenant, he is also subjected to temptation, so that he might become an exemplar for us to imitate: "Because he himself has suffered and been tempted, he is able to help those who are tempted." He is not Superman; he is a man, as Pope Benedict wrote, in whom God is so completely present that we see and experience God when we see and experience him. Thus his miraculous healings are neither magic nor a suspension of the laws of nature but an unveiling of what God had intended nature to be, before the Fall: full of life. Likewise, the raising of Lazarus unveils the truth about the divine intent in creation, which is to offer a share in the divine life, fully and forever. The same dynamic is at work in today's gospel reading: in the man Jesus and his exercise of authority (which includes authority over the Law strictly interpreted), we see, not the Law's abrogation, but the superiority of the divine mercy, which offers sinners a new opportunity at righteous living. In Jesus, and in his miracles, the End—the fulfillment of creation—is reaching into the here-and-now.

In early Christian biblical commentary, the innocent Susanna of today's first Mass reading was presented as a type of the unjustly persecuted Church. Thus the assignment of the Susanna story to today's liturgy is particularly appropriate given today's *statio* at St. Chrysogonus, who, like Sebastian and George, was a soldier-martyr of the Diocletian persecution in the early fourth century. Veneration of St. Chrysogonus was so widespread in Rome that his name was inscribed in the Roman Canon (Eucharistic Prayer I). Chrysogonus conformed himself to the sacrifice of Christ on Calvary by offering his own life in witness to the grace of God that had transformed him. So did St. John Fisher, who provides the second selection in today's Office of Readings. Fisher reminds Lenten pilgrims that the imitation of Christ, while perfected in martyrdom, also takes place in many other ways: "All who have embarked on true contrition and penance for the sins they have committed, and are firmly resolved not to commit sins again for the future but to persevere constantly in that pursuit of virtues which they have now begun, all these become sharers in [Christ's] holy and eternal sacrifice."

St. Chrysogonus: *Madonna and Child with St. Chrysogonus and St. James* (Pietro Cavallini, 1300)

S T. CHRYSOGONUS IS a stone's throw from one of ancient Rome's main wharves. Sailors, merchants, and foreigners abounded here, and the site's Christian history most likely began with a third-century house church: a *titulus* crammed amid shops, homes, and a laundry in a bustling, cosmopolitan neighborhood. That structure was transformed into a proper church in the fourth century: a large, single-nave edifice with no side aisles and a wide apse facing west. Much of it remains underground, but a 1907 archaeological exploration discovered considerable remnants of frescoes on its walls.

As Constantine unified the empire, relics began to travel from place to place; thus, the relics of St. Chrysogonus were brought to Rome with those of his companions, Sts. Anastasia and Rufo. The *titulus* was first mentioned in 499, but archaeological evidence suggests that the church had been here for well over a century. The complex included a large basin to the side of the church, likely a primitive baptistery for the new converts who entered the Church at this multicultural crossroads.

The relics were placed in an annular crypt in the eighth century, when the church was frescoed with stories from the patron saint's life, but the building's proximity to the river eventually led to flooding and severe damage. The basilica was saved in 1129 by its cardinal-titular, Giovanni da Crema, one of the architects of the Concordat of Worms, which brought hostilities over the Investiture Controversy to a (temporary) close.

Cardinal de Crema built the new church of St. Chrysogonus seventeen feet above and slightly to the right of the former structure and donated the pavement, one of Rome's oldest and best-preserved Cosmatesque floors. The church was enhanced with a bell tower, a squat structure lightened by its elegant arched openings. Twenty-two granite columns were recycled and capped with plaster capitals to line the nave, and the church's relics were placed in the inlaid stone altar. Shimmering mosaic decoration was also added; the remnant framed behind the altar displays the *Madonna and Child with St. Chrysogonus and St. James*.

The church owes its present appearance to Cardinal Scipione Borghese, who commissioned his favorite architect, Giovanni Soria, to lead a major restoration in 1623. Soria built the canopy over the altar and placed medallions of the Borghese family's coat of arms (a dragon surmounted by an eagle) in the floor. The Bolognese painter Guercino designed the ceiling with his fresco of *St. Chrysogonus in Glory*; his work bears some similarity to the coffered ceiling of St. Mary in Trastevere, designed by Guercino's more famous contemporary, Domenichino. (The fresco visible today is a copy, the original having been taken in 1808.)

The Trinitarians, founded in the twelfth century to ransom Christians from their Muslim captors, were given charge of the church in the mid-nineteenth century, and the beautiful, inlaid-wood choir stalls date from that period. A chapel on the left contains the relics of Anna Maria Taigi (1769–1837), a Third Order Trinitarian mystic who was beatified in 1920. [E.L.]

St. Mary in Via Lata: High Altar, *Mary Our Advocate* (Gian Lorenzo Bernini, 1636)

TUESDAY OF THE FIFTH WEEK OF LENT

Station at St. Mary in Via Lata

Holy Mass

Numbers 21.4–9

Psalm 102

John 8.21–30

Office of Readings

Hebrews 3.1–19

St. Leo the Great: Sermon on the Lord's Passion

THE AUTHOR OF THE Letter to the Hebrews teaches today that those who imitate Christ are the household of God, and does so in terms that hearken back to the beginning of the Lenten pilgrimage and its call to conversion:

Christ was faithful over God's house as a son. And we are his house if we hold fast our confidence and pride in our hope.

Therefore, as the Holy Spirit says,

"Today, when you hear his voice,

do not harden your hearts as in the rebellion,

   on the day of testing in the wilderness,

where your fathers put me to the test . . ."

The same theme is reiterated in the first responsorial of the Office of Readings, which combines Hebrews 3.6 with Ephesians 2.21 in order to extend the imagery from the familial (household) to the sacramental (the Temple):

Christ was faithful over God's house as a son;
—and we are that house.
Through him the whole structure is joined together,
And grows into a holy temple in the Lord.
—And we are that house.

Evocations of the Temple bring us to the gospel reading at today's Mass, drawn again from the Johannine narrative of Jesus's dramatic mission during the Feast of Tabernacles at the Temple in Jerusalem. This pilgrimage festival included a ceremony of light, celebrated around four great menorahs erected in the Temple's court of women. There, pious Jews danced every night for a week while the psalms were chanted. As biblical scholar Francis Moloney noted in his commentary on John, this ceremony may have been intended to evoke the pillar of fire by which YHWH led Israel in the wilderness, a pillar that many thought would return at the end of ages. The ceremony thus heightened the sense of salvific expectation at this annual ingathering of the chosen people in the Holy City; in doing so, it gave the Temple a future-oriented character.

So when Jesus declares that "I am the light of the world" and that "he who follows me will not walk in darkness, but will have the light of life" [John 8.12], and does so within the Temple in the midst of the Feast of Tabernacles, he is making two radical, history-changing claims: he is identifying his person and mission with the God who led Israel through the night desert as the blazing, light-giving Presence described in Exodus 13.21; and he is identifying his destiny with Israel's hope that the return of the pillar of fire will signal the redemption of the nation and the inauguration of the end time. In today's gospel reading, those claims are distilled into an even bolder identification between Jesus and the God of Abraham, Isaac, Jacob, and Moses, who revealed himself out of the burning bush as "I AM" [Exodus 3.14]. Jesus says: "When you have lifted up the Son of Man, then you will know that I am he, and that I do nothing on my own authority but speak thus as the Father taught me." Some translations render this as "you will know that I AM," an even closer and more radical identification of the Son of Man with the Father that Jesus will make unmistakably explicit in Thursday's gospel reading.

For the moment, though, it is enough to reflect on the drama of the claims that Jesus is making, sometimes overtly ("*I am the light of the world*"), sometimes more elliptically ("I am he"). During the pilgrimage feast that had come to embody Israel's expectation of a world-changing divine event that would vindicate the chosen people's faith and hope, Jesus announces, at the Temple that is God's dwelling among men, that God will now be found when the Son of Man is "lifted up": which can only mean lifted up on the Cross. The Cross will be the new center of the world, the *axis mundi* where all humanity will encounter the Holy One who named himself to Moses as I AM. In the past, the chosen people were instructed to look at the bronze serpent cast by Moses in order to be healed of the affliction caused by poisonous serpents, as recalled in the first reading of today's Mass. Now, the chosen (who include, potentially, all of humanity) are called to look up at the Cross, and at the Son of Man who is lifted up there, in order to be healed of the illnesses caused by the seraph serpents—the demons—that wound every life. Jesus's challenge to accept the gift of new life found in him or risk being lost—"Unless you believe that I am he"—is addressed not only to those attending the Feast of Tabernacles in Jerusalem two millennia ago, but also, as Francis Moloney put it, "to people of all times."

The imitation of Christ to which this phase of the Lenten pilgrimage of conversion summons us thus includes an entirely new way of looking at humanity's story over time. When it is approached in a classic, linear fashion, world history is taught under chapter headings that run something like this:

Ancient Civilizations; Greece and Rome; the Dark Ages; the Middle Ages; Renaissance and Reformation; the Age of Revolution; the Age of Science; the Space Age; the Digital Age. The challenge posed by Jesus's dramatic and radical claims at the Feast of Tabernacles is to understand that this rendering of history, while true enough, remains on the surface of things. It's history as outlined by a neutral, unengaged observer who records the flow of events.

History read through the eyes of faith—history as His-story—has a different texture and is organized under different chapter headings: Creation; Fall; Promise; Prophecy; Incarnation; Redemption; Sanctification; the Kingdom of God (or, if you prefer, the Wedding Feast of the Lamb). This is history read in its true depth and against its most ample horizon. This is the story that "begins" when God the Holy Trinity freely brings into being that which is not-God, so that God may share with his creation the superabundance of the Trinitarian life. This is the story that "ends" when God is all-in-all: "When all things are subjected to him, then the Son himself will be subjected to him who put all things under him, so that God may be everything to every one" [1 Corinthians 15.28].

The Lenten itinerary of conversion is an opportunity to deepen our understanding that these two readings of history do not run on parallel tracks, as if there were "world history" *here* and "salvation history" *there*. Rather, salvation history *is* world history read "in spirit and in truth" [John 4.24]. Salvation history is the seed of the Kingdom being sown throughout history, a sowing that provides the true dynamic of history.

Looking on the Son of Man lifted up and seeing in him the Light of the world, Christians come to know how the story—our personal stories, and the world's story—is going to come out. "The story" will not end in cosmic entropy; nor will it end in a cosmic black hole (no matter what happens to the physical universe as we now understand it). "The story" will end with the Wedding Feast of the Lamb. That is what St. Cyriacus (the early fourth-century martyr whose *statio* was transferred to today's basilica by Pope Sixtus V) saw as his eternal destiny, which he embraced by conforming his own life to the logic of the Cross. To see that destiny as available through faith in the Son of Man lifted up is the conversion to which Lent calls every Christian, every year.

Today's *statio* was relocated to the Basilica of St. Mary in the Via Lata when Michelangelo transformed the ruins of Diocletian's baths into the Basilica of St. Mary of the Angels and Martyrs—an architectural expression of salvation history transforming the world's story. Such transformations can be difficult to discern amid the flux of time. Thus at Holy Mass today, Preface I of the Passion of the Lord is a prayer of thanksgiving to the Father for empowering us to discern in history the unfolding of the divinely authored story of salvation:

> For through the saving Passion of your Son
> The whole world has received a heart
> To confess the infinite power of your majesty,
> Since by the wondrous power of the Cross
> Your judgment on the world is now revealed
> And the authority of Christ crucified.

St. Mary in Via Lata: *Sts. Peter, Paul, Martial, and Luke*
(Cosimo Fancelli, 1640)

T HE BASILICA OF
St. Mary in Via Lata is
laden with memories of Christian antiquity. Pious traditions
have Sts. Paul, Luke, Peter,
and John all living here at one
time or another. What little
is known of the site's history
from archaeology begins with
a cluster of first-century rooms
that in the third century were
transformed into a warehouse
fronted by a portico. In either
the fifth or the sixth century,
the site's ideal location on the
Via Lata, the principal road
leading to the city from the
northern gate, led to its designation as a *diaconia*, a place where Christians cared for the poor
and needy.

The *diaconia* stood next to the Arcus Novus, a triumphal arch dedicated to Diocletian in
303 that spanned the Via Lata. In 1149, Pope Eugenius III built a church above the *diaconia*.
Both the Basilica of St. Mary in Via Lata and its neighbor, the Basilica of St. Marcellus, faced
away from Diocletian's arch (and today's Via del Corso) in what may have been a deliberate
gesture of disdain for imperial Rome's most vicious persecutor of Christians. Innocent VIII's
modifications in 1492 included turning the church to face the Corso; at the same time, the apse
was expanded into the property of the convent and church of St. Cyriacus next door. The
seventh-century frescoes from the *diaconia* were removed a few years ago to a nearby museum.

The Baroque era gave the church its distinctive interior: a luminous ceiling; twenty-four
red jasper columns; and Rome's most beautiful organ, handsomely veneered with silver. In
1650, Innocent X began to enfold the structure into the Doria Pamphili Palace, his family
residence, while his successor, Alexander VII, who was a member of the Chigi banking family,
lavished the church with embellishments: the new façade was designed by the pope's favorite
architect, Pietro da Cortona, the high arch of its upper story evoking memories of the triumphal arch that once stood nearby. When St. Mary in Via Lata replaced St. Cyriacus (which was
demolished as part of Alexander's urban renewal project) as today's station, the crypt, which
was all that remained of the earlier church, was redesigned by Pietro da Cortona, who engaged
Cosimo Fancelli to carve an elegant marble relief of Sts. Peter, Paul, Martial, and Luke. Viviano
Codazzi, trompe-l'oeil painter par excellence, completed the ceiling with a false perspective

(*continues*)

(continued)

gallery poised above the transept: one lithe figure straddles a fictive balustrade, while an angel hangs a garland above him.

Designed by Gian Lorenzo Bernini and surmounted by a seventeenth-century fresco of the Assumption by Andrea Camassei, the altar contains one of the church's oldest images: *Mary Our Advocate*, set in a heavy gilt frame. Many miracles have been attributed to prayer before this icon, which a pious tradition holds to have been one of seven images of the Madonna painted by St. Luke. The altar holds the relics of St. Cyriacus and a third-century deacon-martyr, Agapitus.

The elegant neoclassical tombs were created for members of the Bonaparte family: Zénaïde Bonaparte, niece to the French emperor, and her son, Joseph Lucien Charles Napoléon Bonaparte, who was born, incidentally, in Philadelphia. Pius VII, former prisoner of Napoleon, gave the deposed monarch's family permission to live in Rome in their post-Waterloo exile from France. [E.L.]

St. Marcellus: Counterfaçade, *The Crucifixion* (Giovanni Battista Ricci, 1613)

WEDNESDAY OF THE FIFTH WEEK OF LENT

Station at St. Marcellus

Holy Mass
Daniel 3.14–20, 91–92, 95
Canticle: Daniel 3.52–56
John 8.31–42

Office of Readings
Hebrews 6.9–20
St. Augustine: Exposition on the Psalms, 85

THE DEBATE BETWEEN JESUS and those participating in the Feast of Tabernacles continues in today's gospel reading, with the focus now on God's truth and the breadth of its reach. Jesus declares that those who hold fast to his word "will know the truth, and the truth will make you free." His listeners—some puzzled, some indignant—respond that, as they are of the stock of Abraham, they "have never been in bondage to anyone." How is it, they demand, "that you say, 'You will be made free'?" The discussion deteriorates from there, with Jesus's interlocutors mistakenly imagining that he is calling them bastard children. Yet, in their confusion and misapprehension, they bring us to the heart of the matter, proclaiming, "We have one Father, even God." To which Jesus responds that, in that case, they ought to esteem him, for "I proceeded and came forth from the Father; I came not of my own accord, but he sent me."

The Son, the Light of the world, is teaching those in the Temple, and us, that salvation history has entered a new phase: while Israel remains in the truth that belongs by right to the descendants of Abraham (for God does not renege on his covenantal promises), the truth first revealed to Abraham is now being offered universally. And in the Kingdom that is breaking into history in Jesus's person and mission, abiding in covenantal truth will no longer be a matter of lineage but of faith—an act of faith that, in principle, is open to everyone, thanks to the grace of God offered to all by the Son of God. The power of Trinitarian love and the truth about God's relationship with his human creation cannot be confined, even if the distinctive role of Israel in witnessing to this truth will remain an essential part of salvation history. Now, however, there will no longer be "Jew or Gentile . . . slave or free" [Galatians 3.28]. All who adhere to the Son, who reveals the truth about the Father, will be one.

This truth that Jesus offers is not something his disciples possess—as, for example, Peter, Andrew, James, and John "possess" certain "truths" about fishing on the Sea of Galilee. On the contrary, the truth of God in Christ seizes and possesses the disciples, reshaping their lives, reordering their priorities, configuring those who embrace it in the imitation of the Son. This is truth with power, and its power is evangelical: this is a truth that must be offered to others and lavishly expended in mission. For the paradox of the truth that Jesus offers is that his presence within us conforms us more closely to him, and its grasp upon us increases the more we give his truth to those who have not yet received it. There are no zero-sum games in the economy of salvation, which is the expression in time of the ever-giving, ever-receiving truth, goodness, and beauty of the Holy Trinity.

This *statio* at Pope St. Marcellus, who died in difficult political and ecclesiastical circumstances in the early fourth century, is an appropriate place along the Lenten itinerary of conversion to begin a deeper reflection on Christ the High Priest, a principal theme in the Letter to the Hebrews that is introduced in today's Office of Readings and continues tomorrow. In a striking phrase, the author of Hebrews urges his fellow Christians to "seize the hope that is before us." For this hope has, in a figure redolent of the Holy of Holies in the Temple, entered "the inner shrine behind the curtain, where Jesus has gone as a forerunner on our behalf, having become a high priest for ever after the order of Melchizedek."

Hebrews thus extends today's Johannine reflection on the new phase of salvation history that has begun in Jesus. The priesthood that Jesus exercises is not Levitical, a priesthood conferred by heredity and, according to the customs of Jesus's time, exercised in a preeminent way by the high priest, who served a year-long term. Rather, Jesus's priesthood, being the priesthood of the Son, is eternal and universal in its mediating scope: the Son, who is the unique mediator with the Father, is a priest forever, and his priesthood is universal in its efficacy. In that sense, his priesthood resembles that of the mysterious figure of Melchizedek in the Book of Genesis, the "king of Salem . . . [and] priest of the Most High God" [Genesis 14.18], who is not of the tribe and heritage of Abraham, but who offers true worship to the true God by gifts of bread and wine, and to whom Abraham in turn offers tithes.

The priesthood of the New Covenant is not founded on Aaron and his sons, but on Jesus, who, like Melchizedek, is "ordained" by God to his priestly identity and mission. In his 1992 apostolic exhortation *Pastores Dabo Vobis* [I Shall Give You Shepherds], Blessed John Paul II explored this crucial aspect of the Church's priesthood (which continues the unique priesthood of Christ) by reference to a biblical drama that has already been part of our Lenten reflection: the episode at the synagogue of Nazareth at the outset of Jesus's public ministry, where Jesus declares to his startled fellow-townsmen that Isaiah's messianic prophecy is being fulfilled in their midst, because he, the son of the carpenter, has been consecrated by an anointing of the Holy Spirit.

Here, John Paul wrote, Jesus is proclaiming the essence of a new kind of priesthood—a priesthood of perfect mediation between God and humanity. Understanding this, he continued, "is absolutely necessary for understanding the nature of the Church's ordained ministry, which is a unique participation in the unique priesthood of Christ." Through the Church's bishops and priests, whose ordination conforms them to Christ and his priesthood in a unique way, the grace of the sacraments is conferred upon the people of the Church: the grace of conversion in Baptism; the grace of the divine mercy in Penance; the grace of participation in Christ's sacrifice through the reception of the Holy Eucharist; and so forth.

The ministerial priesthood, in turn, empowers the people of the Church to exercise the priestly character bestowed on them in Baptism. Through that character, the new People of God who are the Body of Christ can offer true worship to the Father through prayer and through their participation in the Eucharistic sacrifice (which is why the congregation is incensed at a solemn Mass). The unique, mediating priesthood of Christ, bestowed on the priests of the Church through the sacrament of Holy Orders, in turn offers to all the baptized their own form of participation in the sanctification of the world. St. Augustine wrote of this in his fifth-century commentary on Psalm 85, which the Church reads today:

> When we speak to God in prayer we do not separate the Son from [God the Father], and when the body of the Son prays it does not separate its head from itself: it is the one Savior of his body, our Lord Jesus Christ, the Son of God, who prays for us and in us and is himself the object of our prayers.
>
> He prays for us as our priest, he prays in us as our head, he is the object of our prayers as our God.
>
> Let us then recognize both our voice in his, and his voice in ours. . . . We pray then to him, through him, in him, and we speak along with him and he along with us.

St. Marcellus: *Madonna and Child; The Nativity and the Presentation in the Temple* (Francesco Salviati, 1563)

THE PRESTIGE OF THE VIA del Corso, the ancient Via Lata, was reflected in the monuments that once lined its length. Augustus's Ara Pacis (Altar of Peace) stood along this road; Marcus Aurelius's column, honoring his victories in Germany, is the only remaining vestige of the three triumphal arches that formerly spanned the great roadway's breadth. The Basilica of St. Marcellus cuts a fine figure alongside the elegant architecture of this stylish avenue, but its origins were much humbler: according to the *Liber Pontificalis*, a history of the popes until the fifteenth century, this was the site of the imperial postal service's stables, from which dozens of horses were dispatched daily to carry letters throughout the empire.

Pope Marcellus was elected in 306 toward the end of a terribly difficult period for the early Church. The bloody persecution by Diocletian began in 303; two years later, the Dalmatian-born emperor abdicated and the Christian community's fate hung in the balance as various claimants sought the throne. Moreover, the Christians themselves were divided, with Donatists insisting that the sacraments performed by those who had wavered under persecution be declared invalid. Pope Marcellus fell afoul of both Church and state, permitting apostates to be reconciled to the Church (after a suitable penance) and refusing to sacrifice to the divinity of the emperor Maxentius. Maxentius sentenced Marcellus to penal servitude in these imperial stables, where the pope died in 309.

Although an oratory in honor of the martyr-pope likely stood here, the first mention of a church on this site is from 418—yet another period of ecclesiastical division, this time triggered by the election of the antipope Boniface IV. Nevertheless, the church grew in size and importance; excavations under the apse have located a fifth-century baptistery. The care of the Basilica of St. Marcellus was given to the Servites in 1368, after which the church was endowed with several chapels. In 1519, however, the basilica burnt to the ground, leaving intact only its great fourteenth-century wooden crucifix—a treasured artifact that became the central icon of the "Day of Pardon" that Blessed John Paul II celebrated in St. Peter's on the First Sunday in Lent in 2000.

The Medici pope, Leo X, provided funds to rebuild the church and hired the Venetian Jacopo Sansovino as architect. Slowed by the 1527 Sack of Rome, the work was completed by the mid-sixteenth century and decorated by some of Rome's finest post-Renaissance painters. Carlo Fontana's curving façade, from 1686, heralds the exuberant Baroque painting inside. The interior of Fontana's structure boasts an unusual Roman church decoration: a colorful, multifigured image of the Crucifixion, painted by Giovanni Battista Ricci, spans the entire counter-façade.

(*continues*)

(continued)

The chapels alternate Baroque panache with Renaissance grandeur. The first on the right contains a brightly painted wooden *Pietà*. The altar in the second contains the relics of Sts. Degna and Merita, surmounted by Pietro Barbieri's dramatic rendition of their martyrdom. The third chapel houses a fourteenth-century fresco of the Madonna and Child; Francesco Salviati, one of the finest painters of the Roman Restoration, executed the side panels of the Nativity and the Presentation in the Temple.

The next chapel contains the St. Marcellus cross, venerated for centuries in processions through the city. Raphael's collaborator, Perin del Vaga, frescoed the *Creation of Eve* above; his work bears a strong resemblance to Michelangelo's efforts in the Sistine Chapel.

On the left, Taddeo Zuccari, a giant of Counter-Reformation art, painted the Chapel of St. Paul with stories of the saint's life. The altarpiece, a rare example of a work executed on slate, depicts the *Conversion of Saul*. [E.L.]

St. Apollinaris: Stational Mass

THURSDAY OF THE FIFTH WEEK OF LENT

Station at St. Apollinaris

Holy Mass

Genesis 17.3–9

Psalm 105

John 8.51–59

Office of Readings

Hebrews 7.1–10

Second Vatican Council:
Dogmatic Constitution on the Church, 9

THE JOHANNINE NARRATIVE OF Jesus at the Feast of Tabernacles reaches its dramatic climax in today's gospel reading. Here, Jesus identifies himself completely with the Father by the radical claim that "before Abraham was, I AM." His relationship to the God who named himself to Moses in this way is unique. As biblical scholar Francis Moloney put it in his commentary on John, that relationship is "before and beyond" the "time" in which Abraham appears. Jesus is the embodiment of the hope for God's saving action in history that was central to the Feast of Tabernacles: that hope existed before Abraham, in the design of salvation history; it continued to exist after the death of Abraham; it is now being fulfilled in Jesus.

The drama of salvation history thus takes a decisive turn in this passage. Fidelity to the divine master plan, not genealogical descent, is the new criterion of adherence to the God of Abraham, who, Jesus says, "rejoiced that he was to see my day." Abraham understood himself to be a servant of the divine plan, not its master; Jesus suggests that Abraham understood that his service to the one true God would eventually be transcended by the One who would bring God's plan to fulfillment. This is the challenge put before those at the Feast of Tabernacles, and to everyone since: Do you recognize in Jesus the unique fulfillment of the salvific history that began with Abraham, but is now brought to its climax in the One who can say, without either blaspheming or confirming that he is mad, "before Abraham was, I AM."

Jesus's claims about himself and his relationship with the Father during this entire Tabernacles narrative coincide precisely with the chief characteristics of that pilgrimage festival, Father Moloney noted. In his person and mission, Jesus reveals the true God—and does so with singular authority because he has been with the Father from before time began. Jesus fulfills, while transcending and universalizing, Israel's expectation of a climactic divine intervention in history in the person of the Messiah. Jesus is the Living Water celebrated at Tabernacles. He is also the true Light of the world, a light he radiates universally, not only to those who celebrate the Ceremony of Light in the Temple.

There is another striking claim made in today's gospel reading: Jesus's unique identification with the Father enables those who become his disciples to live beyond death: those whom he calls, and who accept his call, "will never see death." They will, of course, die physically. But because they will have already been living in Kingdom-time, through the eternal life that Jesus makes available now, death for Jesus's disciples loses its fearsome quality. Now it signals, not final catastrophe, but transition to a new mode of eternal life, the path to which has been blazed by the Son in his obedient self-sacrifice to the will of the Father. And if the reign of death is no more, so, too, the reign of sin is ended by Jesus's messianic mission, for death came into the world through sin.

Life has changed, and so has history, through the inbreaking of the Kingdom in the person and mission of Jesus, who is one with the Father.

The Fathers of the Second Vatican Council explored one of the consequences of this shift in the templates of history in Vatican II's Dogmatic Constitution on the Church (fittingly entitled, in Latin, *Lumen Gentium* [Light of the Nations]). There they wrote, and the Church reads today, that the New Covenant in Christ created "a people that was to form a unity, not in human fashion but in the Spirit, as the new people of God," composed of both Jews and Gentiles. "Those who believe in Christ, reborn not of corruptible but of incorruptible seed through the word of the living God, not from the flesh but from water and the Holy Spirit, are constituted in the fullness of time as 'a chosen race, a royal priesthood, a holy nation, God's own people . . . once . . . no people but now God's people' [1 Peter 2.9–10]." The Messiah forms from himself, and for himself, a messianic people united in spirit and in truth: a people whose mission is to proclaim that the Kingdom has come in Jesus and that eternal life is now available, without cost, to all.

In the world's terms, the Council Fathers continued, this messianic people may not seem much; it "often seems to be a tiny flock." Yet, whatever its size, it is "the enduring source of unity, hope, and salvation for the whole human race . . . established by Christ . . . [and] sent out into the whole world as the light of the world and the salt of the earth." The Church, this messianic people drawn from every corner of the human world, is thus the "visible sacrament" of the unity of the human race.

The imitation of Christ to which Lent calls pilgrims is an imitation within the Body of Christ that is the Church. The Church is not an add-on, something secondary or incidental to my personal relationship with the Lord. The Church, this messianic people, is of the essence of the divine master plan, and to imitate Christ is to deepen one's adherence to the Church.

What, though, does it mean to call the Church a "sacrament"?

The term is used here by way of analogy. As the *Catechism of the Catholic Church* puts it, the "mystery of salvation" is "revealed and active in the Church's sacraments (which the Eastern Churches also call 'the holy mysteries'). The seven sacraments are the signs and instruments by which the Holy Spirit spreads the grace of Christ the head throughout the Church which is his Body. The

Church, then, both contains and communicates the invisible grace she signifies . . . [and] . . . in this sense . . . is called a sacrament."

The "sacramentality" of the Church thus extends in two directions, vertical and horizontal. The Church is the "sacrament" of the Holy Trinity's communion with men and women: the vertical dimension. And the Church is the "sacrament" of the unity of the human race, which will be achieved in the unity of being "one People of God . . . one body of Christ . . . one temple of the Holy Spirit": the horizontal dimension.

This "sacramentality" of the Church—the Church's sign-character as the visible expression of God's invisible grace at work, bringing salvation history to its end in the Wedding Feast of the Lamb—thus has a radical orientation toward the future, and toward the final vindication of God's creating, salvific, and sanctifying purposes. The *Catechism* puts it this way, describing that future where the Church of today will meet the Church of the martyr-bishop Apollinaris of Ravenna, today's *statio*, and all the saints in glory:

> At the end of time, the Kingdom of God will come in its fullness. . . .
>
> Sacred Scripture calls this mysterious renewal, which will transform humanity and the world, "new heavens and a new earth."
>
> In this new universe, the heavenly Jerusalem, God will have his dwelling among men. "He will wipe away every tear from their eyes, and death shall be no more, neither shall there be mourning nor crying nor pain any more, for the former things have passed away" [Revelation 21.4].
>
> . . . This consummation will be the final realization of the unity of the human race, which God willed from creation and of which the pilgrim Church has been "in the nature of a sacrament" [*Lumen Gentium* 1]. Those who are united with Christ will form the community of the redeemed, the "holy city" of God, "the Bride, the wife of the Lamb" [Revelation 21.2, 9]. She will not be wounded any longer by sin, stains, self-love, that destroy or wound the earthly community. The beatific vision, in which God opens himself in an inexhaustible way to the elect, will be the ever-flowing well-spring of happiness, peace, and mutual communion.

To be conformed to Christ means to become a living member of his Body, the Church: not in the sense of "membership" in a club, but in the deeper sense of participating in the life of a living organism. This Body's head is the one who could say, without blasphemy or lunacy, "before Abraham was, I AM." To be conformed to the head is to be a member of the Body, and to be a member of the Body is to enter, here and now, into the communion of the Holy Trinity, in anticipation of the full communion in Trinitarian life and love that is the Wedding Feast of the Lamb.

That is the truth Jesus proclaimed at the Feast of Tabernacles. Adherence to that truth is the "imitation" of the Holy One of God to which Lent calls us.

St. Apollinaris: *The Glory of
St. Apollinaris* (Stefano Pozzi, 1746)

IN THE SEVENTH CENTURY, Greek influence spread through Italy as the Byzantine emperor claimed nominal sovereignty over the remnants of the ancient Roman empire. Ravenna, where the first-century Syrian-born martyr-bishop Apollinaris lived and died, was home to the Byzantine exarch who held authority over Naples, Calabria, Perugia, Venice, and Rome. Through this portal, Eastern customs and devotions found their way to Rome. The Basilica of St. Apollinaris dates from this period, when many popes were of Eastern origin, and was welcomed as one of the Roman station churches shortly after its construction. Situated in the ruins of Nero's baths, it was likely first cared for by Basilian monks who fled Constantinople during the Iconoclast Controversy.

Little of this Eastern Christian heritage remains in today's church, which was completely rebuilt in 1478 by Cardinal Guillaume d'Estouteville as part of Sixtus IV's great urban reorganization; a fresco fragment inside the front door is a reminder of this Renaissance patronage. The antechapel, turned perpendicularly to the entrance, is now used for Eucharistic adoration; above the tabernacle is an image of the Madonna and Child flanked by Sts. Peter and Paul. The fresco was covered with a thin layer of plaster in the late fifteenth century, but in 1647 some of the plaster cracked and fell, and the fresco was revealed. The image was then crowned in 1653 by the Chapter of St. Peter's Basilica, becoming one of only 1,300 images of Mary worldwide so honored by the Vatican chapter.

D'Estouteville's small but elegant church included a Cosmatesque pavement, a slim tower, a porch, and a marble frieze of Sts. Apollinaris and Peter amid garlands and birds (now housed in the Vatican grottoes). Given to the newly formed Jesuits in 1575, the parish became home to the first "Sunday School" of Christian doctrine, founded by Marco Cusani. The Jesuits hired Niccolò Circignani, also known as Pomarancio, to fresco the interior with stories of the life of St. Apollinaris. The Jesuits also turned the church into a school for sacred music, in the 1650s commissioning a spectacular organ (later destroyed) by the Dutch master Willem Hermans.

In 1714, Pope Benedict XIV publicly lamented the "indecorous darkness and dankness of the church, which, for its antiquity, was shameful." The Pope offered to pay for a new high

(continues)

(continued)

altar—and offered the services of his architect, Ferdinando Fuga (who was then designing the new façade of the Basilica of St Mary Major). Today's Basilica of St. Apollinaris is the fruit of that papal rebuke and of his architect's genius.

The porch was transformed into an antechapel, and the church was rebuilt with a luminous vault leading to a low dome. Frescoed in 1746 by Stefano Pozzi in a Rococo style, it shows St. Apollinaris being presented to God the Father by St. Peter amid billowing clouds and adorable angels.

The side chapels are well lit but deeply recessed from the nave, causing no distraction from the main altar. Their decoration was done by some of the eighteenth century's most prominent artists. Pierre Legros the Younger, the principal sculptor for the tomb of St. Ignatius, sculpted St. Francis Xavier with a golden crab at his foot. The crustacean recalls the story that the saint, caught in a storm at sea during a missionary voyage, threw his crucifix into the ocean to calm the waters; but after Xavier safely made landfall, a crab scuttled onto the beach with his cross.

The oval crypt beneath the high altar and the triumphal arch holds the relics of the martyrs Orestes, Eugenius, Auxentius, and others. In 1990, the church was given into the custody of Opus Dei, which dedicated a chapel to Opus Dei's founder, St. Josemaria Escriva. [E.L.]

St. Stephen on the Caelian Hill: Stational Mass

FRIDAY OF THE FIFTH WEEK OF LENT

Station at St. Stephen on the Caelian Hill

Holy Mass
Jeremiah 20.10–13
Psalm 18
John 10.31–42

Office of Readings
Hebrews 7.11–28
St. Fulgentius of Ruspe: Treatise on Faith

I N THE FIRST CENTURIES of Christianity, reception of the sacraments of initiation at the Easter Vigil marked the conclusion of the catechumenate, the elementary school of faith. Yet the Church continued to instruct those who had just been baptized, confirmed, and admitted to the celebration of the Holy Eucharist during a postbaptismal catechetical period known as *Mystagogy*, an instruction on "the mysteries" of Christ and how they are present through the sacraments that aimed to deepen the newly baptized's sense of the riches of the faith. This instruction continues in the twenty-first-century Church every year when, in the months after the Easter season, the Church reads *On the Mysteries*, a fourth-century catechesis for the newly baptized by St. Ambrose of Milan.

There are some aspects of the faith, Ambrose explained, that those who have not been enlightened by Baptism simply cannot grasp. Baptismal regeneration and illumination are necessary in order to comprehend "the mysteries," of which the sacraments are the visible sign and the Bible is a witness: the baptismal bath that is "the holy of holies" of the New Covenant; the priest whose priesthood continues the new high priesthood of Christ; the water that is no longer mere water, but the instrument for cleansing sin; the dove who came back to Noah's ark with an olive branch, whom we now see as "the one in whose likeness the Holy Spirit descended" on Jesus at his baptism—the same Spirit who breathes into the newly baptized "peace of soul, tranquillity of mind."

Baptism, Ambrose taught his new Christians, breaks open the enduring truths of the Bible in a new way. Remember Naaman the Syrian, about whom you heard during the catechumenate? Ambrose asked. Then see him, and your-selves, in a new light: "Here was a man who doubted before being made whole. You are already made whole, so ought not to have any doubt." Or consider another figure from the catechumenate, the man at the pool of Bethesda who was waiting for a cure: "The paralytic at the pool was waiting for someone. Who was this if not the Lord Jesus, born of a virgin? At his coming, it is not a question of a shadow healing an individual, but Truth himself healing the universe."

Similarly, the baptismal rite unites Word and Sacrament in a profound mys-tery of grace. You were clothed in white garments at your baptism, Ambrose reminds his listeners. Understand now that "when Christ sees his Church clothed in white . . . he cries out, 'How beautiful you are, my beloved, how beautiful you are; your eyes are like the eyes of a dove' [Song of Songs 4.1], for it was in the likeness of a dove that the Holy Spirit came down from heaven." You were told about the manna in the desert and the water flowing from the rock. See in these miracles images of the even greater miracle in which you have just participated: the bread from heaven and the blood that flowed from Christ, both of which you have now received in the Eucharist.

And considering all this, Ambrose urges his new Christians—and Chris-tians today—to remember the mystery that has happened within the baptized: "Remember . . . that you have received a spiritual seal, 'the spirit of wisdom and understanding, the spirit of knowledge and reverence, the spirit of holy fear' [Isaiah 11.2]. Keep safe what you have received. God the Father sealed you,

Christ the Lord strengthened you and sent the Spirit into your hearts as the pledge of what is to come."

Today's station, St. Stephen on the Caelian Hill, is also known as "St. Stephen in the Round," for unlike the classic, rectangular basilica form of most of the Lenten *stationes*, here we are in a circular space. Those two configurations of sacred space represent the complex truth Ambrose taught his Milanese congregation 1,600 years ago: the itinerary of conversion, the Christian pilgrimage of faith, is both a movement *toward* and a movement *within*. The Lenten journey leads *toward* Calvary, then *toward* the night watch of the Easter Vigil, then *toward* the empty tomb and the appearances of the Risen One. At the same time, and along the same linear path, Lenten pilgrims are also journeying *within*, penetrating more deeply into the mysteries, the profound and saving truths, that these places and events embody and convey. The life of faith is a life that is deepened over time, coming by degrees to greater clarity—a clarity made possible by a deeper conformation of our lives to the imitation of the Messiah who declared himself the "Light of the world" [John 8.12].

Thus the circular space of this unique station church evokes something quite different from the image of the self-celebrating community conveyed by some twenty-first-century church buildings. The *statio* at St. Stephen on the Caelian Hill evokes the memory of that ancient mystagogical catechesis by which new Christians were empowered to plunge more deeply into the wonders of creation, redemption, and sanctification and enabled to see salvation history at work within world history. The journey forward from Baptism is also a journey into the depths of grace. So it was for Ambrose's new Christians in ancient Mediolanum; so it is for all those undergoing the annual catechumenate of Lent in every time and place.

The Office of Readings today deepens the Lenten pilgrim's reflection, which began yesterday, on the mystery of the high priesthood of Christ—and, by extension, on the nature of the ordained ministry in the Church.

As the Letter to the Hebrews teaches, the priesthood of the New Covenant that is inaugurated in Jesus is a priesthood conferred "not according to a legal requirement concerning bodily descent but by the power of an indestructible life." The new form of priesthood is announced at those moments, previously considered along the Lenten pilgrimage path, when the Spirit descends on Jesus and the Father declares him to be his Beloved Son: at Jesus's baptism in the Jordan and at his Transfiguration on Mt. Tabor. Jesus is then anointed High Priest of the new and eternal covenant through the Paschal Mystery of his suffering, death, and resurrection: here, the obedient Son is constituted the perfect mediator between God and humanity by the Father who raises him from the dead, so that, in the Spirit, he may be "the first-born among many brethren" [Romans 8.29]. And that mediation extends throughout history because the high priesthood of Christ, the Risen One who dies no more, is permanent and unending: "He is able for all time to save those who draw near to God through him, since he always lives to make intercession for them," as the Letter to the Hebrews puts it.

The sixth-century North African bishop St. Fulgentius of Ruspe takes us further into the Trinitarian depths of the mystery of salvation by reflecting in today's Office of Readings on this unique priesthood of the Son:

> He is at once priest and sacrifice, God and temple. He is the priest through whom we have been reconciled, the sacrifice by which we have been reconciled, the temple in which we have been reconciled. He alone is priest, sacrifice, and temple because he is all these things as God in the form of a servant; but he is not alone as God, for he is this with the Father and the Holy Spirit in the form of God.

The priesthood of the New Covenant, continued in the ordained ministry of the Church, is essentially ordered to "the mystery": as "servants of Christ and stewards of the mysteries of God" [1 Corinthians 4.1], priests are ordained to lead the people of the Church into an experience of the mystery of Jesus Christ, crucified and risen, the Savior of the world who reveals both the face of the merciful Father and the truth about our humanity.

St. Stephen on the Caelian Hill: *Sts. Primus and Felician* (seventh century)

ROMAN GENERALS OFTEN marked their triumphs with victory temples "in the round"; like the crown of valor earned in battle, the circular temple evoked enduring fame. Constantine adopted this architectural conceit and chose a circular form for the Church of the Holy Sepulcher in Jerusalem; Rome built its first round church in honor of the Church's first martyr.

The Basilica of St. Stephen "in the Round" was built on the Caelian Hill in the early fifth century, a golden era of Roman church construction, when noble families sponsored such dazzling edifices as the basilicas of St. Sabina, St. Mary Major, and St. Paul Outside the Walls. St. Stephen's may have been financed by the aristocratic Valerian clan, whose daughter, St. Melania, was a frequent pilgrim to the Holy Land. When the protomartyr's relics were rediscovered in 415 and translated to Rome, St. Stephen's was designed as a noble reliquary.

Built atop a military barracks, the main chapel rests upon a Mithraic shrine. The original construction was innovative, consisting of three radiating circular arcades intersected by four arms, which in turn form a Greek cross. From the outer rung, the play of light increased toward the center, where, above the altar, a wide dome rested on twenty-two windows, flooding the interior with light.

This unique and refined architectural marvel suffered badly from the fifth-century barbarian invasions, and then from neglect during the centuries that the Caelian Hill lay dormant. The church enjoyed a brief revival in the sixth century, when it was embellished with mother-of-pearl and marble veneers by two canonized popes, John I and Felix IV. Pope St. Gregory the Great preached here; remnants of his episcopal throne are still visible.

In 640, Pope Theodore brought the relics of Sts. Primus and Felician to the church and built a chapel in their honor. The two brothers had been buried on the Via Nomentana; their relics are believed to be the first brought inside the city walls from the catacombs. The chapel glows with a mesmerizing gold apse mosaic; the brothers appear in purple and white togas flanking a jeweled cross, similar to that which the Persians stole from Jerusalem in 614. A border of poppies springs up by the martyrs' feet, symbols of their earthly suffering; at the apex of the cross, Christ looks calmly outward, pleased with the brothers' steadfastness.

Pope Innocent II restored the badly decayed building in the twelfth century, adding the central traverse arcade for extra support; despite this intervention, the roof eventually collapsed. The restorations undertaken by Pope Nicholas V for the Jubilee of 1450 likely saved the building, but a contemporary chronicler wrote that "he ruined it considerably as well": the basilica's exterior rung was destroyed; the spaces between the second rungs were filled in; and the ornamentation disappeared.

During the Reformation, Christianity's protomartyr inspired members of the new religious orders that had been founded to combat heresy—thus they themselves became the progenitors of a new generation of martyrs. Pope Gregory XIII gave the church to the Jesuits, who hired Niccolò Circignani (Pomarancio) to fresco the walls with twenty-four large images of martyrdom. Despised by art historians for their violent imagery, these frescoes underscore the centuries of sacrifice during which Christians were brutalized by an empire determined to eradicate them.

The cycle, which opens with Christ's crucifixion and Stephen's stoning, is organized by imperial reign: 360 degrees of witness that recall human cruelty, human fortitude, and the fragility of tolerance. [E.L.]

St. John Before the Latin Gate: Stational Mass

SATURDAY OF THE FIFTH WEEK OF LENT

Station at St. John Before the Latin Gate

Holy Mass
Ezekiel 37.21–28
Canticle: Jeremiah 31
John 11.45–56

Office of Readings
Hebrews 8.1–13
St. Gregory Nazianzen: Homily 45

D ELIVERANCE, RESTORATION, RENEWAL, true worship, peace: these Kingdom themes are lifted up in today's liturgical readings, as if to keep the glorious end of the drama of salvation history before the eyes of Lenten pilgrims on this day before Palm Sunday, as we prepare with the apostles to go up to Jerusalem "that we may die with him" [John 11.16]. Today's *statio*, which honors the Beloved Disciple and is the farthest station from the center of ancient Rome, is similarly evocative: it is built near the spot where tradition says that St. John survived an attempt to kill him by boiling him in oil (hence the station's secondary name in Italian, San Giovanni in Olio).

In the first reading at today's Mass, Ezekiel, from the depths of Israel's Babylonian captivity, conveys God's promise to restore the exiles to their land and make of them a reunited people, freed from sin in a new epoch of holiness: "I will make a covenant of peace with them; it shall be an everlasting covenant with them; and I will bless them and multiply them, and will set my sanctuary in the midst of them for evermore. My dwelling place shall be with them; and I will be their God and they shall be my people. Then the nations will know that I the LORD sanctify Israel, when my sanctuary is in the midst of them for evermore." Even in the midst of exile and confronted by temptations to despair, prophetic faith can "see" a future of divine redemption.

Unity after the fragmentation of exile and deliverance from oppression are also themes in today's responsorial canticle, drawn from the prophet Jeremiah and evocative of the Good Shepherd theme of Eastertide:

Hear the word of the LORD, O nations
>and declare it to the coastlands far off;
say, "He who scattered Israel will gather him,
>and will keep him as a shepherd keeps his flock."

For the LORD has ransomed Jacob,
>and has redeemed him from hands too strong for him.
They shall come and sing aloud on the height of Zion,
>And they shall be radiant over the goodness of the LORD.

The gospel reading of the day, which includes Caiaphas's blunt statement that "it is expedient . . . that one man should die for the nation," is often interpreted as the epitome of pragmatic political intrigue trumping principle. Yet in John's gospel, God and his Anointed One are always sovereign, and events are always guided toward the fulfillment of the Father's saving will; thus the gospel narrator is not quite so harsh about the alleged cynicism here. Yes, Caiaphas, as high priest, is worried that this miracle-working rabble-rouser from Galilee will bring the wrath of Rome down on Jerusalem and imperil the people, and is thus prepared to sacrifice him to the demands of realpolitik. Yet, by saying that it would be "expedient" for Jesus to die so that the nation might live, he evokes the memory of the Jewish martyrs of the Maccabean period, who were widely venerated at the time of Jesus. Moreover, Caiaphas, as biblical scholar Francis Moloney put it, "rightly prophesied that Jesus would die for the nation." As Father Moloney also observed, "the benefits of Jesus's death could not be limited to the nation[,] as was the case with the deaths of the Maccabean martyrs. Jesus will die for Israel, but his death will also gather into one the children of God who are scattered abroad."

In the divine plan, even Caiaphas's calculations are turned to God's ends. Jesus dies for others, so that all those who are lost, Jews and Gentiles alike, may be gathered into the Kingdom of God. Everything that is about to happen during Holy Week, the gospel of John is telling us, is happening for a divinely authored purpose. Be not afraid. As Blessed John Henry Newman once said of God, the scriptwriter of the drama of salvation history, "He knows what he is about."

In today's Office of Readings, the author of the Letter to the Hebrews continues the theme of ingathering by quoting from the same passage in the book of the prophet Jeremiah from which today's responsorial canticle is taken: "Behold the days are coming, says the LORD, when . . . they shall all know me . . . for I will forgive their iniquity and I will remember their sin no more" [Jeremiah 31.31, 34]. St. Gregory Nazianzen then deepens this part of the day's reflection on the Kingdom-life that next week's events will make available to all by reflecting on the New Life in a way that is reminiscent of St. Ambrose's mystagogical teaching yesterday. The imitation of Christ on which Lenten pilgrims have been reflecting, Gregory preaches, should lead us to "put on," imaginatively and in our Holy Week prayer, the characters in the drama that begins to unfold tomorrow on Palm Sunday:

Let us take our part in the Passover . . . according to the teaching of the Gospel. . . .

If you are a Simon of Cyrene, take up your cross and follow Christ. If you are crucified beside him like one of the thieves, now, like the good thief, acknowledge your God. . . .

If you are a Joseph of Arimathea, go to the one who ordered his crucifixion, and ask for Christ's body. Make your own the expiation for the sins of the whole world. If you are a Nicodemus, like the man who worshipped God by night, bring spices and prepare Christ's body for burial. If you are one of the Marys, or Salome, or Joanna, weep in the early morning. Be the first to see the stone rolled back, and even the angels perhaps, and Jesus himself.

Jesus's sacrifice, Gregory continues, should empower his disciples to similar acts of radical self-donation, which are made possible by coming to the new Temple and the new Holy of Holies, which is Christ himself: "We must sacrifice ourselves to God, each day and in everything we do, accepting all that happens to us for the sake of the Word, imitating his Passion by our sufferings, and honoring his blood by shedding our own. We must be ready to be crucified." Like the narrator of the gospel, who has been leading us from the Feast of Tabernacles to the climax of the drama of salvation history, we, too, must imitate the sovereign Jesus by deepening our faith in the divine plan, however strangely or mysteriously it is at work in our own lives. "He knows what he is about."

The grace of God, not our own striving, makes this kind of radical self-gift possible. At the end of today's gospel reading, the confused crowds, gathering for Passover and looking for Jesus, ask, "What do you think? That he will not come to the feast?" There are doubtless times when we, too, wonder whether the Lord is present, or even en route. The lesson to be learned during the week ahead—the lesson toward which the Lenten itinerary of conversion has been leading us for over five weeks—is that Jesus the Lord *is* "the feast." He has come and remains with his people forever, for his is the new Passover that liberates, not simply from human bondage, but from sin and death. By clinging to him and conforming our lives to the pattern of his life, we can live the life of his Kingdom here and now. Be not afraid of what is coming next, along this pilgrim road. God "knows what he is about."

St. John Before the Latin Gate:
Interior, Oratory of St. John in Olio
(Lazzaro Baldi, 1657)

THE TRADITION SURROUNDING the Roman trials of John the Evangelist originates with Tertullian, the prolific second-century Christian author, who wrote that John was arrested in Ephesus and brought to Rome for trial before the emperor Domitian, builder of the Colosseum and implacable enemy of Christianity. Domitian first tried to shame John into renouncing his faith; when that failed, he ordered the evangelist thrown into a pot of boiling oil outside the Latin Gate. John submitted willingly, but as the tradition has it, the oil left him untouched. Domitian then exiled John to Patmos, where he wrote the Book of Revelation.

The Basilica of St. John Before the Latin Gate is well outside the ancient city center, close to the Aurelian Walls. The path to the basilica goes past the Baths of Caracalla to a small, round oratory that was rebuilt in 1509 by Pope Julius II (its whimsical dome was added by Borromini in the Baroque era). The oratory marks the site of John's witness, the circular form evoking both the cauldron of oil and the saint's victory over his persecutors.

The church's arched portico is a few steps away. Thin red bricks date from the reign of the Ostrogoth king, Theodoric, who in 525 gave the Basilica of Sts. Cosmas and Damian to the Christian community; many scholars therefore date today's church to the pontificate of St. Gelasius I (492–496). The triple apses and polygonal form of the central apse, however, reflect Byzantine design; thus, a later date of 550, the time of the emperor Justinian, seems more appropriate.

Although archaeological evidence verifies the church's antiquity, there are no literary sources until 790, when Pope Hadrian I commissioned a restoration; the marble wellhead in the forecourt dates from this period. The stone carver, a certain Stephen, added the inscription, "In the name of the Father, of the Son, and of the Holy Ghost. . . . All you who are thirsty come to the water."

Despite the small windows in the clerestory and the side walls, the church is astonishingly luminous when morning light floods the apse through the large windows of yellow onyx. The sun plays off the whitewashed lower walls, fruit of a 1940s restoration by the Rosminian Fathers.

The impression of modernity in the interior soon dissipates amid the many ancient artifacts found here: the mismatched nave columns were culled from imperial monuments, while the lectern is decorated with a medieval inscription and one of Theodoric's roof tiles.

Pope Celestine III's extensive 1191 redecoration animates the space with dazzling streaks of color. Purple porphyry and green serpentine form patchwork swaths of Cosmatesque pavement. The restorations of 1914 and 1940 brought to light fifty biblical scenes along the nave; they begin with Genesis and conclude, in the triumphal arch above the altar, with scenes from Revelation—offering a rare opportunity to ponder a complete medieval fresco-cycle.

A few frescoes were added during the Renaissance, but only the *Madonna and Child* in the Lady Chapel remain from that period. The dramatic fresco over the altar, depicting the failed execution of St. John amid a swirling mass of women, children, soldiers, and angels, is Baroque. [E.L.]

Holy Cross
in Jerusalem:
Reliquary of the
True Cross

HOLY WEEK

St. John Lateran: Apse mosaic (Jacopo Torriti and Jacopo da Camerino, thirteenth century)

PALM SUNDAY OF THE LORD'S PASSION

Station at St. John Lateran

Holy Mass

Procession of Palms	Liturgy of the Word	
[A] *Matthew 21.1–11*	*Isaiah 50.4–7*	[A] *Matthew 26.14–27.66*
[B] *Mark 11.1–10 or*	*Psalm 22*	[B] *Mark 14.1–15.47*
John 12.12–16	*Philippians 2.6–11*	[C] *Luke 22.14–23.56*
[C] *Luke 19.28–40*		

Office of Readings

Hebrews 10.1–18

St. Andrew of Crete: Sermon on Palm Sunday

I N 1925, AS THE shadows of totalitarianism began to lengthen across Europe, Pope Pius XI instituted the Feast of Christ the King and placed it on the last Sunday of October. In 1969, as secularism advanced rapidly throughout Christianity's historical European heartland, Pope Paul VI moved the celebration to the last Sunday of the Church year and redesignated it as the Solemnity of Our Lord Jesus Christ, King of the Universe—thus laying increased stress on the feast's cosmic, or Kingdom, dimension. In both its Pian and Pauline forms, the liturgical celebration of Christ the King links the reign of Christ over space and time to his Passion and Death through the gospel read on that day. Thus Palm Sunday—the first day of Holy Week, the day on which the Church remembers and reenacts the Lord's triumphal entry into Jerusalem, and the day on which the Church first reads one of the Passion narratives from the gospels—is the prototypical feast of Christ the King.

T oday's liturgical texts are best read allegorically or, to borrow a term used in the latter part of Lent, as a catechesis in *mystagogy*. Here, the Church ponders the central mystery of salvation history: the redemptive sacrifice of the Son, who, in obedience to the will of the Father, offers himself freely, thus embodying what John the Baptist (one of the patrons of today's station) first called him: the "Lamb of God who takes away the sins of the world" [John 1.29].

In all three years of the Lectionary cycle, the Church reads today from the third of Isaiah's songs of the Suffering Servant. In this passage, the Servant, whom the Church has identified with Christ since the apostolic age, suffers "shame and spitting," but nonetheless sets his "face like a flint," for he knows that he will "not be put to shame." In his freely accepted humiliation—"I gave my back to the smiters, and my cheeks to those who pulled out my beard"—the Church sees an anticipation of the mockery of Christ that she will remember in the Passion narratives of today and Good Friday. The text can also be read mystagogically: to strike the Just One as if he were an idiot or a fool is to reject the divine Wisdom through which the world was created. In the brutality that hard men imagine as an exercise of power over a weakling, the Church sees the folly of humanity throughout the ages, falling time and again into sin. In the humiliation of the one considered a simpleton, who does not strike back but sets his face "like a flint," the Church discerns the depths of the divine love for creatures whose pride brings about their own misery. As the events of the week ahead will show, the suffering of the Just One does not indicate rejection, but election, for it is through a demonstration of the radical gift of self that God will effect the world's cure from the death-dealing character of self-love and self-assertion.

Psalm 22, which follows the reading of the third song of the Suffering Servant, anticipates the Lord's cry from the Cross—"My God, my God, why hast Thou forsaken me?"—while reminding the Church that this psalm, evoked by the dying Messiah, ends on a note of triumph:

Yea, to him all the proud of the earth bow down;
> before him shall bow all who go down to the dust,
> and he who cannot keep himself alive.

Posterity shall serve him;
> men shall tell of the Lord to the coming generation,

and proclaim his deliverance to a people yet unborn,
> that he has wrought it.

The day's second reading, the Christological hymn from St. Paul's Letter to the Philippians, also recurs every Palm Sunday, as it does regularly in the Liturgy of the Hours (alternating with the Christological hymns from the "pastoral letters" to the Ephesians and the Colossians and from the First Letter of Peter). Although originally framed in the context of a Pauline admonition to his Macedonian congregation against self-interestedness and conceit, the Christological hymn in Philippians has been read by the Church for two millennia as a profound meditation on the transformation of history and the cosmos wrought by the Incarnation of the Son of God, his sacrificial and atoning death, his Resurrection, and his exaltation. In Paul's sweeping vision, the Passover of the New Covenant begins with the self-emptying of the Son of any semblance of his "equality with God," passes through the agony of the Cross, and is completed in the Resurrection and Ascension: a drama in which Christ, having descended in humility "to the form of a servant, being born in the likeness of men," ascends in glory from degradation to exaltation, "so that at the name of Jesus every knee should bow, in heaven and on earth and under the earth, and every tongue confess that Jesus Christ is Lord, to the glory of God the Father."

Witnessing that drama, the truly converted disciple cannot remain a mere bystander or observer. As St. Andrew of Crete teaches in today's Office of Readings, the profound humility of the Son of God in entering history for the sake of saving humanity from its own folly ought to inspire an equally profound imitation of those who once hailed him with palms, albeit with a difference that derives from our standing on the far side of the act of redemption, which makes us new creatures:

Let us run to accompany him as he hastens toward his passion, and imitate those who met him then, not by covering his path with garments, olive branches, or palms, but by doing all we can to prostrate ourselves before him by being humble and by trying to live as he would wish. Then we shall be able to receive the Word at his coming, and God, whom no limits can contain, will be within us. . . .

So let us spread before his feet, not garments or soulless olive branches, which delight the eye for a few hours and then wither, but ourselves, clothed in his grace, or rather, clothed completely in him. We who have been baptized into Christ must ourselves be the garments that we spread before him. . . . Let our souls take the place of the welcoming branches as we join today in the children's holy song: "Blessed is he who comes in the name of the Lord. Blessed is the king of Israel."

The Synoptic Passion narratives, all of which were once read during Holy Week, are now read sequentially on Palm Sunday throughout the three years of the Lectionary cycle, while John's Passion narrative is read annually on Good Friday. Each of the three Synoptic accounts offers distinctive insights into the drama of salvation that is played out between the Last Supper and the sealing of the tomb.

In Matthew's account, the agony of Jesus in the garden, which is real, is also, according to biblical scholar Gianfranco Ravasi, a perfect form of prayer and an abiding image of the demanding search for God's will that is part of every disciple's life. Having conformed his own will to the Father's, the Son then offers himself on the Cross in an act of radical obedience that has multiple and dramatic effects. The sacrifice of the Son signals the beginning of a new covenant in his blood (" . . . the curtain of the Temple was torn in two, from top to bottom"). It shakes the cosmos (" . . . the earth shook and the rocks were split"). It inspires acts of faith ("The centurion and those who were with him . . . were filled with awe and said, 'Truly this was a son of God!'"). And, most profoundly, it liberates humanity from the bondage of death that entered the world through sin ("The tombs were also opened, and many bodies of the saints who had fallen asleep were raised").

In Mark's account, the "messianic secret" that has been one of the leitmotifs of Jesus's public ministry ("And he strictly charged them that no one should know this") is revealed. Jesus declares openly who he is, with what mission he has been charged, and what that mission's results will be: "Again the high priest asked him, 'Are you the Christ, the Son of the Blessed?' And Jesus said, 'I am; and you will see the Son of Man sitting at the right hand of Power, and coming with the clouds of heaven.'" There is no ambiguity here, no secret, and certainly no coyness: Jesus, his person and his mission, demands a decision. That Peter, who was to be the rock, fails the first test of this new moment of clarity and denies his Master suggests the weakness of the sons and daughters of the Church throughout history. That Peter then repents (" . . . he broke down and wept") bears witness to the power of repentance and of the divine mercy throughout time: he who failed his first test of courage becomes the one whom the angel at the empty tomb calls to Galilee, where he will see the Risen One and be sent in mission to the world.

Luke's Passion narrative is structured, observed Ravasi, according to a "personal-moral perspective": to follow Jesus in his suffering and death is to conform one's life to him in such a radical way that this act of faith reshapes the entirety of life. The Lord pours himself out completely and unreservedly; his disciples are to do the same. The Lord offers a final lesson in forgiveness and reconciliation by asking the Father's mercy on those who crucify him, not knowing what they are doing, and by promising the repentant thief admission to the Kingdom of God; his disciples are to be similarly generous, not out of calculation but out of love. In dying with the words of Psalm 31 on his lips—"Into thy hand I commit my spirit"—Jesus completes, as Ravasi put it, the "great catechesis" on divine providence that he began in his discourse on the lilies of the field: "Fear not, little flock, for it is your Father's good pleasure to give you the kingdom" [Luke 12.32]. Now, he lives that great catechesis to the last extreme by invoking confidently, at the very end, the one whom he calls "Father."

Palm Sunday is thus redolent with imagery. Its central image—the procession with palms—is reenactment with a difference. By reliving the joy of the crowds who greet Jesus on his entrance into Jerusalem because (in the Johannine account) they have been amazed by the raising of Lazarus from the dead, the Church begins Holy Week in anticipation of the Resurrection that will be celebrated a week hence. We walk the way to Calvary in sorrow, but with confidence that what will seem like a catastrophe is in truth the Passover of the Lord to exaltation—and the key to our own salvation.

St. John Lateran: Colonna heraldry
and Cosmatesque floor

I N THE PAPAL ARCHBASILICA
of St. John Lateran, Catholic history unfolds
through an eclectic decorative scheme. Unlike
St. Peter's Basilica, with its seamless ornamentation, this papal cathedral displays a dis-
jointed and even jarring mix of styles in what
may serve as a reminder that tranquillity has
not always been the hallmark of the Church's
voyage through two millennia.

Constantine's fourth-century donation of
silver altars and golden chandeliers earned
the Lateran the nickname Basilica Aurea
(Golden Church). A century later, Genseric
sacked Rome and looted these treasures; the
denuded structure then fell to an earthquake in 477. Yet the fledgling basilica proved resilient. Its
walls were rebuilt, and rather than investing in ornaments, the Lateran began to amass the world's
greatest collection of relics. Originally housed in the Sancta Sanctorum, the pope's private chapel,
the collection was catalogued in a mosaic list that is found today outside the sacristy.

Pope St. Leo III (795–816) added an elaborate dining hall to the residential part of the Lateran complex; its mosaic apse is visible from the street. In 896, amid the contest for southern Italy
between the Church and Islam, another earthquake struck St. John Lateran; the basilica had to be
rebuilt from the ground up by Pope Sergius III (904–911). Happily, this was an age in which Rome
produced the world's finest stone carvers. The basilica floors were laid by the Cosmati family, who
invented the cleverest of medieval recycling techniques: taking shards of precious stones from the
rubble of imperial Rome, the Cosmati laid them into the colorful geometric patterns familiar from
other station churches in a style that came to be known as "Cosmatesque."

The basilica's golden apse mosaic was a gift of Pope Nicholas IV in 1292. To the left of the
bejeweled Cross stand Mary, Peter, and Paul; John the Baptist and John the Evangelist (to whom
the church was dedicated in 905 and 1145, respectively) approach on the right, while Andrew
brings up the rear. The two smaller figures are Francis of Assisi and Anthony of Padua, new saints
from the thirteenth century. The Franciscan love of nature may have influenced the design, as flora
and fauna fill the grass below and the water is alive with sea creatures. The two deer evoke Psalm
42: "As a hart longs for flowing streams, so my soul longs for thee, O God."

Between 1100 and 1500, the Lateran Basilica hosted five ecumenical councils. Here, too, Pope
Boniface VIII declared the inaugural jubilee year, 1300: that proclamation is memorialized in a
scene depicted on the first right-hand pier in a fresco fragment attributed to Giotto, the artist
who first "translated the art of painting from Greek to Latin," as Giotto's contemporary Cennino

(continues)

(continued)

Cennini noted, meaning that he moved away from the enigmatic stylization of Byzantine art to a more straightforward naturalism.

Shortly after the papacy decamped for Avignon in 1308, the basilica suffered another fire. The *baldacchino* above the altar was erected by Giovanni di Stefano in 1367, a small compensation after yet another conflagration in 1360. In 1376, the pope returned to Rome and to a devastated cathedral and Lateran Palace; popes would never live in the Lateran complex again. The Colonna pope, Martin V, restored the basilica, leaving the family heraldic symbol, a column, on the floors; Martin V, the pontiff who resolved the Great Schism, is buried in the *confessio* in a bronze tomb.

Pope Sixtus V (1585–1590) restructured the entire site, making it more accessible to pilgrims, while Clement VIII (1592–1605) added the colorful transept with its painted tapestries of Constantine. Francesco Borromini transformed the nave of the church with his lofty, white, undulating style in preparation for the Jubilee of 1650.

The papacy lost much of its temporal patrimony in 1870; Leo XIII responded by enlarging the basilica's choir, anticipating a future in which the priesthood would again thrive. In 1993, a Mafia bomb exploded outside the transept; repairs were completed in time for John Paul II to open the Holy Door and lead the Church into the third millennium. [E.L.]

St. Praxedes: Triumphal arch and apse (ninth century)

MONDAY OF HOLY WEEK

Station at St. Praxedes

Holy Mass
Isaiah 42.1–7
Psalm 27
John 12.1–11

Office of Readings
Hebrews 10.19–39
St. Augustine: Sermon 3 from Codex Guelferbytanus

TODAY'S STATIONAL CHURCH, WHICH houses the Chapel of St. Zeno and its exceptionally beautiful mosaics, offers an apt occasion for reflection on one of the most difficult of pieces to fit into the mosaic of discipleship: patience—a recurring theme in today's Mass and Office of Readings. According to the traditional catalogue of "fruits of the Holy Spirit," patience is one of those perfections into which Lenten pilgrims must grow, as the itinerary of conversion gradually equips us to become the kind of people who can enjoy the glory of eternity within the light and love of the Holy Trinity. "Gradually," of course, suggests that growth in patience is, more often than not, an exercise in patience.

The theme is introduced in the first reading at Mass, the first of the four Suffering Servant songs in Isaiah. Here, the chosen servant of the Lord is depicted as a man of godly forbearance, familiar with the weakness of humanity, who will reshape history according to the patient rhythms of the divine mercy:

> Behold my servant, whom I uphold
>> my chosen, in whom my soul delights;
> I have put my spirit upon him,
>> he will bring forth justice to the nations.
> He will not cry or lift up his voice,
>> or make it heard in the street;
> a bruised reed he will not break,
>> and a dimly burning wick he will not quench;
>> he will faithfully bring forth justice.
> He will not fail or be discouraged
>> till he has established justice in the earth;
>> and the coastlands wait for his law.

Patient waiting for the working out of the divine plan of salvation history is also the lesson taught by the psalmist in response to Isaiah's portrait of the noble Servant of YHWH. As sung by the Church, the first and last verses of Psalm 27 are a confession of faith in the coming Kingdom—no matter how long delayed its advent may seem—and an admonition to patient, courageous, watchful waiting along the pathways of history:

> The Lord is my light and my salvation;
>> whom shall I fear?
> The Lord is the stronghold of my life;
>> of whom shall I be afraid?
>
> . . .
>
> I believe that I shall see the goodness of the Lord
>> in the land of the living!
> Wait for the Lord;

be strong, and let your heart take courage;

yea, wait for the LORD!

The gospel reading for the day continues the story of Jesus's friendship with Martha, Mary, and Lazarus, which, read through the prism of today's theme, appears as an ongoing lesson in patience. At their first encounter in Luke's gospel, when a family disagreement breaks out over whether the duties of hospitality are being ignored, Jesus teaches Martha and Mary patience with each other: there is a place for work and there is a time for contemplation, but listening to the Lord should always inform the active life. Now, Mary anoints the feet of Jesus with a precious substance and dries them with her hair, and Judas complains about the waste of money this extravagance represents. Jesus tries—in vain, as the gospel of John has it—to teach Judas patience; seen with the eyes of faith, Mary's anointing is not a waste of money, but a preparation for Jesus's burial.

In the Office of Readings, the author of the Letter to the Hebrews teaches his readers that patience is required to align our lives with the divine master plan, which, from our perspective, can sometimes seem stalled: "You have need of endurance, so that you may do the will of God and receive what is promised." What can seem to us delay is in truth the divine patience at work within history; what can seem a lengthy delay is but a "little while" when we remember that the Lord of history is in charge of history.

The English word "patience" comes from the Latin verb *patior* [to suffer], so that, etymologically, "patience" means "to suffer with" or "to bear with." If patience is one of the fruits of the Holy Spirit [Galatians 5.22], given in Baptism and Confirmation, then, for the Christian, the ultimate source of patience—the power to "bear with" and "suffer with" others—is the Cross. For nowhere is the divine patience more strikingly manifest than at Calvary. In the patristic selection in today's Office of Readings, St. Augustine reflects on this theme: "The Passion of our Lord and Savior Jesus Christ," he preaches, "is the hope of glory and a lesson in patience." The Word through whom the cosmos was created patiently takes a human nature precisely so that he might "suffer with" those desperate for forgiveness and redemption. As he shares in our humanity, so his burning desire to "bear with" us by bearing the Cross empowers us to share in his divinity, through the blood and water that evoke Baptism and the Holy Eucharist. Therefore, Christians should not regard the Cross as something shameful, but as something in which to boast:

> The death of the Lord our God should not be a cause of shame for us; rather, it should be our greatest hope, our greatest glory. In taking upon himself the death that he found in us, he has most faithfully promised to give us life in him. . . .
>
> Brethren, let us then fearlessly acknowledge, and even openly proclaim, that Christ was crucified for us; let us confess it, not in fear but in joy, not in shame but in glory.

Pope Benedict XVI's 2011 Lenten message to the Church offered a similar challenge. Reflecting on the Second Vatican Council's teaching that the Church ought to recover the baptismal character of Lent, the Pope noted St. Paul's teaching, in his Letter to the Philippians, about the transformation that begins in us through our baptismal participation in the events of Good Friday and Easter. The life of grace, the Apostle wrote, is one in which we are constantly being conformed to the patiently suffering Christ of Calvary, so that we might be strengthened in our hope of sharing in his resurrected glory: as Paul prayed that he may "come to know him and the power of his resurrection, and partake of his sufferings by being molded to the pattern of his death, striving towards the goal of resurrection from the dead" [Philippians 3.10–11], so twenty-first-century Christians, according to Benedict XVI, must allow the power of Baptism to inform our "entire existence," which thereby becomes an "encounter with Christ . . . imparting divine life."

Deep conversion means being molded into "the pattern of [Christ's] death," so as to share in the glory of his Resurrection. There are neither accidents nor coincidences in the economy of salvation. The patience of the Suffering Servant on Good Friday is the necessary prelude to the exaltation of that same Servant on Easter.

St. Praxedes (St. Zeno Chapel):
Pillar of the Flagellation

T UCKED BEHIND ST. MARY MAJOR, the little Basilica of St. Praxedes is a surprising treasure chest, its dingy portal opening into an interior of dazzling mosaics.

Pope St. Paschal I (817–824), whose efforts to return beauty to the Eternal City led to the creation of many examples of luminous art in the "Dark Ages," rebuilt this church near an earlier *titulus* (documented in 491) dedicated to St. Praxedes. Paschal's entrance still exists in the portico facing Via San Martino ai Monti; remnants of the antique church remain in the sixteen granite columns lining the nave and in an architrave of carved Roman cornices. The powerfully articulated nave leads to a mosaic-encrusted triumphal arch, the gateway to the apse, altar, and crypt, into which Paschal transferred the remains of 2,300 martyrs from the suburban catacombs.

Paschal's architectural aesthetic focused on light: thus the nave was lined with twenty-four clerestory windows through which the sun's rays streamed before dancing off the small glass tiles of the ornamentation. The apse mosaic took its inspiration from the Basilica of Sts. Cosmas and Damian: against a mesmerizing blue sky, a golden-robed Christ floats under the hand of God. Peter and Paul flank him, wearing senatorial togas; Praxedes and her sister Pudenziana, holding their crowns of martyrdom, are embraced by the apostles and guided toward Christ. St. Zeno is on the far right, while Paschal (wearing the blue nimbus of the living) stands under a palm tree next to a phoenix, symbol of the Resurrection.

This celestial gathering is surmounted by apocalyptic imagery: the Lamb of God, flanked by seven candlesticks and the symbols of the four evangelists. Scores of white-robed figures offer their wreaths. Their procession concludes at the arch's summit, where the apostles, Mary, and John the Baptist point toward Christ, flanked by angels. The entire work is an invitation to look through this world into the *Civitas Dei* (City of God).

Structural instability forced Pope Innocent III to reconfigure the building in 1198, and at that time many of the clerestory windows were closed. St. Charles Borromeo, as cardinal-titular, tried to rectify the interruption of what Paschal had intended as a unified space, but without lasting success. Echoes of Borromeo's efforts remain: the table where he dined with Rome's poor is in the third chapel on the left, while the second chapel preserves his chair.

Alexander de Medici, cardinal-titular until his election as Pope Leo XI in 1605, commissioned the nave frescoes from Paris Nogari and Baldassare Croce: a counterclockwise cycle of the Passion.

(continues)

(*continued*)

The apostles, pillars of the church, are painted on faux marble bases; above, angels hold open scrolls recounting the Creed.

Great Italian artists worked on the tombs here. Arnolfo di Cambio's *Tomb of Cardinal Pantaleone Anchier*, Andrea Bregno's sepulcher of Cardinal Alain de Coëtivy, and a funerary monument for Giovanni Santoni by a young Gian Lorenzo Bernini, which inspired nineteenth-century poet Robert Browning to write "A Bishop Orders His Tomb."

Paschal I built the glorious St. Zeno Chapel in honor of his mother, Theodora. Its unique, wall-to-wall mosaics create a golden vision of heaven; precious columns line the four corners, capped with golden capitals from which angels seem to reach to the vault's summit, where Christ Pantocrator looks serenely down. The glass-encased marble fragment to the side, a gift from Cardinal Giovanni Colonna in 1223, has long been venerated as the column of Christ's flagellation.

The sarcophagus of the two sister-martyrs, under the altar, inspired a young Italian student, Giovanni Battista de Rossi, to begin exploring the catacombs; in 1864, de Rossi published the first scientific work of Christian archaeology. [E.L.]

St. Prisca: Fresco fragment (fifteenth century)

TUESDAY OF HOLY WEEK

Station at St. Prisca

Holy Mass
Isaiah 49.1–6
Psalm 71
John 13.21–33, 36–38

Office of Readings
Hebrews 12.1–13
St. Basil the Great: On the Holy Spirit, 15

THE GOSPEL READINGS AT Mass today and tomorrow center on Judas's betrayal, which sets in motion the last act of the drama of Jesus's life. Matthew's account, to be read tomorrow, is perhaps the more familiar of the two: Judas approaches the chief priests and is paid thirty pieces of silver to deliver Jesus into the hands of his enemies. John's account in today's Mass is the more theologically suggestive. Jesus, in sovereign command of the situation, knows what Judas is about. He knows that Satan has tempted this disciple, and that Judas is in mortal danger of being conscripted into the legion of those who violently oppose the Father's design of salvation history, which is being worked out in Jesus's person and mission. In a last act of fellowship and love, Jesus reaches out to Judas and offers him the dipped morsel—at which point, the gospel narrator reports, "Satan entered into him." Yet even here, at the moment of moral betrayal, Jesus bends what seems to be Satan's victory to his own and the Father's purposes, sending Judas off and telling him to "do quickly" what he plans to do.

The contrast between Judas's betrayal and Peter's impending three denials at the interrogation of Jesus is striking. Although Peter denies knowing the Master, his tears of remorse and repentance bring him forgiveness. As with the prodigal son, his filial dignity is restored, and the continued outpouring of the Divine Mercy turns him into the rock, the foundation, on which the Church of the Risen One is built. Judas, as the Church will read on Good Friday, compounds his sin of betrayal by committing the sin of despair. Unable to imagine forgiveness for such a sin as his, he falls into what Pope Benedict XVI once described as his "second tragedy," killing himself. Brought by grace from the darkness of betrayal to the light of repentance, Peter lives, eventually giving his life out of love for his Lord. Rejecting the Light of the world, Judas enters the darkness of those who hate the divine master plan and its bearer, and is ensnared in their death-dealing plots.

The reading from Isaiah in today's Mass, taken from the second of the Suffering Servant songs, speaks of the glorification of the one whom "the LORD called from the womb," whose "mouth [was] like a sharp sword": "It is too light a thing that you should be my servant," says the LORD. Rather, "I will give you as a light to the nations, that my salvation may reach to the end of the earth."

This vindication of the Suffering Servant, whose luminous witness will draw all nations to a knowledge of the one true God who is the God of Israel, anticipates and prefigures what the Church calls the "communion of saints," as does that "great cloud of witnesses" of which the author of the Letter to the Hebrew speaks in today's Office of Readings. Prior to the invocation of this image, the eleventh chapter of Hebrews catalogues the acts of faith by which the "men of old received divine approval" and thus became witnesses to the saving action in history of Israel's God, which would reach its climax in Jesus. Their company includes Abel, the righteous bearer of sacrificial gifts; Enoch, who did not taste death; Noah, who saved humanity from the flood; Abraham, who "sojourned

St. Praxedes: Triumphal Arch, St. Zeno Chapel

St. Praxedes: Ceiling, St. Zeno Chapel

St. Mary "at the Martyrs" (Pantheon): Interior

St. John Lateran: Apse and *Baldacchino*

St. Mary Major: High Altar, Ceiling, and *Baldacchino*

St. Mary Major: *The Enthronement of the Virgin*

St. Peter: Apse

St. Peter: High Altar with Reliquaries; *St. Helena*

St. Peter: Interior of the *Baldacchino*

St. Peter: Interior of the Dome

in the land of promise" and obediently offered his firstborn, Isaac (whose rescue prefigures the Resurrection); Moses, who "considered abuse suffered for the Christ greater wealth than the treasures of Egypt, for he looked forward to the reward." There are judges, kings, prophets, and martyrs here—all these valiant men and women of the covenant with Israel inspire Lenten pilgrims to receive with gratitude the gift that will be given in the sacrifice of the Son and his resurrection from the dead: "Since we are surrounded by so great a cloud of witnesses, let us lay aside every weight, and sin which clings so closely, and let us run with perseverance the race that is set before us, looking to Jesus the pioneer and perfecter of our faith, who for the joy that was set before him endured the cross, despising the shame, and is seated at the right hand of the throne of God" [Hebrews 12.1–2; see also Hebrews 11.4–38].

The "communion of saints," in which the Church professes its belief every time she prays the Nicene Creed and the Apostles Creed, extends the baptismal gift of supernatural charity both through time and beyond the boundaries of time. As Pope Paul VI's 1967 apostolic constitution, *The Doctrine of Indulgences*, puts it, "a perennial link of charity exists between the faithful who have reached their heavenly home, those who are expiating their sins in Purgatory, and those who are still pilgrims on earth. Between them there is . . . an abundant exchange of all good things." This exchange aims at perfecting the entire Church in the *caritas Christi*: the love of Christ that Judas rejected; the love that enabled Peter to confess his denials and receive forgiveness. In the economy of salvation, men and women of every time and place are, by the power of the Holy Spirit, enabled to confess, with St. Paul, that "the Son of God . . . loved me and gave himself for me" [Galatians 2.20]. Putting on that selfless, life-giving love through adherence to the Anointed One of God is what it means to imitate Christ. To love God and neighbor freely and without calculation is to be enumerated among the "great cloud of witnesses," to live within the communion of saints. To love freely is to love as Jesus loved during this week of climax in the drama of salvation history.

And to love freely is to be drawn into worship at the Wedding Feast of the Lamb, as one of the greatest of theological poets, Gerard Manley Hopkins, understood, in his poetic translation of a prayer of St. Francis Xavier:

O God, I love thee, I love thee—
Not out of hope of heaven for me
Nor fearing not to love and be
In the everlasting burning.
Thou, thou, my Jesus, after me
Didst reach thine arms out dying,
For my sake sufferedst nails and lance,
Mocked and marred countenance,
Sorrows passing number,
Sweat and care and cumber,
Yea and death, and this for me,
And thou couldst see me sinning:
Then I, why should not I love thee,
Jesu, so much in love with me?
Not for heaven's sake; not to be
Out of hell by loving thee;
Not for any gains I see;
But just the way that thou didst me
I do love and will love thee;
What must I love thee, Lord, for then?
For being my king and God. Amen.

St. Prisca: Side altar

T HE DISCREET FAÇADE OF THE BASILICA of St. Prisca brings to mind the ancient, incognito house church hailed by St. Paul in the Letter to the Romans as the home of Prisca and Aquila.

The Aventine, Rome's blue-collar neighborhood until the second century A.D., was fertile soil for early Roman Christianity. A multicultural area above the port where wares from across the empire flowed into the imperial capital, the Aventine was home to dockworkers, soldiers, and foreigners. This religious diversity gave St. Prisca, the house church, at least one exotic neighbor—a Mithraeum, the artwork of which remains largely intact. Sadly, the ancient *domus ecclesiae* on the site is difficult to identify amid the archaeological remains.

The first official mention of the church of St. Prisca dates from 499. That fifth-century church was rebuilt by Pope Paschal II in 1100, but his work was completely engulfed by a restoration undertaken by Pope Callistus III in 1455. Callistus added the poetic inscription to the left of the altar, which paints a pleasing literary portrait of the site, which was once home to a temple of Hercules, then home to St. Peter, who "brought many to God through baptism."

The decoration dates from the Jubilee of 1600, when Benedetto Giustiniani, the cardinal-titular, gave the church its present façade, restored the altar, and reopened the subterranean crypt, which contained an altar held by one tradition to have been consecrated by St. Peter. The wall decoration was executed by the Florentine painter Anastasio Fontebuono (whom Cardinal Giustiniani had also commissioned to work at St. Balbina). Fontebuono, anticipating Gian Lorenzo Bernini's angel bridge at Castel Sant'Angelo by half a century, decorated the nave with angels on pedestals holding the instruments of the Passion. Alternating between the angels are the apostles Peter, Paul, John, and Andrew.

Domenico Cresti's apse decoration provides cheerful relief in the austere space. The plaster decoration along the walls seems like confectionary, softly framing the pastel frescos. These light-hearted swirling cornices surround stories of the martyrdom of St. Prisca; her baptism by St. Peter holds pride of place over the altar, while on the left the saint awaits execution in prison, and on the right Pope Eutyches carries her relics in procession.

Many religious orders have left their mark on the church. A few fragments of the chancel screen (now in the baptistery) are reminders of the Greek monks who moved here in the seventh century. A damaged mosaic of St. Peter recalls the eleventh-century arrival of the Benedictines. The Franciscans, coming in the mid-fifteenth century, added an altar to St. Anthony, while the Augustinians later contributed chapels to St. Augustine, St. Monica, and St. Rita of Cascia. [E.L.]

St. Mary Major (Borghese Chapel): Stational Mass

WEDNESDAY OF HOLY WEEK

Station at St. Mary Major

Holy Mass
Isaiah 50.4–9a

Psalm 69

Matthew 26.14–25

Office of Readings
Hebrews 12.14–29

St. Augustine: Tractate 84, On the Gospel of John

FIVE WEEKS AGO, WHEN St. Mary Major first appeared on the station church pilgrimage, the great Marian basilica and the readings of the day prompted a reflection on Jesus's mother as the paradigm of discipleship: the woman of faith whose articulated *fiat*—"Let it be to me according to your word" [Luke 1.28]—set the pattern for all subsequent followers of her son. Mary's articulated *fiat* was the prologue to the Incarnation, to the mission of Jesus, and to the Church; Mary's consent to bearing the Son of God pointed humanity into the two great mysteries of salvation history, the Incarnation and the Trinity.

Now, on "Spy Wednesday," the last full day of Lent, the stational pilgrimage returns to what Romans know as the "Liberian Basilica." On the eve of the Paschal Triduum, the forces of darkness are closing in on the Light of the world, and the Lamb of God is preparing to celebrate his last Passover before he enters into the mystery of the new and definitive Passover of his own death. On this day of lengthening shadows and foreboding, the Lenten pilgrim's attention is naturally drawn to Mary's "second *fiat*": the inarticulate, silent *fiat* at the foot of the Cross, where the *Redemptoris Mater* (the Mother of the Redeemer, as Blessed John Paul II entitled his 1987 encyclical on Our Lady) receives the dead body of her son and conforms her will to the inscrutable will of God once again.

In recent centuries, as other Christian communities have come to a deeper appreciation of Mary's unique role in salvation history, there have also been notable developments of Marian doctrine in the Catholic Church. These developments are both Christological and ecclesiological; they deepen our understanding of the mystery of Christ and of the mystery of the Church. In 1854, Blessed Pius IX, after consulting the world episcopate, declared that Mary had been preserved from original sin in order to be the *Theotokos*, the God-Bearer; this is the doctrine of the Immaculate Conception, the celebration of which, on December 8, is the patronal feast of the United States. In 1950, Pope Pius XII, again after consulting the world episcopate, declared that Mary had been assumed into heaven soul and body; as the *Catechism of the Catholic Church* puts it, Mary's Assumption was "a singular participation in her Son's Resurrection and an anticipation of the resurrection of other Christians." Thus Mary is both the origin of the Church and the icon of the Church in glory—a "sign of certain hope and comfort to the pilgrim People of God," as the Fathers of Vatican II wrote in the Dogmatic Constitution on the Church.

Over two millennia, the Church has honored Mary with many titles, the most beautiful of which are in the Litany of Loretto: "Mirror of Justice," "Seat of Wisdom," "Mystical Rose," "Gate of Heaven," "Refuge of Sinners," "Comforter of the Afflicted," and so forth. Yet while many Christians are aware of these various titles for the Mother of God, few are familiar with the idea of Mary as *martyr*. Today's *statio*, coming two days before that martyrdom is proclaimed in the Johannine Passion narrative, is an apt moment to reflect on this often unremarked aspect of Mary's life and witness.

The idea of Mary as a martyr who, like the Beloved Disciple who stands with her at the foot of the Cross, does not die the typical martyr's death, is a venerable one: St. Bernard of Clairvaux invoked it in the eleventh century in a sermon that the Church reads every year on September 15, the Memorial of Our Lady of Sorrows. There, Bernard reflects on the "sword" (Luke 2.35) that Simeon prophesied would pierce the soul of Mary and identifies it with the soldier's spear that pierced the side of Mary's dead son, bringing forth the blood and water that are signs of Baptism and the Eucharist:

Truly, O blessed Mother, a sword has pierced your heart. For only by passing through your heart could the sword enter the flesh of your Son. Indeed, after your Jesus—who belongs to everyone, but is especially yours—gave up his life, the cruel spear, which was not withheld from his lifeless body, tore open his side. Clearly it did not touch his soul and could not harm him, but it did pierce your heart. For surely his soul was no longer there, but yours could not be torn away. Thus the violence of sorrow has cut through your heart, and we rightly call you more than martyr, since the effect of compassion in you has gone beyond the endurance of physical suffering. . . .

Perhaps someone will say . . . "Did she not expect him to rise again? . . ." Surely. "And still she grieved over her crucified Son?" Intensely. Who are you and what is the source of your wisdom that you are more surprised at the compassion of Mary than at the Passion of Mary's Son? For if he could die in body, could she not be with him in spirit? He died in body through a love greater than anyone had known. She died in spirit through a love unlike any other since his.

Mary's martyrdom is thus a martyrdom of love, born of unfailing fidelity to the designs of Providence.

Nine centuries later, in a small book on the Rosary, *The Threefold Garland*, Hans Urs von Balthasar developed this insight by writing of how the essential form of Mary's discipleship—her *fiat*—shaped her participation in the

Passion and Death of her Son. Mary's suffering on the *Via Crucis*, the Way to Calvary, is greater than anyone's, Balthasar suggested, because it was a suffering built on her "Let it be." There was nothing Mary could do for Jesus; thus, "in her spirit," Balthasar wrote, "she suffers from not being able to relieve her Son of any suffering." The suffering of Mary is a true martyrdom, because "she must leave the entire burden to him . . . and [she] darkly knows that this burden exceeds all the world's weights." In fidelity to the economy of salvation as designed by the Triune God, Mary "has to let it happen, and can only offer [God] this *letting happen* which as such cannot accomplish anything."

Yet it is precisely in this *letting be* that we encounter the essence of Marian martyrdom and Marian sanctity, even as we glimpse the essence of Mary as Mother of the Church:

> [Calvary] is not for her an occasion of despair, because her thoughts do not dwell on her own ability or inability, but wholly on her Son. And she does not stage a revolt either against God, who allows these things to happen, or against mankind, which is torturing her Son. She lets it all happen in the context of a consent which no longer has any active power, but which is like an infinite—eucharistic—dissolution.

The silent *fiat* at the foot of the Cross has become an icon of the reception of the Eucharist, the body and blood of Christ, offered on the Cross for the redemption of the world.

The passage from Hebrews in today's Office of Readings offers a powerful and reassuring vision of that Kingdom where Mary, first of disciples and first of the glorified members of the Church, now lives within the light and love of the Trinity: "You have come to Mount Zion and to the city of the living God, the heavenly Jerusalem, and to innumerable angels in festal gathering, and to the assembly of the first-born who are enrolled in heaven, and to a judge who is God of all, and to the spirits of just men made perfect, and to Jesus, the mediator of a new covenant, and to the sprinkled blood that speaks more graciously than the blood of Abel." This eternal life in the New Jerusalem, whose foundation stones are the apostles of the Lamb, has been made possible because, as we see again in today's gospel reading, Jesus will remain in sovereign command as "the hour" for which the Son has come into the world arrives: he seizes the moment ("My time is at hand . . .") and bends human betrayal to the divine purpose: "I do as the Father has commanded me, so that the world may know that I love the Father" [John 14.31].

As the Letter to the Hebrews reminds us today, the love of God the Father for the Son and for the world is a "consuming fire." Over the next forty-eight hours, and through the sacrifice of the Son in the power of the Spirit, that fire will consume the world's sin, so that death might be no more. The martyrdom of Mary involved her saying, yet again, "Let it be. . . ." Her example—the witness of the enduring prototype of Christian discipleship—prompts Lenten pilgrims to do the same.

St. Mary Major (Borghese Chapel): *Pope Liberius and the Miraculous Snowfall* (Stefano Maderno, 1612)

THE BASILICA OF ST. Mary Major is Rome's Bethlehem. Its dedication to the God-Bearer, the arch mosaics of the Incarnation, and its relic of the crib readily associated the basilica with the Nativity, as did the Christmas stational Mass celebrated here. The Middle Ages strengthened this bond, as St. Jerome's relics were translated here from the Bethlehem cave where he died; Arnolfo di Cambio carved one of the first Nativity scenes (now in the basilica's museum) for the repository. In 1290, Jacopo Torriti decorated the apse with a frieze of stories of the Virgin, above which he depicted Mary crowned in heaven. Like Pietro Cavallini's contemporaneous mosaics in St. Cecelia, Torriti used three-dimensional effects, a kind of proto-perspective, to anchor his scenes in the physical world: as Christ crowns his mother outside of time and space, the saints, their feet amid the plants and animals at the water's edge, rise into a golden background festooned with garlands and an amazing avian array—St. Francis's *Canticle of the Creatures* set to images.

Counter-Reformation Catholicism in Rome reemphasized the Jerusalem-Bethlehem axis of St. Mary Major, St. John Lateran, and Holy Cross in response to Protestant critiques of alleged Catholic antibiblical bias; at the end of the sixteenth century, St. Mary Major was restored and enhanced to affirm the Church's devotion to the Mother of God. Thus, in 1562, Michelangelo, whose Marian piety is evident in his *Pietà*, designed the Sforza Chapel, now the Blessed Sacrament Chapel, his last work before his death in 1564.

Pope Sixtus V built his own burial chapel here in 1585: it is constructed in the shape of a Greek cross, with an octagonal temple for the Blessed Sacrament in the center that is held aloft by four angels. In a cave-like crypt below, Sixtus placed Arnolfo di Cambio's *Nativity* and the relics of St. Jerome (both have since been moved). Cesare Guerra's and Giovanni Nebbia's paintings celebrate Christ's ancestors and Mary's life, another response to Protestant criticisms of Catholic Marian devotion. The pope's tomb is on the right; a triumphal arch frames a sculpture of Sixtus kneeling before the tabernacle. (Opposite his own burial chapel, Sixtus built a tomb for his friend Pope Pius V, who created him cardinal. Pius V was canonized in 1712, the first pontiff so honored since Celestine V in 1315.)

Pope Paul V planned the basilica's Borghese Chapel on an even grander scale. Flaminio Ponzio designed the Borghese pope's resting place in the same shape as Sixtus's chapel, but made it loft-

(continues)

(*continued*)

ier and larger; Rome's best artists—Cavaliere D'Arpino in fresco and Pietro Bernini in sculpture—worked on the decoration. (Here, Scipione Borghese discovered fifteen-year-old Gian Lorenzo Bernini working for his father, Pietro. Gian Lorenzo Bernini's ties to the basilica were such that he asked to be buried here; his simple tomb lies in the floor to the left of the altar.)

Elaborate decoration frames the icon above the Borghese Chapel altar: one tradition claims that this icon, the Madonna *Salus Populi Romani*, was painted by St. Luke. What is more likely is that the panel was here in the sixth century and that Pope St. Gregory the Great carried it in procession through the city to rid Rome of the plague. Thus, for 1,400 years, this Marian image has watched over the health (*salus*) of the Roman people—which in this context means more than physical well-being. Thus, the fresco above the icon shows Mary, St. John the Evangelist, and St. Gregory Thaumaturgus healing people bitten by the serpents of heresy, which cause greater damage than any mortal illness. [E.L.]

St. John Lateran: Stational Mass

HOLY THURSDAY

Station at St. John Lateran

Chrism Mass

Isaiah 61.1–3a, 6a, 8b–9

Psalm 89

Revelation 1.5–8

Luke 4.16–21

Evening Mass of the Lord's Supper

Exodus 12.1–8, 11–14

Psalm 116

1 Corinthians 11.23–26

John 13.1–15

Office of Readings

Hebrews 4.14–5.10

St. Melito of Sardis: Easter Homily

THURSDAY OF HOLY WEEK is a day of transition. The liturgical season of Lent ends this afternoon with the last hour of Midday Prayer; the Church then enters the Paschal Triduum of the Passion, Death, and Resurrection of the Lord, beginning with the Evening Mass of the

Lord's Supper. Yet the "Forty Days" continue through today, Good Friday, and Holy Saturday, and indeed reach their spiritual climax in the Triduum.

The Chrism Mass, at which the local bishop consecrates the holy oils to be used during the next year and celebrates the gift of the priesthood of the New Covenant with his diocesan presbyterate, is best celebrated on Holy Thursday, from a biblical point of view; for reasons of convenience and logistics, however, many dioceses celebrate the Chrism Mass earlier in the week. Although rarely attended by lay Lenten pilgrims, the Chrism Mass, whenever it is celebrated, should be an occasion in every local Church for the people of the Church to give thanks for the gift of Jesus Christ, the "great high priest" of today's reading from the Letter to the Hebrews, and for the gift of the Church's priests.

Through the work of the Holy Spirit in the sacrament of Holy Orders, Christ, the eternal High Priest who "became the source of eternal salvation to all who obey him" [Hebrews 5.9], configures the priests of his Church to himself in a unique way, making them icons of his own priesthood. Thus Thursday of Holy Week is also an opportunity to give thanks for the gift of the priesthood, a unique type of spiritual paternity that continues the mediating priesthood of Christ himself, and a distinctively Christian form of headship that, as Jesus will demonstrate to his disciples in tonight's gospel reading, is exercised through the holiness of pastoral charity. Holy Thursday is also a fitting day on which to thank the Church's priests for their sacrifice and their ministry and to pray for an abundance of vocations to the priesthood.

The Preface of the Chrism Mass beautifully summarizes the theology of priesthood in the Catholic Church, in which the ordained priesthood feeds, blesses, and ennobles the baptismal priesthood of all the faithful, enabling them to go into the world to convert it to Christ:

[By] the anointing of the Holy Spirit you made your Only Begotten Son High Priest of the new and eternal covenant, and by your wondrous design were pleased to decree that his one Priesthood should continue in the Church. . . .

. . . Christ not only adorns with a royal priesthood the people he has made his own; but with a brother's kindness he chooses men to become sharers in his sacred ministry through the laying on of hands.

They are to renew in his name the sacrifice of human redemption, to set before your children the paschal banquet, to lead your holy people in charity, to nourish them with the word and strengthen them with the sacraments.

As they give up their lives for you and for the salvation of their brothers and sisters, they strive to be conformed to the image of Christ himself and offer you a constant witness of faith and love.

The Paschal Triduum of the Lord's Passion and Resurrection is not so much a series of moments—the Last Supper, the agony in Gethsemane, the arrest and trial, the Via Crucis and Calvary, the burial, the discovery of the empty tomb—as it is a single, unfolding event: a sacred journey, the ultimate pilgrimage. In the Triduum, the Anointed One of God, by entering obediently into the Passion that is his divinely appointed destiny, makes that Passion into the axial moment of human history and the inbreaking of the end time. Initiating the Passover of the New Covenant, Jesus passes over from mortal life, through death, into resurrection and exaltation. The new Passover lamb, the Lamb of God, thereby liberates humanity from the burden of sin and opens up, for those who profess faith in him, the possibility of a share in that eternal life where he is now exalted at the Father's right hand.

As the holy bishop from second-century Anatolia, Melito of Sardis, explains in today's Office of Readings, Jesus recapitulated in himself the history of salvation as revealed in the Hebrew Bible. Christ, as St. Melito reads the prophets, *is* the "mystery of the Passover." Through his Incarnation, he "clothed himself in . . . humanity" for the sake of suffering humanity, and "took the pain of fallen man upon himself." Like the Passover lamb, he was "led forth . . . [and] slaughtered," so that his blood might be the sign on the doorposts and lintels of the faithful that they, too, have been "freed from . . . slavery to the devil" and brought "out of darkness into light, out of tyranny into an eternal kingdom," by the new

High Priest "who made us into a new priesthood, a people chosen to be his own for ever."

In all of this, Christ is "the Passover that is our salvation." And because he was with the Father from before time and knows the Father as only the Son can know him, Christ the New Passover shared, in a mysterious way, not only in the design of salvation history, but in its accomplishment, even before the Incarnation. Thus, as St. Melito writes, "it is he who endured every kind of suffering in all those who foreshadowed him. In Abel he was slain, in Isaac bound, in Jacob exiled, in Joseph sold, in Moses exposed to die. He was sacrificed in the Passover lamb, persecuted in David, dishonored in the prophets." In him, the longing of Israel for a Son of David who will bring about the restoration of the kingdom is fulfilled, although in a surprising way and to a radical end: the establishment of the eternal Kingdom of God among Jews and Gentiles alike, such that the "wild olive shoot" is grafted onto the cultivated "richness of the olive tree" of Israel [Romans 11.17]. The resurrection of Israel from the death of slavery in the Passover of old has been completed in the Resurrection of Christ, the New Passover lamb, who makes possible the New Life that is eternal life for all his brethren.

And who are those brethren? In Matthew's account of the Last Supper, read in Year A in the Lectionary cycle, Jesus "took a cup, and when he had given thanks, he gave it to them, saying 'Drink of it, all of you; for this is my blood of the covenant, which is poured out for many for the forgiveness of sins.'" In Mark's account, read in Year B, "he took a cup . . . and said to them, 'This is my blood of the covenant, which is poured out for many.'" In the words of consecration in the Canon of the Mass, the Latin, following Matthew and Mark, has it that the blood of Christ, the blood of the new and everlasting covenant, will be shed *pro multis*—which from 1970 until Advent 2011 was translated into English (and Italian and Spanish) as "for all." As even those with no Latin will easily recognize, this was a translating error and an inappropriate rendering of the gospels' witness to the Last Supper. It was also, as Pope Benedict XVI pointed out, an inaccurate rendering of Jesus's own definition of his mission in Mark 10.45: "For the Son of Man . . . came not to be served but to serve, and to give his life as a ransom for many."

Has the Catholic Church then concluded, as some have suggested, that in his Passion and Death, which is relived at every Mass, Jesus did not die for everyone? No. As Benedict XVI wrote in his commentary on the Passion narratives, the Church gradually grew in its understanding of "the many" for whom Christ died, such that, by the time of Paul's First Letter to Timothy, the apostle could write of Jesus as the one mediator who "gave himself as a ransom for all" [1 Timothy 2.6]. At this juncture, Benedict wrote, "the universal salvific meaning of Jesus's death is . . . made crystal clear"—the Church has grasped that "the many" of Mark 10:45 and of the Last Supper narratives is in truth the "all" for whom Jesus died. But this is a matter of theological development, not of biblical record. The new translation of the words of consecration, "for many," preserves that distinction, which can and should be explained in homilies and in religious education.

Father Raymond de Souza made two important points about these gospel texts, which relate a story central to today's commemoration of the institution of the Eucharist. The first was that the Church does not "hear" the words of the Lord in Matthew and Mark, and in the reformed liturgical translations, with "the ears of the world," in which *for many* is perhaps restrictive. Rather, the Church hears the words of Scripture and the words of the liturgy with "ears" that are formed by faith and by doctrine: that is, the Church hears *for many* with "the ears of the Church's tradition, which understands the universal character of the sacrifice of Christ."

Borrowing from Benedict XVI, Father de Souza then made his second important point: "While Christ's death is offered for all, the sacramental memorial of the same—the Eucharist—does not have the same range. Christ died 'for all' but those who receive the Eucharist are 'many,' not 'all.' Some are not aware of the Gospel, some are not initiated in the sacraments, and some choose not to receive them. Christ died for them, too, but he does not force the sacraments upon them."

It's an important point to reflect upon on Holy Thursday, when Jesus freely embraced his destiny while freely giving the Church his body and blood as a means of sharing in that destiny. What is at issue is the freedom of discipleship. As Father de Souza wrote, "to say 'for many' protects the importance of our human freedom. It leaves room for our response. God counts us among the many. Do we choose to be so counted?"

St. John Lateran, *St. Thomas*
(Pierre Legros, 1711)

THE BISHOP OF ROME typically celebrates two Masses at his cathedral church every year: today's Evening Mass of the Lord's Supper, and Mass for the Solemnity of the Body and Blood of Christ [Corpus Christi]. These papal liturgies at St. John Lateran, like the massive figures of the twelve apostles in the nave, focus attention on the basilica's sanctuary and its ancient altars.

The apostles seem to emerge from confinement, as if on a mission: the dark stone backdrop of each niche, framed with green marble columns donated by Constantine, dramatically highlights the white statuary. Each apostle stands before a doorway, an allusion to the twelve gates of the celestial Jerusalem (Revelation 21.12). Carved between 1705 and 1718, the figures are strikingly individualized, in part because of the unusual circumstances of the commission: Pope Clement XI could not afford to sponsor twelve gigantic marble statues, so other notables stepped into the philanthropic breach. (Peter II of Portugal paid for St. Thomas, while Cardinal Benedetto Pamphilj donated the statue of St. John.) Two of the sculptors were particularly noteworthy. Italy's Camillo Rusconi carved the powerful St. Matthew, in the second niche on the right: the evangelist, absorbed by the inspired gospel before him, stands on a sack of coins, renouncing his previous life. Directly opposite is St. Bartholomew, carved by Pierre Legros: the apostle offers the skin flayed from his body during his martyrdom—a ghostly face and hand hang from his robe; though, in his resurrected body, they have been restored to him.

The stucco reliefs above the statues, designed by Alessandro Algardi in 1650, are a parade of biblical stories that link the Old and New Testaments. Jonah, regurgitated from the whale, faces the Resurrection of Christ; Joseph, sold by his brothers, looks across at Christ's betrayal by Judas; the sacrifice of Isaac points toward the Crucifixion.

Halfway down the nave, a hand reaches out of a niche, a finger pointing decisively toward the altar: here is St. Thomas, who first doubted but then proclaimed, "My Lord and my God." Thomas propels our attention toward the sanctuary—where the Renaissance *baldacchino* contains relics of Peter and Paul, and a table-altar, said to have been used by Peter, is at the center of the high altar.

The basilica's recollection of the institution of the Eucharist continues in the Blessed Sacrament Chapel to the right of the *baldacchino*. Antique golden columns frame the opulent marble chapel and the exquisite ciborium; a bronze relief copy of Leonardo da Vinci's *Last Supper*, above the tabernacle, contains what tradition holds to be a fragment of the table used in the Upper Room by Jesus and the Twelve.

The chapel's design and decoration anticipate the Resurrection, as the Last Supper was a prelude to Easter. Thus, dark marbles and shadows lead upward to an explosion of light. Cavaliere D'Arpino's *Ascension* (painted in 1595) borrowed much from Raphael's *Transfiguration*, painted over seventy years before. But where Raphael used shadows to emphasize the light of Christ, D'Arpino employed a pure golden aura: Christ appears suddenly and dominates the composition, a reminder of his presence in the tabernacle below; his outstretched arms recall the Crucifixion, but are now victorious in the new life to which he invites others in the Eucharist. [E.L.]

Holy Cross in Jerusalem: Good Friday procession with relic of the True Cross

GOOD FRIDAY

Station at Holy Cross in Jerusalem

Celebration of the Lord's Passion
Isaiah 52.13–53.12

Psalm 31

Hebrews 4.14–16, 5.7–9

John 18.1–19.42

Office of Readings
Hebrews 9.11–28

St. John Chrysostom: Catechesis 3

T HE LITURGIES OF THE Paschal Triduum are one continuous act of worship. There was no dismissal from the Evening Mass of the Lord's Supper last night. There is no formal beginning of today's Celebration of the Lord's Passion, nor is there a dismissal at its end. Tomorrow, the Easter Vigil of Easter will simply begin, with the Service of Light. It is all one action, this commemoration of the axial point of human history and the beginning of the end time—the time of fulfillment.

Today, at the midpoint of the Triduum, the Lenten pilgrimage comes at last to Calvary, where the Church ponders the judicial murder of Jesus of Nazareth, whose obedience to the will of the Father, even to the last extremity of a cruel and degrading death, reveals him to be, in truth, the Son of God. Pope Benedict XVI's reflections on the royal dimension of Good Friday—in which the Cross becomes the coronation throne of the Messiah acclaimed by the crowds on Palm Sunday—serve as an apt introduction to the liturgical texts of the day:

> Christ's execution notice became with paradoxical unity the "confession of faith," the real starting-point and rooting-point of the Christian faith, which holds Jesus to be the Christ: as the crucified criminal this Jesus is the Christ, the King. His crucifixion is his coronation; his coronation or kingship is his surrender of himself to men, the identification of word, mission, and existence in the yielding up of this very existence. His existence is thus his word. From the Cross faith understands in increasing measure that this Jesus did not do and say *something*; that in him person and message are identical, that he always already is what he says.

The first reading at today's commemoration of the Passion is the fourth and greatest of Isaiah's Suffering Servant songs. Read through the eyes of Christian faith, the fourth song becomes the Church's reflection at the foot of the Cross, where two millennia of believers have stood beside Mary, John, and the holy women. Isaiah's harsh descriptions of the Servant—"His appearance was so marred, beyond human semblance, . . . he had no form or comelinesss that we should look at him, . . . he was despised and rejected by men, . . . and we esteemed him not"—is all the more striking for its following hard upon a comforting vision of messianic expectation: "How beautiful upon the mountains are the feet of him who brings good tidings, and who publishes peace, who brings good tidings of good, who publishes salvation . . . for the LORD has comforted his people, he has redeemed Jerusalem" [Isaiah 52:7]. At the foot of the Cross, the Church wonders how it could have come to this: how did the messianic fervor of Palm Sunday yield, in less than a week, the condemnation and brutalization of the promised deliverer? The answer of faith is given at the end of the fourth Servant song: death is not the Servant's final destination, for the Just One "shall make many to be accounted righteous," for he will have borne "their iniquities" while making "intercession for the transgressors."

While meditating upon this divinely ordained destiny of the Suffering Servant, the Church prays, with her crucified Lord, a confession of trust in God through Psalm 31. Then the author of the Letter to the Hebrews reflects on the radical, history-changing redemption won by Jesus: the Suffering Servant who has become the High Priest of the New Covenant, sealed in his blood, is the mediator through whom we can "with confidence draw near to the throne of grace, that we may receive mercy." The Letter to the Hebrews is an extended meditation on the unity of God's salvific purposes in calling Israel to be his chosen people and in sending his Son as Redeemer of the world; today's reading falls squarely within that unity of Old and New Testaments. The Exodus of Israel from Egypt, begun with the Passover meal, was a deliverance from political bondage into freedom and nationhood, and the paradigmatic sign of an even greater liberation to come. In the Passover of the New Covenant, Jesus, passing over from death to resurrected life, offers humanity an eternal and definitive liberation—freedom from sin and its consequence, death; freedom for life within the light and love of the Trinity; freedom lived now within the fellowship of the People of God, composed of both Jews and Gentiles; freedom lived for all eternity in the communion of saints, at the Wedding Feast of the Lamb.

The Johannine Passion narrative read today displays in its most dramatic form a key feature of the fourth gospel with which Lenten pilgrims have become familiar over the past two and a half weeks: Jesus's sovereign command of his destiny. The Passion is emphatically not something that happens *to* Jesus. The Passion is the destiny that Jesus embraces. At every moment in today's narrative, it is Jesus who drives the drama forward: in the garden, where he is arrested; at his interrogation by the Temple aristocracy; in the quasi-judicial proceeding before Pilate; in addressing Mary and John from the Cross; in declaring his mission finished and giving over his spirit.

Jesus's testimony to truth before Pilate is particularly striking in the cultural circumstances of the early twenty-first century, in which, for many, the only secure truth is that there is no such thing as *the* truth, only partial and personal truths. Pilate can stand for those with an insecure grasp upon the truth today:

What, he asks, is truth? The only "truth" that counts here is that I, Pilate, have absolute power over you, Jesus. Not so, Jesus replies. I have told the truth about myself and my mission; the truth is that this mission poses no threat to you; and yet for reasons of expedience you are prepared to condemn me—a condemnation that would not be possible unless this were, in ways you cannot understand, part of the divine plan. You ask, thinking it an argument-stopper, "What is truth?" I answer: *This* is the truth, it is embodied in me, and I spoke it at the very beginning of my public ministry—"God so loved the world that he gave his only Son, that whoever believes in him should not perish but have eternal life" [John 3.16]. And all of this is of the will of God, who is Truth: "You would have no power over me unless it had been given you from above. . . ."

John's account of the crucifixion is deeply ecclesiological, arising as it does from the faith and experience of the Church. For John, reflecting the way in which the first Christian generations understood the drama of Calvary, the Church is born at Calvary. From the earliest days of Christian faith, the water and blood that issued from the pierced side of Christ were understood to be signs of Baptism and the Eucharist, the sacrament from which Christians are born and the sacrament by which Christians are fed. The Fathers of the Church in the first Christian centuries understood the "tunic . . . without seam" that is stripped from Jesus before his crucifixion—the seamless garment that cannot be torn—as a sign of the indestructible unity of the Church. That unity is also embodied in the *dramatis personae* of the Johannine Passion narrative: Mary, John, the holy women; Peter in his denial; those who are *not* present at Calvary, including the disciples who are cowering somewhere in fear or shame or both; Joseph of Arimathea and Nicodemus, who arrive on the scene late; the centurion moved to faith, who is the beginning of the Gentile Church. All of these figures are uniquely touched by the divine mercy radiating from the Cross; all of them, whatever their behavior on Good Friday, are united in the Church.

Station church pilgrims may also see themselves in this drama, for, as Pope Benedict XVI pointed out in *Jesus of Nazareth—Holy Week*, the soldiers at the Cross are not the only ones who offer the dying Jesus sour wine or vinegar: "It is we ourselves who repeatedly respond to God's bountiful love"—that "thirst" of which Jesus spoke to the Samaritan woman weeks ago—"with a sour heart that is unable to perceive God's love. 'I thirst': this cry of Jesus is addressed to every single one of us."

As Pope Benedict's interpretation reminds us, the Passion according to St. John invites us to "see" what is happening today against a transcendent and salvific horizon, not simply a historical horizon. These things happened; but they are pregnant with meaning, and the interplay of event and meaning is the key to grasping that this is indeed the axial moment, the turning point of human history. Moreover, this "moment" is so rich in meaning that it will continue to resonate throughout history. Today's station, the Basilica of the Holy Cross in Jerusalem, houses many of the relics of the Passion that Helena, mother of Constantine, brought from Jerusalem to Rome in the early fourth century. The basilica is in the midst of a busy Roman neighborhood where, Christians believe, the work begun on Calvary (of which the relics of the Passion are the tangible, physical evidence) continues—as it continues around the world.

This aspect of the Passion—the continuing presence of the crucified Lord in our lives—was captured well in the Way of the Cross celebrated in downtown Toronto during World Youth Day 2002, when half a million young people imaginatively walked Jerusalem's Via Dolorosa by walking from City Hall to the Ontario Provincial Parliament up tree-lined University Avenue. The WYD-2002 souvenir album captured the spiritual intensity of the moment, an intensity that in fact began on a rocky hillside outside Jerusalem two millennia ago:

Jesus moves through the heart of the city. He carries the Cross past air-conditioned skyscrapers filled with the busy and the powerful. He walks past the sick in the hospitals that line University Avenue. He shares their suffering, the young and old, male and female.

He makes his way, station after station, through the believers and the atheists, the hopeful and the despairing, the rich and the poor, the happy families and the forlorn individuals. He is the object of scrutiny by curious onlookers, excited children, contemplative crowds. He passes through a gathering of nations, languages, and cultures, sowing on his way the question that every

Christian must answer: "And who do you say that I am?" He is nailed to the cross, then placed in the tomb. The crowd disperses into the night, each person looking for the last station—the station that manifests itself in life's many twists and turns.

Tonight Jesus passes among us on the Way of the Cross—just as he does every day on the streets of the world.

Holy Cross in Jerusalem: Gate to the relics of the Passion

THE RELIC CHAPEL OF the Basilica of the Holy Cross in Jerusalem is reached by a flight of stairs; dingy gray walls and green pilasters mark the steps of this imaginative journey to Calvary. Along the stairs, inset niches contain modern bronze reliefs of the Stations of the Cross, cast in the 1930s when the relic chapel was built.

A small antechamber, recently redecorated in veneers of green and white marble, precedes the relic chapel proper. Stained-glass angels lead the way toward the relics of the Passion, arranged in a niche at the back of a marble enclosure. At the center is the golden reliquary of the True Cross.

According to Eusebius, fourth-century bishop of Caesarea and the first Christian historian, Helena, mother of Constantine and a Christian convert, went on pilgrimage to the Holy Land to visit the sites of the Passion. There, on May 2, 326, she discovered the Cross, hidden underground, 293 years after the Crucifixion. By the late fourth century, St. Cyril of Jerusalem claimed that "the whole world was filled with fragments of the True Cross." The wooden relic Helena brought to this basilica, her home chapel, was broken up by the Barberini pope, Urban VIII. A large piece of it is housed in a chapel at St. Peter's, above the great statue of St. Helena beneath the basilica's dome.

The nails of the crucifixion also have a long history of veneration: mentioned by fifth-century Holy Land pilgrims (along with the crown of thorns, which Paulinus of Nola placed in Jerusalem's Basilica of Mt. Zion in 409), these relics were transported to Constantinople during the Persian destruction of Christian Holy Land sites and were eventually brought to Italy when Byzantium was consumed by the Iconoclast Controversy.

To the right of the piece of the True Cross on display at the Basilica of the Holy Cross in Jerusalem is a plank from the cross of Dismas, the "Good Thief" who asked Jesus to remember him when he came into his kingdom [Luke 23.40–43]. Fragments of the column of the scourging rest in another reliquary, but the eye is caught by a rough wooden board: this is the "title" of the cross, placed above Christ's head during the crucifixion and reading, as all four gospels attest, "Jesus of Nazareth, King of the Jews," in Hebrew, Latin, and Greek. This piece was discovered in 1492, hidden behind a brick in the basilica's triumphal arch. Once dismissed as a medieval imposture, its claim to authenticity was strengthened by the nineteenth-century discovery of the diary of Egeria, the fourth-century Holy Land pilgrim who wrote of devotion to the *titulus* during her visit to Jerusalem. The headboard is also striking in that all three inscriptions are written from right to left, in the Hebrew style.

This singular gathering of relics, on this singular day, evokes memories of the words of another Jerusalem pilgrim (and hermit), St. Jerome, first of Christian biblical scholars: "By devoutly respecting the instruments of Christ's Passion, we profess our faith in him who suffered for us, we excite our hope in his merit, enkindle his love in our breasts, and renew the grateful remembrance of his death." [E.L.]

HOLY SATURDAY

Office of Readings
Hebrews 4.1–13
Ancient Holy Saturday Homily

THIS MORNING THE CHURCH'S "station" is not at a particular basilica made holy by the relics of martyrs and the prayers of those who have venerated them; rather, the Church's Holy Saturday "station" is her religious imagination. There is no Mass during the day, so there is neither a *collecta* where the Church gathers nor a *statio* to which the Church processes. In the evening, as the sun sets, the Church will gather at St. John Lateran, the "mother and head of all the churches in the city and the world," to await the dawn of Resurrection. Now, before the Easter Vigil, is a time to enter reflectively into the divine rest.

In today's Office of Readings, the author of the Letter to the Hebrews ponders this moment by reference to the Sabbath that God decreed on the seventh day, so that he might rest "from all his work which he had done in creation" [Genesis 2.3]. The divine promise, in creation, was that humanity might also enter that Sabbath rest. Sin changed, not the promise, but its realization, which required human cooperation. Our ancestors "did not benefit" from God's word and fell away from the righteous path God had pointed out, arousing the divine wrath: "Therefore I swore in my anger that they should not enter my rest" [Psalm 95.11].

The God of creation—the God of Abraham, Isaac, and Jacob, whom Jesus calls "Father"—does not renege on his promises, however; nor is his anger the essence of his being. He is the Father of mercies, who welcomes the prodigal son back from his foolishness, restores to him the dignity of his squandered sonship, and invites him to reenter his family home, where he may be at rest. And so, the author of Hebrews writes, God "again . . . sets a certain day," a new day of Sabbath rest: that rest is the Kingdom of God come in its fullness, the Kingdom announced in the person and mission of Jesus. The key to opening the gates of that Kingdom is the Son's obedience to the Father's will, which makes sonship possible for all who believe in the Son.

In this moment of rest and reflection, the Letter to the Hebrews invites us to begin our reflection on the cosmic drama of creation and redemption that will be continued tonight at the Easter Vigil, and to ponder, in the silence of this day, the rest—the eternal Sabbath—that awaits the faithful.

The unknown author of the ancient Greek Holy Saturday homily that follows in today's Office of Readings also remarks on the silence of this day that is in-between: "There is a great silence on earth today, a great silence and stillness. The whole earth keeps silence because the King is asleep." Stunned by the epic drama that took place yesterday, when "the curtain of the Temple was torn in two, from top to bottom, and earth shook and the rocks were split" [Matthew 27.51], nature itself is quiet: "The earth trembled and is still because God has fallen asleep in the flesh."

Yet the King, while asleep in the tomb, is not inactive. Rather, as our anonymous Greek preacher puts it, "he has gone to search for our first parent, as for a lost sheep." As centuries of Christian iconography, following the Apostles Creed, have depicted the scene, Jesus at his death descended into the land of the dead. But as the *Catechism of the Catholic Church* makes clear, "he descended there as Savior, proclaiming the good news to the spirits imprisoned there." Today's ancient homilist, exercising the Church's religious imagination, suggests the message he brought:

At the sight of him Adam, the first man he had created, struck his breast in terror and cried out to everyone: "My Lord be with you all." Christ answered him: "And with your spirit." He took him by the hand and raised him up, saying: "Awake, O sleeper, and rise from the dead, and Christ will give you light."

I am your God, who for your sake have become your son. . . . I did not create you to become a prisoner in hell. Rise from the dead, for I am the life of the dead. Rise up, work of my hands, you who were created in my image. Rise, let us leave this place, for you are in me and I am in you; together, we form one person and we cannot be separated. . . .

Rise, let us leave this place. The enemy led you out of earthly paradise. I will not restore you to that paradise, but I will enthrone you in heaven. . . . The throne formed by the cherubim awaits you, its bearers swift and eager. The bridal chamber is adorned, the banquet is ready, the eternal dwelling places are prepared, the treasure houses of all good things lie open. The kingdom of heaven has been prepared for you from all eternity.

What happened yesterday touches and transforms all of history, including the past. There is nothing in the human condition that Jesus did not share, and there is nothing in the human condition that Jesus did not redeem.

This day of rest is also an opportunity to reflect upon the nature of the atonement that Jesus effected yesterday by his obedient death on the Cross. Few aspects of Christian doctrine are more misunderstood than the doctrine of the atonement. In its liberal Protestant forms, mid-twentieth-century Christian theology was so off-put by the idea of the divine wrath and the atoning death of Christ that it ended up stripping salvation history of its cosmic and redemptive drama; such smiley-face Christianity was famously parodied by H. Richard Niebuhr in biting terms: "A God without wrath brought men without sin into a kingdom without judgment through the ministrations of a Christ without a cross." Traces of this biblical hollowness can be found in various Christian communities today, again because of a misunderstanding of the doctrine of atonement.

In *Jesus of Nazareth—Holy Week*, Pope Benedict XVI explained the true doctrine of the atonement, not in terms of a divine vengefulness that must be appeased, but in terms of a divine love that must be displayed and a divine image that is thereby restored. Pope Benedict was not hesitant in describing the horror of the Cross, a horror that was in fact beyond anything we can imagine: "In Jesus's Passion, all the filth of the world touches the infinitely pure one, the soul of Jesus Christ and, hence, the Son of God himself." But now, there is a difference:

> While it is usually the case that anything unclean touching something clean renders it unclean, here it is the other way around—when the world, with all the injustice and cruelty that make it unclean, comes into contact with the infinitely pure one, then he, the pure one, is the stronger. Through this contact, the filth of the world is truly absorbed, wiped out, and transformed in the pain of infinite love. Because infinite good is now at hand in the man Jesus, the counterweight to all wickedness is present and active within world history, and the good is always infinitely greater than the vast mass of evil, however terrible it may be.

Here, Benedict suggested, is the answer to the charge often made against the Christian doctrine of atonement: that "it must be a cruel God who demands infinite atonement." Such a doctrine, the critics charge, disfigures the image of God; it must be abandoned. Precisely the opposite is true, Benedict replied. The evil and injustice that disfigure the world also distort and disfigure the image of God; we cannot see God clearly through "the filth of the world." This distortion cannot be ignored; it has to be dealt with. And that is exactly what God does:

> [The doctrine of atonement] is not a case of a cruel God demanding the infinite. It is exactly the opposite: God himself becomes the locus of recon- ciliation, and in the person of his Son takes the suffering upon himself. God himself grants infinite purity to the world. God himself "drinks the cup" of

every horror to the dregs and thereby restores justice through the greatness of his love, which, through suffering, transforms the darkness.

In the silence of this day, the Church ponders the Good News that some considered a folly and others a stumbling block, but that nonetheless changed the world: in the crucified Christ, now in the tomb, the eyes of faith see not absurdity and divine vengeance, but the ultimate demonstration of divine love.

St. John Lateran: Coffered ceiling with instruments of the Passion

THE EASTER VIGIL

Station at St. John Lateran

Genesis 1.1–2.2
Psalm 104 / Psalm 33

Genesis 22.1–18
Psalm 16

Exodus 14.15–15.1
Canticle: Exodus 15.1–6, 13, 17–18

Isaiah 54.5–14
Psalm 30

Isaiah 55.1–11
Canticle: Isaiah 12.2–6

Baruch 3.9–15; 3.32–4.4
Psalm 19

Ezekiel 36.16–17a, 18–28
Psalm 42–43 / Canticle: Isaiah 12 / Psalm 51

Romans 6.3–11
Psalm 118

[A] *Matthew 28.1–10*
[B] *Mark 16.1–7*
[C] *Luke 24.1–12*

DURING THE EASTER VIGIL, the Church awaits its "blessed hope, the appearing of the glory of our great God and Savior, Jesus Christ, who gave himself for us to redeem us from all iniquity and to purify himself a people of his own who are zealous for good deeds" [Titus 2.13–14]. The Church's waiting is both historical and eschatological, both "then" and "future": with the holy women, we await the dawn of Resurrection and the announcement that the Lord is risen indeed; as the Church today, we await his return in glory, which will complete the drama of salvation history and inaugurate the Wedding Feast of the Lamb in its full splendor.

The readings at the Easter Vigil, which follow the lighting of the paschal candle and the singing of the *Exultet*, make present in word and imagination the crucial moments in salvation history: Creation, culminating in the breath of life being given to man and woman, images of the Creator in themselves and in their communion; the testing of Abraham, whose obedience made him our "father in faith"; the exodus from Egypt and the liberation of the chosen people from slavery and its death-dealing habits; Isaiah's visions of a world made aright in justice and peace, a world of bounty freely given and gratefully received; Baruch's testimony to the divine wisdom in giving humanity the law that liberates; Ezekiel's exilic prophecy of a people of God cleaned from impurity, whose "heart of stone" will be replaced by a "heart of flesh."

After these readings, best proclaimed with the lights dimmed, the Church anticipates the proclamation of the Lord's Resurrection by singing the *Gloria*, during which bells are rung and the church fully illuminated. Now, in anticipation of the baptismal liturgy that will shortly follow, the Church reads Paul's reminder to the Romans that "all of us who have been baptized into Christ Jesus have been baptized into his death." This dying with Christ is no mere recapitulation; rather, it is a sacramental living out of what the Church has pondered throughout this day and anticipates in its Easter celebration: "We were buried therefore with him by baptism into death, so that as Christ was raised from the dead by the glory of the Father, we too might walk in newness of life."

The gospel reading at the Easter Vigil varies according to the three-year Lectionary cycle. Each of these Synoptic gospel selections ends on a note of surprise and puzzlement: it will take time for the holy women and the remaining eleven disciples to understand the meaning of the empty tomb and the angelic message there. Read today, with the eyes of faith, the initial incomprehension of those closest to Jesus is a reminder that every disciple must grow in a knowledge of the Resurrection and in an appreciation of what Easter faith truly means.

Pope Francis stressed this note of surprise in his first Easter Vigil homily as Bishop of Rome, noting that, as it was with the apostles and the holy women, "*Newness* often makes us fearful, including the newness which God brings us, the newness that God asks of us." Easter calls us beyond such fears, though: "Dear brothers and sisters, let us not be closed to the newness that God wants to bring into our lives! Are we often weary, disheartened, and sad? Do we feel weighed down by our sins? Do we think that we won't be able to cope? Let us not close our hearts, let us not lose confidence, let us never give up." For Easter faith teaches us that "there are no situations which God cannot change, there is no sin which he cannot forgive if only we open ourselves to him."

The journey of Lent has ended. Yet the itinerary of conversion continues in the journey beyond Easter, in which travelers along the pathways of the Forty Days go from Galilee to the ends of the earth, bringing the news of humanity's redemption. In the words of Pope Benedict XVI:

> Faith in the resurrection of Jesus says that there is a future for every human being; the cry for unending life which is a part of the person is indeed answered. Through Jesus we do know "the room where exiled love lays down its victory." He himself is this place, and he calls us to be with him and in dependence on him. He calls us to keep this place open within the world so that he, the exiled love, may reappear over and over in the world. . . . God exists: that is the real message of Easter. Anyone who even begins to grasp what this means also knows what it means to be redeemed.

St. John Lateran: Tomb of Pope Leo XIII
(Giulio Tadolini, 1907)

THE SANCTA SANCTORUM, the private chapel of the Bishops of Rome for a thousand years, stands across the street from St. John Lateran in the same building as the Scala Sancta, the Holy Stairs. Here, popes once began the celebration of Easter by opening the doors of an ancient triptych, the *Anastasis* icon, to reveal the image of Christ risen from the tomb. To go from the Sancta Sanctorum to the Lateran Basilica, where the symbols of the Passion are arrayed in gilt among the ceiling coffers, is to see torture instruments transformed into triumphant trophies.

The last Roman chapel to be endowed by a noble family, given by Prince Alessandro Torlonia in 1850, is on the left side of the basilica and is dedicated to the deposition from the Cross. Its neoclassical style is in harmony with the somber yet expectant mood of Holy Saturday, the Church's day of silent waiting. Here, the violence, pain, and grief of Good Friday give way to quiet meditation, exemplified by Pietro Tenerani's masterful marble relief of the deposition. The body of Jesus drapes gently across the arms of his mother, Nicodemus, and St. John. No signs of suffering mar the elegant form; he appears to sleep peacefully, his head resting against Mary's brow. The composure of Mary and John is striking: no distracting tears or dramatic gestures electrify the scene; only the weighty folds of drapery, slowly falling downward, hint at sorrow. Golden light permeates the chapel from its Pantheon-like dome; warm and enveloping, it creates a space to keep vigil. To the left and right of the altar are the Torlonia tombs: altars, sarcophagi, and effigies stacked inside triumphal arches; the hope of resurrection artistically embodied amid reminders of the reality of death.

The Lateran Basilica's side aisles are lined with sepulchers of popes and princes, royal and ecclesiastical. Some are flamboyant; one tomb, erected in 1650 by Cardinal Cesare Rasponi for himself and his mother, features the lithe figure of Fame holding aloft the prelate's portrait. Another, dedicated to Pope Sylvester III, contains a twentieth-century relief donated by Hungary atop the pope's medieval funerary inscription. (Roman legend knows this slab of marble as the "sweating stone," said to become damp when a pope dies.)

The thirteenth-century tomb of Cardinal Giussano sparkles with golden Cosmatesque inlay, while a few steps away, the effigy of Cardinal Pietro Gasparri, whose negotiation of the 1929 Lateran Treaty created Vatican City State, kneels in prayerful expectation of the day of Resurrection.

Among the popes buried in this papal cathedral, Innocent III and Alexander III represent the Middle Ages and the height of papal temporal power; Leo XIII, creator of the modern papacy of moral witness (and the last pope buried outside of St. Peter's) rests opposite Innocent III to the left of the apse. [E.L.]

St. Paul
Outside the Walls:
Apse mosaic detail
(1220)

EASTER WEEK

St. Mary Major: Nave and ceiling

EASTER SUNDAY

Station at St. Mary Major

Holy Mass

Acts 10.34a, 37–43

Psalm 118

Colossians 3.1–4 or 1 Corinthians 5.6b–8

John 20.1–9

T HE EASTER NARRATIVES IN the New Testament are so familiar that something quite surprising in them may pass unnoticed: the early Christian Church incorporated into its proclamation of the risen Lord Jesus the fact that the friends of the Crucified One didn't immediately understand what had happened to him, and to them, after the discovery of the empty tomb on Easter Sunday morning.

This is all the more striking when we remember, with biblical scholar N. T. Wright, that there is no evidence of *any* form of primitive Christianity that did not believe in the Resurrection—despite the fevered imaginings of some novelists. *That* Jesus had been raised from the dead was the rock-solid foundation of Christian faith. *What* "resurrection" meant, for Jesus and for those who would come after him, took time to understand.

That understanding came, however, and it changed everything. The earliest written witness to the Resurrection, which Wright judges to be 1 Corinthians 15, puts it at the very foundations of Christian faith. Belief in the Resurrection is not one tenet of faith in a catalogue of Christian convictions. Rather, 1 Corinthians 15.3–8 proclaims the Resurrection as that on which the entire structure of Christian faith is built; without belief in the Resurrection, the entire edifice crumbles:

> For I delivered to you as of first importance what I also received, that Christ died for our sins in accordance with the scriptures, that he was buried, that he was raised on the third day in accordance with the scriptures, and that he appeared to Cephas, then to the twelve. Then he appeared to more than five hundred brethren at one time, most of whom are still alive, but some of whom have fallen asleep. Then he appeared to James, then to all the apostles. Last of all, as to one untimely born, he appeared also to me.

This, Paul is saying, is the bottom of the bottom line. And, as Wright put it, this is the first and best answer to the question posed to first-generation Christians and to Christians today: "Why *are* you?" To which the answer then, and now, is, "We *are* because Jesus was raised from the dead."

Faith in the Resurrection was thus so securely planted in the life-experience of the first generation of Christians that they could admit that it took time for them to understand what had happened, and *how* what-had-happened had exploded all previous expectations of what God's saving action in history would look like. The primitive Christian community, in other words, grew in its understanding of the Resurrection; the stories of that growing comprehension will occupy the Church's reflection throughout the Octave of Easter. The holy women are instructed at the tomb by the Risen One himself, although in one account, Mary Magdalene does not initially recognize him. Two disciples cannot recognize the Jesus they had known while talking with one they regard as a stranger on the road to Emmaus; only in the breaking of bread do they see that the one with whom they had traveled is the Risen Lord. At one appearance, the eleven disciples at first think that they're seeing a ghost. Even later, up along the Sea of Galilee, it takes a while for John and Peter to recognize that "It is the Lord!" This sequence of growing comprehension and understanding concludes on the Octave of Easter; there, the Church recalls the story of Thomas, who first refused to believe, but who, on encountering the Risen One personally, offers the Church's confession of faith: "My Lord and my God."

As N. T. Wright (in *The Challenge of Jesus*) and Pope Benedict XVI (in *Jesus of Nazareth—Holy Week*) analyze this process, the first believers in the Resurrection came to understand that their every expectation of how God would act in history to redeem Israel had been transformed by God's unprecedented action in raising his servant, Jesus, from the dead.

Their view of history changed. The "last days" had indeed come and had been inaugurated in the Resurrection of the Son of God. But history continued, such that life in the Kingdom could be lived *now*, not just after some final cataclysm—for the cataclysmic act that reveals what God had intended "in the beginning" had taken place in the Resurrection. Contrary to the expectations of all those who (like Martha at the tomb of Lazarus) looked forward to the dead being raised, the Resurrection had taken place—not at the end of time, but *within* time—and it had dramatically changed the texture of all of time.

Their view of "resurrection" changed. The Resurrection of Christ was not the kind of "resurrection" that many pious Jews expected at the time of Jesus's public ministry. It did not involve the resuscitation of a corpse, but neither did it involve the decomposition of the corpse of the man who had been crucified at Calvary. The Risen Lord has a transformed body, in which he appears to his friends; but the tomb is empty.

Their understanding of how the Risen Lord was present to his followers changed. The Resurrection appearances continued for a period. But then the Risen Lord was "present" to the community of believers in a new, sacramental way: in Baptism, in the breaking of bread in the Eucharist, and so forth.

Their understanding of their responsibilities and their prospects changed. The unexpected and expectation-shattering Resurrection of Jesus is not about Jesus alone, the first generation of believers came to see; it demonstrated what the resurrection of the faithful would be. Thus the Resurrection became the warrant of hope for the future (and a warrant of such power that it would lead many of that first generation to embrace martyrdom with confidence). At the same time, the Resurrection was the inspiration for the Church's mission here-and-now: this is Good News that demands to be shared.

Their understanding of worship and its relationship to time changed. Those who experienced the presence of the Risen Lord were all pious Jews, for whom the Sabbath was sacrosanct; the Sabbath had been established by God himself as part of the act of creation, and its importance had been reaffirmed by the Ten Commandments. Yet, the first generation of Christians quickly fixed Sunday, not Saturday, as "the Lord's Day," because it was on Sunday, the "third day," that Jesus was raised from the dead. Benedict XVI explained what this revolution implies:

> Only an event that marked souls indelibly could bring about such a profound realignment in the religious culture of the week. Mere theological speculations could not have achieved this. . . . [The] celebration of the Lord's day, which was characteristic of the Christian community from the outset, is one of the most convincing proofs that something extraordinary happened that day—the discovery of the empty tomb and the encounter with the Risen Lord.

Christ, risen, changes everything. Creation, promise and prophecy, time and expectation, vocation and worship now come into clearer focus. The unity of God's revelation of himself to the people of Israel and his revelation in his Son is confirmed. The Church is born.

Thus there is no explaining the Church and its proclamation without the Resurrection, which is one of the strongest historical warrants for the truth of the united witness of the early Church: the conviction that "Jesus of Nazareth was raised bodily to a new sort of life, three days after his execution" (to use N. T. Wright's succinct formula). Yet there are dimensions to the Resurrection that remain in the realm of mystery: in the realm of realities that can only be grasped in love, for to comprehend them fully is beyond our present capacities while we remain "in the world" and in "this age." That the Risen Lord is neither a ghost nor some other form of spirit is the united testimony of the gospels; yet we cannot really grasp the reality of this new, risen, transphysical body that can be touched, and that eats and drinks, but that also appears and disappears, unobstructed by obstacles like doors. All we can say is what this means: as Pope Benedict XVI put it in an interview just before Easter 2011, the Resurrection teaches us that the body has an eternal destiny, although it will be a transformed body, no longer subject to decay and death. Jesus now lives in a new dimension, a new circumstance, to which all those who will share in the resurrection of the dead will be called. But we cannot describe the properties of this new world in any detail, and we must therefore be content with biblical images, such as the Wedding Feast of the Lamb, or with the poetic imagination of great believers like Dante.

That having been said, it is also worth recalling with Benedict XVI that the New Passover we have marked in the Paschal Triduum replicates in some respects the "form" of the Passover of Israel. As Pope Benedict put it in his 2010 Easter message: "Easter does not work magic. Just as the Israelites found the desert awaiting them on the far side of the Red Sea, so the Church, after the Resurrection, always finds history filled with joy and hope, grief and anguish. And yet this history is changed, it is marked by a new and eternal covenant, it is truly open to the future." That is why, Benedict concluded, we can continue the pilgrimage of conversion and mission after Easter. Having been saved by hope, the Church carries the message of the Risen Lord into the future, "bearing in our hearts the song that is ancient and yet ever new: 'Let us sing to the Lord: glorious his triumph!'"

A nd why today's station at St. Mary Major? A great early twentieth-century student of the liturgy, Blessed Ildefonso Schuster, offered a practical reason and a more theological explanation in *The Sacramentary*. The practical reason was that the popes of the mid-first millennium, having celebrated a lengthy service at St. John Lateran on Holy Saturday night, would not have been eager to go all the way to the Vatican Basilica from the papal residence in the Lateran Palace for Easter Sunday, but chose instead to celebrate Easter Sunday Mass at the nearer Liberian Basilica. The more theological rationale Schuster offered takes us from the practicalities of first-millennium Roman commuting to the realm of salvation history: "After the paschal vigil at the Lateran the first basilica to be visited is that of the Mother of God on the Esquiline, for it is fitting that to her, before any other, the joys of the Resurrection should be announced, to her who more intimately than any other shared the Passion of Jesus."

Writing decades after Schuster, Hans Urs von Balthasar addressed one of the puzzles of the Resurrection stories in the gospels: Why is there no mention of Mary, Jesus's mother? Following St. Ignatius of Loyola, Balthasar, in *The Three-fold Garland*, suggested an answer to be found in the *regula fidei*, the structure of the faith: "Without doubt it was to her . . . that the Son first appeared" as the Risen Lord. Why? Because Mary is "the very core of the Church," and as the Church is the community that must take the Gospel of the Resurrection out into the world, she who was first "visited by the Spirit and conceived the Body of the Word" should by all rights be the first to meet the Lord Jesus on the far side of his death, to see what God had wrought in raising Jesus from the dead, and to experience Easter joy.

Mary's silent *fiat* at the foot of the Cross, we are permitted to imagine, was vindicated in the filial embrace given her by the Risen One.

St. Mary Major: Triumphal arch mosaic detail (fifth century)

THE CHURCH CELEBRATES Easter Sunday in Rome's Bethlehem: the birth of Christ in the flesh, and the birth of the New Life made possible by the Resurrection, are linked architecturally and aesthetically in the Liberian Basilica of St. Mary Major.

Blessed Pius IX entrusted the decoration of the basilica's *confessio* to Virginio Vespignani, who employed seventy different types of marble in his work. The statue of Pius IX in prayer expresses Pio Nono's deep devotion to the Mother of God; the pontiff looks up, smiling gently at Mary's image in the apse.

Ferdinando Fuga, architect of the basilica's façade, designed the *baldacchino* over the high altar using four columns made of porphyry, a precious stone reserved in antiquity for the use of Roman emperors. The altar, also of porphyry, contains relics of St. Matthew, St. Jerome, and the martyrs Simplicius, Faustinus, and Beatrice, while the altar stone holds relics of the protomartyr Stephen and the great Roman deacon Lawrence.

At the keystone of the triumphal arch, the mosaic depiction of an empty throne, studded with jewels and supporting the cross, symbolically evokes Christ's Easter victory over death and his future coming in glory at the consummation of history. The time between those two epochal moments is the time of the Church, and the basilica is replete with images of the Church's universality.

On the left side of the triumphal arch, the three wise men—the first Gentiles to be enfolded within salvation history—offer their gifts to Christ. In this exquisite mosaic, Christ sits enthroned in majesty, while the brightly colored, polka-dot-clad Magi suggest exotic, distant places that are yet part of the drama of salvation. Two women flank the youthful Christ, one dressed as a princess, one heavily shrouded by her mantle: images, scholars believe, of the Church of the Jews and the Church of the Gentiles, now united through the life, death, and Resurrection of Christ, the universal Savior. The same theme continues on the opposite side of the arch: there, the mosaics depict an apocryphal account of the Holy Family's arrival in Egypt, where the local governor pays homage to the Christ Child, recognizing his divinity.

Viewed "in reverse" from the high altar, the basilica is suffused with light pouring through a stained-glass rose window that was installed in 1995. Twenty feet in diameter, the window is the work of Hungarian artist Janos Hajnal. In the window, Mary, robed in royal purple, holds the Christ Child, both overflown by a dove. To one side, the Ten Commandments and a menorah represent the Old Testament; on the other, the Eucharist evokes the New Covenant sealed at Calvary and confirmed by the Resurrection.

The statue of Mary, *Regina Pacis* [Queen of Peace], past which pilgrims enter and leave St. Mary Major, was sculpted by Guido Galli in 1918 and given to the basilica by Pope Benedict XV, the pope who tried in vain to stop Europe's self-immolation in World War I. [E.L.]

St. Peter: Chapel, St. Helena Pier

MONDAY WITHIN THE OCTAVE OF EASTER

Station at St. Peter

Holy Mass

Acts 2.14, 22–33

Psalm 16

Matthew 28.8–15

Office of Readings

1 Peter 1.1–21

St. Melito of Sardis: Easter Homily

ACCORDING TO ST. JOHN'S Passion narrative, Pilate presents the bloody and battered Jesus to the frenzied mob that is seeking his blood with the ironic, even sarcastic, line, *Ecce homo!*—"Here is the man!" [John 19.5]. Whatever his intent, Pilate spoke far more truth than he knew.

Throughout the Octave of Easter, which is really Easter extended for seven more days, the Church proclaims that this, indeed, *is* "the man." This is the man in whom the world's destiny is embodied. This is the firstborn to be raised from the dead, not to die again, but to a new and eternal mode of superabundant life, which is in fact the divine life. This is he who, being Son of God as well as son of Mary, is the one in whom humanity is reborn, with a future completely open to glory and to divinization. This is he who, by the will of God the Father and in the power of the Holy Spirit, has overcome death, trampled the powers of hell underfoot, and restored hope to suffering humanity. *Ecce homo!*

During the Easter Octave, the Church reads the First Letter of Peter, written to young churches that were suffering various trials for the faith. At the very beginning of his exhortation to fidelity, the author, who writes with the authority of the apostle whose Vatican Basilica is today's *statio*, summarizes in a canticle all that the Church marks this week in the liturgy:

> Blessed be the God and Father of our Lord Jesus Christ!
> By his mercy we have been born anew to a living hope
> through the resurrection of Jesus Christ from the dead,
> and to an inheritance which is imperishable, undefiled, and unfading,
> kept in heaven for you,
> who by God's power are guarded through faith
> for a salvation ready to be revealed in the last time.

Christ has been raised from the dead; here is the sure foundation for a living hope (which is far stronger than mere optimism); here is the pledge of future glory for all who believe in the Risen One; here is the "end time" bursting into history. All of this, the apostle continues, is cause for continual, constant rejoicing. For despite the trials of life between the "now" of the Church's earthly existence and the unlimited future of life in the Kingdom, all that is happening "now" is happening for the glory of God and ought to be perceived through that truth. What the Church endures now, it endures "so that the genuineness of your faith, more precious than gold which though perishable is tested by fire, may redound to praise and glory and honor at the revelation of Jesus Christ." History continues, but history has been decisively changed through the Resurrection. Of this, we have witnesses. So "without having seen him, you love him; though you do not now see him you believe in him and rejoice with unutterable and exalted joy."

Every day during the Easter Octave, at Mass and in the Liturgy of the Hours, the Church sings, *Haec dies quam fecit Dominus; exultemus et laetemur in ea!* [This is the day the Lord has made; let us rejoice and be glad in it!]. That antiphon, which is sung at Mass every Sunday at the Holy Sepulcher in Jerusalem, is a reminder that the power of the Resurrection is a power that endures throughout time. It is the power of the Triune God at work in history, redirecting the drama of creation toward the saving ends that God intended "in the beginning." Its potency is not exhausted after the Easter Octave. Yes, the Cross remains. But now there is Easter, and the Cross does not have the final word. Christians die; but Christians live and die in the sure hope of sharing in the Lord's Resurrection.

Things have changed: decisively, radically, eternally.

The First Letter of Peter also reminds the Christians of the Roman provinces of Pontus, Galatia, Cappadocia, Asia, and Bithynia that they are living in a "time of . . . exile." While this has been literally true of some Christians over two millennia, it is, in a deeper, paschal sense, true of all Christians in every time and place. Christians are what the Letter to Diognetus (a second-century work of apologetics) calls "resident aliens." Christians are people for whom every foreign country is a homeland and every homeland a foreign country. Living in the promised future that has burst into history through the Resurrection, Christians nonetheless live in the "now" of quotidian life. Living in and through that future, Christians live in a somewhat unsettled, but always hopeful, condition: Christians know how the story of history is going to turn out, for that is what has been displayed in the Risen Lord. But in the meantime there is "now," and "now" is full of surprises and challenges.

Today's *statio* is a reminder of that, and of the Easter faith that changed the world. Insofar as forensic science can tell, the bones of Simon, son of John, renamed Peter—a fisherman from the far edges of the Roman imperium—are buried under Gian Lorenzo Bernini's magnificent *baldacchino* and beneath Michelangelo's dome in a basilica that is one of the world's masterpieces of art and architecture (and engineering). How did this happen? What could have propelled a man from mending nets on the Sea of Galilee to the center of world power? Why would this man be remembered and honored for over two millennia? Why did he rate the world's most magnificent headstone?

The answer the Church gives is straightforward: Peter is *here* because Peter met the Risen Lord, in whom he recognized the resurrected life of the one who had called him from his Galilean nets to become a "fisher of men" [cf. Matthew 4.19]. Peter testifies to this himself in today's Mass reading from the Acts of the Apostles. Peter will continue to testify to this life-changing and history-remaking truth throughout the Book of Acts, which the Church will read in its entirety during the Easter season. There will be no more hesitation; there will be no more denials; Peter has become a radically converted Christian disciple, and while there will be more temptations to infidelity (as in the *Quo vadis* legend of Peter's flight from Nero's persecution), they will ultimately be resisted.

Peter has seen the Risen Lord. That is why he is *here*. That is why he is honored as he is. That is why the Church is here today, singing *Haec dies quam fecit Dominus; exultemus et laetemur in ea!*

St. Peter: Holy water font detail
(Agostino Cornacchini, 1720)

THE VATICAN BASILICA on Easter Monday is radiant with color. The great piazza and the *sagrato*, the stone platform or porch of the basilica, are filled with flowers. Inside, bronze monuments glow warmly from a pre-Easter burnishing: a renewal reflecting the spirit of the Easter Octave.

The Blessed Sacrament Chapel, on the right, is the Baroque jewel of the basilica. Its bronze tabernacle, in the form of a round victory temple, was designed by Gian Lorenzo Bernini in 1674 to resemble Bramante's celebrated *Tempietto* in San Pietro in Montorio on the Janiculum: a tiny church, built for the Jubilee of 1500 on what was then believed to have been the site of Peter's crucifixion. Bernini's miniature *Tempietto*, gilt and inlaid with lapis, is flanked by two kneeling angels in bronze, who bow as they gaze at the Blessed Sacrament; they remain still, but their robes appear to waft around them as if they have just alighted.

Wrought-iron doors designed by Borromini lead back to the main body of the basilica, and to the "latitude" that Michelangelo intended for the basilica's façade before his Greek Cross plan (with its four equal sides) was altered to a Latin Cross by Carlo Maderno in 1612. Maderno's alteration, made to accommodate pilgrims, nonetheless distorted Michelangelo's theologically driven architectural idea, which was to inspire through the dome's soaring verticality.

The dome (which the Greek Cross plan would have made easily visible from both the piazza and the basilica's interior) was intended to draw everyone to the tomb of St. Peter—and to ponder what it meant that this Galilean fisherman came to be buried *here*. The tomb, beneath the high altar in the *confessio*, is surrounded by one hundred bronze oil lamps, which blaze day and night. A ninth-century mosaic directly above the tomb depicts Christ, his hand raised in blessing, watching over the grave of his friend and follower; the casket beneath his hand holds the *pallia*, the woolen liturgical collars the pope gives to newly appointed metropolitan archbishops every year on June 29, the Solemnity of Sts. Peter and Paul.

In 1600, painter Giuseppe Cesari was given the daunting task of decorating Michelangelo's dome, an assignment completed by that era's finest mosaic artists. Concentric bands structure the design, beginning with representations of sixteen popes buried in the basilica (in the lunettes) and continuing with Christ, the Blessed Virgin, St. Joseph, St. John the Baptist, and the apostles. Angels are prevalent throughout the vertical ascent to the dome's apex: some hold the instruments of the Passion; others watch over Peter's tomb among the winged heads of the cherubim and seraphim, who know and adore the Lord. At the summit, inside the lantern, God reaches down in blessing to those gathered at the papal altar.

Against a golden ground, black letters stream across the niches of the relics of the True Cross, expressing the evangelical essence of the papacy as an office of unity: *Hinc una fides mondo refulgent* [From here a single faith shines throughout the world]. [E.L.]

St. Paul Outside the Walls: Side chapel with frieze of papal portraits

TUESDAY WITHIN THE OCTAVE OF EASTER

Station at St. Paul Outside the Walls

Holy Mass

Acts 2.36–41

Psalm 33

John 20.11–18

Office of Readings

1 Peter 1.22–2.10

St. Anastasius of Antioch: Discourse, 4

T HE STATIONAL CHURCHES OF the Easter Octave invite us to traverse a great highway of Christian sanctity, which in turn prompts a reflection on the effects of the Resurrection throughout history. Today's *statio* at the great Pauline basilica on the Ostian Way reminds pilgrims of the importance of the Apostle of the Gentiles in shaping the understanding and mission of the primitive Church according to the deep meaning of Easter faith.

It was Paul who first grasped in depth the new ecclesial reality of which the First Letter of Peter speaks today, describing the Church as formed by "living stones . . . built into a spiritual house": before the Resurrection, Peter writes, "you were no people, but now you are God's people"; before the Resurrection, "you had not received mercy, but now you have received mercy." Understanding the radically new situation of those who believed in the Risen Lord was a communal exercise, and not without its tensions. Saul of Tarsus, renamed Paul, played the pivotal role in shaping that new understanding and in defining the mission that flowed from it.

It was Saul, the learned Pharisee who encountered the Risen One on the road to Damascus, who had to think through the perspective-shattering meaning of the Resurrection for Jews and Gentiles alike. It was Saul, the former student of Gamaliel, who had to reread the Hebrew Bible and "the promises" in light of what he had seen and heard when meeting Jesus, whom he had been persecuting. It was Saul, whose fervor in the observance of the Law outstripped the fervor of his contemporaries, who, as Paul, grasped that the mission *ad gentes*, the mission to the nations, required the new community of the Church to embrace those who were not bound by the Law and who were previously regarded as heathens. It was Saul, the zealot who approved stoning Stephen the Protomartyr, who, as Paul, would join Stephen in the noble fellowship of martyrdom by giving his life in testimony to the truth of God in Christ.

The Galilean fisherman, Peter, and the scholarly Pharisee, Paul, may or may not have embraced along the Ostian Way, shortly before their Roman martyrdoms, as a contemporary plaque along the roadside attests; that is more a matter of pious legend than history. What *is* history, manifest as *His*-story, is that faith in the Resurrection led these two utterly unlikely brothers-in-Christ to the center of the Roman world, where they shared the same glorious destiny—and thereby became the foundation stones of the world Church's center of unity.

Today's gospel reading from St. John demonstrates just how difficult it was, even for those closest to Jesus, to grasp what had happened to him during the Paschal Triduum—in this instance, by relating Mary Magdalene's difficulty in grasping the meaning of the empty tomb and her subsequent journey from what Francis Moloney, in his commentary on John, describes as "the darkness of unfaith through a partial faith into perfect belief."

As the scene opens, Mary is standing at the empty tomb, immobile and in tears, after Peter and John have left and returned to their homes. Her weeping recalls the incomprehension that Jesus faced over his delayed arrival in Bethany, when neither his disciples nor Martha and Mary could understand why he had not come earlier and saved Lazarus from death. Mary's inability to understand deepens, Moloney notes, when she turns to face Jesus, but doesn't recognize the One she sees as Jesus, thinking him a gardener from whom she can discover the location of a corpse—"Tell me where you have laid him, and I will take him away." Then Jesus, the Good Shepherd who calls each of his own by name, calls her by name: *"Mariam"* [Mary].

The initial response is one of partial faith: *"Rabbouni"* [My master, or Teacher]. Something has happened, Mary grasps, but she still holds onto the past, to the Jesus whom she had known as a powerful teacher before his crucifixion. It is this Jesus to whose feet she clings, not recognizing the full, startling truth about the Risen One: that the Jesus who died has now been raised to an entirely new dimension of human existence—life beyond death, life no longer under the shadow of death. That is why the Risen Lord instructs her: "Do not hold me." In holding onto the feet of the Risen One, Mary, in her partial faith, is holding onto the past. But this will not do, for that past has now been transformed into a present that is pregnant with the new future made available by Jesus's "hour"—the "hour" of the New Passover that encompasses his dying, his rising, and his new mode of life.

Then the Risen One gives Mary a glimpse of what that future will be: "Go to my brethren and say to them, I am ascending to my Father and your Father, to my God and your God." Before this, as Father Moloney points out, only Jesus was "Son" to the "Father." Now, he tells Mary, those who believe in him as the Risen Lord will also be able to call God "Father," for they will be the "brethren" of the Son whom the Father has raised from the dead into the fullness of New Life. The Church is being formed in Jesus's "hour": his disciples, Moloney writes, have become his brothers and sisters.

Thus Mary, who does what she has been commanded and goes to the disciples, has come through partial faith to radical belief: "I have seen the Lord." As Father Moloney observes, Mary has passed from incomprehension—from a limited and partial faith that clings to a past that is no more—to a more mature faith—a faith that transforms her, turning her into the first messenger of the

Good News. And this "passover" in Mary has been made possible by Jesus's passover from death to life, which changes everything.

The Easter appearances to the holy women are a parallel to the presence of the holy women at Calvary, Pope Benedict XVI noted in *Jesus of Nazareth—Holy Week*, and they shed light on relationships and offices in the Church of the twenty-first century: "Just as there were only women standing by the Cross—apart from the beloved disciple—so too the first encounter with the Risen Lord was destined to be for them. The Church's juridical structure is founded on Peter and the Eleven, but in the day-to-day life of the Church it is the women who are constantly opening the door to the Lord and accompanying him to the Cross, and so it is they who come to experience the Risen One."

In the new People of God—those "living stones" who, as 1 Peter testifies, constitute "a chosen race, a royal priesthood, a holy nation, God's own people"— the fundamental reality is discipleship, and the first responsibility is mission ("Go . . . and say . . ."). The brothers and sisters of the Risen One have been "called . . . out of darkness into his wonderful light" so that they may "declare the wonderful deeds" of the Father, who has changed everything by raising Jesus from the dead to New Life.

St. Paul Outside the Walls:
Triumphal arch detail (fifth century)

THE 1823 FIRE that consumed the Basilica of St. Paul Outside the Walls came at a low point in the city's fortunes: the Napoleonic storm had despoiled Rome of her art, money, and citizens; funds for rebuilding were unavailable locally; and it seemed unimaginable that the secularizing world of Europe would take much interest in building another Roman church. Yet the tomb of Saul of Tarsus, which had already suffered sacks, floods, collapses, and neglect, continued to inspire benefactors all over the world; their contributions led to a new basilica being built a quarter-century later.

The golden light of the façade's shimmering mosaic sets the Ostian basilica apart from its rather drab neighborhood. Its polished nineteenth-century surface enhances the ancient iconography of Christ enthroned between Sts. Peter and Paul, the two foundation-stones of Christian Rome; the Lamb of God stands above four prophets, Isaiah, Jeremiah, Daniel, and Ezekiel. In the atrium, the luminously white marble statue of St. Paul by Giuseppe Obici symbolizes the clarity of the apostle's writings; the sword is an allusion not only to his martyrdom, but to the "sword of the Spirit, which is the Word of God" [Ephesians 3:17].

The bell tower, rising above the church, is a striking new mix of several old styles. Built by Luigi Poletti in 1860, it stands 213 feet tall and is divided into five stories. The first two recall the square blocks of medieval bell towers; the third, articulated with Doric columns, seems like a temple façade. The fourth story is octagonal, the form of ancient baptisteries and symbol of regeneration. The crowning section is an open circular rotunda like the victory temples of old.

The splendid entrance portal was cast by Antonio Mariani in 1931. Intended to recall the 1,000-year-old doors of Pantaleone, cast in Constantinople, these are also inlaid with silver. Stories of St. Paul are paired with the life of St. Peter in ten panels sheltered under the arms of a silver cross, traced through the doors as a curling vine. Christ appears twice in the doors, reflecting light as he endows Peter with the keys of the Kingdom and converts Saul on the Damascus road.

The basilica's sleek surfaces confer a modern sheen to St. Paul's, while its spaciousness—and the warmth from the amber glow of the alabaster windows—makes for a welcoming atmosphere.

Rome's most prestigious painters vied to decorate the nave; Pope Pius IX hired twenty-one artists to each contribute a panel of a story of St. Paul—and in the case of a few celebrity artists, offered them two panels. Pietro Gagliardo, who frescoed the interior of St. Augustine, executed the *Martyrdom of St. Stephen* and the *Conversion of Saul*; Francesco Podesti took charge of the stories of Saul-become-Paul and Ananias. The great decorative series of papal portraits, begun by Leo the Great, was re-created by the Vatican mosaic laboratory and is beneath the fresco cycle; it includes mosaic medallions of every pope from Peter to the incumbent. [E.L.]

St. Lawrence Outside the Walls (*confessio*)*:* Sarcophagus of St. Lawrence

WEDNESDAY WITHIN THE OCTAVE OF EASTER

Station at St. Lawrence
Outside the Walls

Holy Mass

Acts 3.1–10
Psalm 105
Luke 24.13–35

Office of Readings

1 Peter 2.11–25
An Ancient Easter Homily

TODAY'S GOSPEL READING, in which St. Luke tells of the Risen Lord's encounter with two disciples on the road to Emmaus, is one of the literary gems of the New Testament. It also summarizes neatly the long and sometimes difficult path the first witnesses to the Resurrection had to walk in order to arrive at the fullness of Easter faith.

As Luke sets the scene, there is, at first, bewilderment: things had gone terribly wrong; the one whom these disciples had hoped would "redeem Israel" had died a shameful death in which Israel's leaders were complicit, because they regarded him as a blasphemer. Bewilderment then gives way to deeper confusion: these two anonymous disciples had heard the women's tale of an empty tomb and a vision of angels who "said that he was alive." But they could not grasp what this "being alive" meant, or what it had to do with the still-incomprehensible suffering and death of the one who was to "redeem Israel."

The stranger—the Risen One—then begins to make things clear: "Beginning with Moses and all the prophets, he interpreted to them in all the scriptures the things concerning himself," including the necessary passage through suffering of the redeemer of Israel. And yet they still did not grasp what had happened, or who this stranger was. It is only when "he took the bread and blessed, and broke it, and gave it to them" that "their eyes were opened and they recognized him." At which point "he vanished out of their sight." Stunned at their own blindness—"Did not our hearts burn within us while he talked to us on the road, while he opened to us the scriptures?"—they rush back to Jerusalem to make their profession of Easter faith, where they are greeted with a parallel act of faith by the Eleven and their companions: "The Lord has risen indeed, and has appeared to Simon!"

Empty tomb *and* appearances; Word *and* Sacrament; the Cross *and* the Resurrection: in its corporate memory of the beginnings of Easter faith, to which Luke bears witness in this marvelously crafted narrative, the Church held fast to everything that had shed light on the radically new situation of those who had met the Risen One—and those who believed the testimony of their friends who had. The Scriptures had to be read afresh, with new eyes; messianic expectations had to be recast; common acts that had once indicated table fellowship, like the breaking of bread and its blessing, now took on deeper meanings; the very idea of "history" changed, as did the idea of God's "redemption" of Israel, which now seemed to extend beyond the familiar boundaries. Although they certainly would not have put it in these terms, the first witnesses to the Resurrection were grasping for an understanding of what Pope Benedict XVI would later describe, in *Jesus of Nazareth—Holy Week*, as an "evolutionary leap" in the human condition: a qualitatively new mode of living was being revealed in the vibrant, manifestly human, but utterly different life of the Risen Lord. And that, as the Octave of Easter has taught again and again, changed *everything*.

In an Easter sermon with the suggestive title "The Heart of Stone Beats Again," Hans Urs von Balthasar suggests that this particular Resurrection appearance ought to resonate in a special way with those living in late modernity, who might well recognize themselves in the disciples who wandered down the Emmaus road some two millennia ago. All of us, Balthasar notes, are in a hurry—but to where? We are all beset by "a constant stream of images"—meaning what? "There is so much hustle and bustle. What we can contain in our heads is so little, and the more that forces its way in, the less we can hold." Busyness, we discover sooner or later, is no substitute for purposefulness. Busyness, we may even begin to suspect, is one of the psychological tricks we play on ourselves to avoid confronting the fact that we are all destined for the grave.

What, then, are we looking for, in this often aimless wandering? We are looking, the Swiss theologian suggests, for what those two confused and perplexed disciples found on the Emmaus road: "the tangible reality of resurrection from the dead." And this is what Christians have found:

One man has come back, not as a spiritist phenomenon but in flesh and blood: "Touch me and see; for a spirit has not flesh and bones as you see that I have." He did not come back as a projection of the living faith of his disciples, for he came when none of them had the least idea of such a possibility, and he had a hard battle against their stubborn unbelief. This One Man has brought back with him from the realm of the dead the hope and certainty of eternal life for all. He brings us the very thing we need, although we cannot see how, namely, a continuing life that is not simply a continuation of the old life. . . . A continuing life, but not *totally* new and different either—a new form of cosmic life on some other planet, for instance—for that would be no solution and we would no longer be ourselves. It is both things at the same time, therefore, and in a way that is beyond our imagining: both a transition into God's eternity and at the same time the transfiguration and fulfillment of all that remained hopelessly unfulfilled and unfulfillable on earth. *This* wonderful, unique, earthly life, purified of all its slag, is to be lifted up to the plane of the eternal.

The challenge today, as for the disciples en route to Emmaus, is to overcome our disbelief that anything could be so good, so true, so beautiful. That radical quality of the New Life promised by Easter faith, Balthasar suggests, is why

Christians are dangerous, and why Christians are persecuted. "Right from the beginning," he writes, "Christianity was seen as a total, highly dangerous revolution." Once, in the days of St. Lawrence, whose major station is revisited today, it challenged Roman authorities, who were convinced that the cult of the gods was necessary for public order. Now, it challenges cultures committed to skepticism and its moral offspring, relativism.

One might think that, because Christianity proclaims what Balthasar calls "meaning's revolt against the meaninglessness of dying," its proclamation would be eagerly embraced. But to imagine that is to misgauge the darkening of mind and hardening of will that is humanity's enduring legacy from our first parents. The "revolt of the Resurrection against the finality of bodily disintegration" suggests that the body has an eternal destiny and is not merely a tool to be used as whim dictates here and now; and that very concept challenges the hedonism of the twenty-first century. The "revolt of love's absoluteness against any resignation on the part of the heart" challenges twenty-first-century cynicism, which confuses love with pleasure and finds it hard to imagine permanence in love.

The Emmaus story ought also to be reassuring to Christians at those moments when faith falters. As pilgrims have discovered along the Lenten itinerary of conversion, the momentum in Luke's gospel is always *toward* Jerusalem; thus, the two disciples in today's Easter story are walking in the wrong direction—away from Jerusalem, and away from the Cross. Yet their misdirection is repaired by the Risen One, who walks with them as he walks with us, even when we are headed in the wrong direction. He walks with us in the Scriptures and in the Holy Eucharist; he walks with us into the confessional; and in that pastoral accompaniment, he points us back to the right path—the path to the New Jerusalem.

The Resurrection changes *everything*. Little wonder that it took so long for the disciples to recognize the Risen One and to grasp what had happened to him, and to them. Little wonder that it takes a lifetime of faith to begin to grasp the meaning of Easter faith today. Amid that struggle to understand, how-ever, the Risen Lord walks with those whose hearts burn within them, yearning for the embrace of the love that can never die again because, as suffering love, it has passed through death and has conquered.

That is the testimony in the First Letter of Peter in the Office of Readings, and it remains as true today as when the first leaders of the Church preached to the newly baptized two millennia ago: "Christ . . . suffered for you, leaving you an example, that you should follow in his steps. He committed no sin. . . . He himself bore our sins in his body on the tree, that we might die to sin and live to righteousness. By his wounds you were healed. For you were straying like sheep, but have now returned to the Shepherd and Guardian of your souls."

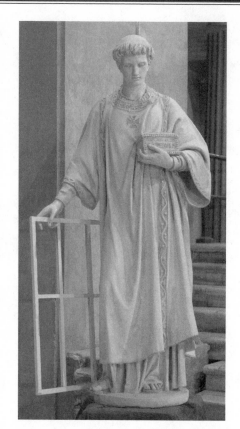

St. Lawrence Outside the Walls:
St. Lawrence (Stefano Galleti, 1865)

THE HIERARCHIC ITINERARY of sanctity in the Easter Octave—Christ; the Virgin Mary; Sts. Peter and Paul—continues in today's station, a cemetery of martyrs gathered around the Roman deacon-martyr, Lawrence.

The great marble casket of St. Lawrence is housed under the altar in a sturdy iron cage within the *confessio*. Over the centuries, relics of other heroes of the early Church came to rest along with those of the third patron of Rome. According to the inscription on the tomb, the martyr Cyriaca and a priest named Justin (who had taken charge of Lawrence's burial) are interred here. Later, the remains of St. Lawrence's jailer, St. Hippolytus, another convert-martyr, found their way to this tomb. In the sixth century, Pope Pelagius brought the relics of the protomartyr Stephen here. According to a charming tale in the *Golden Legend* (the greatest of medieval "Lives of the Saints"), Lawrence rolled over to make room for his fellow-martyr when the sarcophagus was opened. Over the centuries, the pairing of Stephen and Lawrence has inspired great artists, most notably Fra Angelico (the patron of artists), who painted the stories of the two great martyrs in the Nicholas V Chapel of the Apostolic Palace.

Anti-Christian persecution in the classical world was vicious and brutal: the men and women buried here were roasted, stoned, scourged, and torn apart by wild horses for their fidelity. And as a tangible reminder of the cost of conviction, the far side of the sarcophagus includes a marble slab covered with perforations: according to tradition, a part of the grill used to roast St. Lawrence. Yet these gruesome deaths were the seed of much of Rome's beauty: the splendid nineteenth-century tomb of Blessed Pius IX is nearby, a witness to his devotion to the early martyrs and a magnificent example of modern mosaic work.

In the thirteenth century, at the apogee of the high Middle Ages, a stately episcopal throne was constructed above the crypt; it faces the sixth-century mosaic of Christ

(*continues*)

(continued)

imparting his blessing while seated on a turquoise orb. Fresco fragments from that same period, the time of Pope Pelagius, remain in the basilica's Chapel of St. Cyriaca; amid the faded pigment, Sts. Catherine, Andrew, John the Baptist, and Lawrence are still recognizable.

Meticulous attention to detail is a hallmark of the Basilica of St. Lawrence Outside the Walls. The capitals of the exotic marble columns are inventively carved with leaves, female figures, and the occasional suit of armor, a sampling of Romanesque inventiveness. Ancient sarcophagi with exquisitely sculpted mythological scenes now hold the remains of medieval prelates; a floral pattern in the floor or an intricately wrought bronze grate catches the eye. Against the simple timbered ceiling and the rustic brick archways, centuries of embellishment have transformed the basilica into a unique aesthetic time capsule, whose raison d'être is the preservation of the memory of the martyrs as witnesses to salvation history. [E.L.]

Twelve Holy Apostles: High altar, *Martyrdom of the Apostles Philip and James the Less* (Domenico Maria Muratori, 1716)

THURSDAY WITHIN THE OCTAVE OF EASTER

Station at the Twelve Holy Apostles

Holy Mass
Acts 3.11–26
Psalm 8
Luke 24.35–48

Office of Readings
1 Peter 3.1–17
Jerusalem Catecheses: Mystagogica 3

D EATH IS, IN A SENSE, UNNATURAL. The body resists death, such that the bodies of terminally ill people and severely wounded soldiers resist the inevitable until the end. From the perspective of biblical faith, this innate, physical resistance to death is a trace of what theologians call "original innocence," the condition of the first parents before the Fall: which is to say, before sin and death entered the story.

In pondering, during the Easter Octave, just what the Resurrection wrought, it is well to keep that natural resistance-to-death in mind, for it sheds light on another dimension of Easter faith: the Church's conviction, evident in some of the later Pauline letters, that the Resurrection wrought a great change in the order of nature as well as in the order of history—a great change in the structure of reality itself. In *Jesus of Nazareth—Holy Week*, Pope Benedict XVI tried to describe those changes (which are, in the final analysis, indescribable) in these terms:

> On the basis of . . . this biblical evidence, what are we . . . is a position to say about the true nature of Christ's Resurrection?
>
> It is a historical event that nevertheless bursts open the dimensions of history and transcends it. Perhaps we may draw upon analogical language here . . . [and think of] the Resurrection as something akin to a radical "evolutionary leap," in which a new dimension of life emerges, a new dimension of human existence.
>
> Indeed, matter itself is remolded into a new type of reality. The man Jesus, complete with his body, now belongs to the sphere of the divine and eternal. From now on, as Tertullian once said, "spirit and blood" have a place within God. . . . Even if man by his nature is created for immortality, it is only now that the place exists in which his immortal soul can find its "space," its "bodiliness," in which immortality takes on its meaning as communion with God and with the whole of reconciled mankind. This is what is meant by those passages in St. Paul's prison letters (cf. Colossians 1.12–23 and Ephesians 1.3–23) that speak of the cosmic body of Christ, indicating thereby that Christ's transformed body is also the place where men enter into communion with God and with one another and are therefore able to live definitively in the fullness of indestructible life. . . .
>
> [Thus] . . . Jesus's Resurrection was not just about some deceased individual coming back to life at a certain point. . . . [An] ontological leap occurred, one that touches being as such, opening up a dimension that affects us all, creating for all of us a new space of life, a new space of being in union with God.

Keeping in mind the magnitude of the change wrought by the Resurrection—a divine action in history and nature that changed history and nature in a radical way, opening new possibilities of life beyond the reach of death—we can perhaps ponder with a bit more patience yet another gospel reading in which the disciples don't, at first, get it. Today's gospel account, read, appropriately enough, at the station of the Twelve Holy Apostles, picks up where yesterday's gospel reading ended. The two disciples who recognized the Risen One in the breaking of bread (and, restrospectively, in his breaking open the Scripture for them in a new way) have returned to Jerusalem, where they have shared their experience with other friends of Jesus. Both the Emmaus disciples and the disciples in Jerusalem believe that Jesus has been raised; they accept the testimony of their own eyes and of other witnesses. But they still cannot grasp what this "being raised" *means*. So when the Risen One appears among them, their first reaction is to think that this is a "spirit," a ghost.

The Lord chastises them mildly, pointing out that he has "flesh and bones" that a "spirit" would not have—and still they do not get it, although St. Luke tells us that they "disbelieved for joy": that is, this is too good to be true. So the Lord asks for something to eat; they give him broiled fish, which he eats before them. Then, as he had done on the Emmaus road, he shows them from Scripture that the Anointed One of God had to suffer; that he then had to rise from the dead to a new form of life; and that repentance should be preached in his name "to all nations, beginning from Jerusalem." They are, he concludes, "witnesses to these things"—which is to say, they have a mission, for which they will be equipped in due course by "power from on high," in the gift of the Holy Spirit.

This pattern—incomprehension followed by divine instruction and example, and then by a gradual emerging of Easter faith in its fullness—has now occupied the first four days of the Easter Octave. It is striking that the Church made its own dullness and initial lack of understanding a central part of its preaching of the Resurrection—which is not precisely what modern marketers would recommend. Why? Why was this slowness to grasp the meaning of the New Life remembered? Why was it enshrined in the holy books of the New Covenant?

Benedict XVI, once again, suggested an answer. This was done, he wrote, because it accurately reflected the ways of God with humanity. Why didn't God do things the way we would have done them—smiting the enemies of God with power, coming down from the Cross, revealing the Truth of the world and of history to the powerful and influential, rather than to a small band of illiterates, peasants, and pious women? Because, Pope Benedict reflected, God's ways are not our ways:

It is part of the mystery of God that he acts so gently, that he gradually builds up *his* history within the great history of mankind; that he becomes man and so can be overlooked by his contemporaries and by the powers that shape history; that he suffers and dies and that, having risen again, he chooses to come to mankind only through the faith of the disciples to whom he reveals himself; that he continues to knock gently on the doors of our hearts and slowly opens our eyes if we open our doors to him.

And yet—is this not the truly divine way? Not to overwhelm with external power, but to give freedom, to offer and elicit love. And if we really think about it, is it not what seems so small that is truly great? Does not a ray of light issue from Jesus, growing brighter across the centuries, that could not come from any mere man and through which the light of God truly shines into the world? Could the apostolic preaching have found faith and built up a worldwide community unless the power of truth had been at work within it?

And because of that, nature and history, the material self and the soul, the world and the cosmos have been transformed: they have been brought into communion with God, who is both Creator and Redeemer. Because of that, we can see, with St. John (if more dimly than he saw), where all of this is heading:

Then I saw a new heaven and a new earth; for the first heaven and the first earth had passed away, and the sea was no more. And I saw the holy city, new Jerusalem, coming down out of heaven from God, prepared as a bride adorned for her husband; and I hear a great voice from the throne saying, "Behold, the dwelling of God is with men. He will dwell with them, and they shall be his people, and God himself will be with them; he will wipe away every tear from their eyes, and death shall be no more, neither shall there be mourning nor crying nor pain any more, for the former things have passed away."

And he who sat upon the throne said, "Behold, I make all things new . . ." [Revelation 21.1–5a].

Twelve Holy Apostles:
Crypt, *Magi* (1877)

T HE WARMTH OF THE BASILICA of the Twelve Holy Apostles dates from an elaborate redecoration financed by Duke Giovanni Torlonia in 1827. The family—silk merchants turned bankers—made their fortune during the Napoleonic occupation of the city. When the papacy returned to Rome after Pius VII's French exile, the Torlonia family dedicated itself to restoring Roman basilicas, and specifically to today's station (next to the generalate of the Conventual Franciscans) and to the Gesù, mother church of the Jesuits. *Giallo di Siena*, a deep yellow marble, is the signature style of Torlonia interventions and gives the basilica's interior its golden aura.

The *confessio* contains the relics of two early witnesses to the Resurrection, the apostles Philip and James the Less; Philip was martyred in Hierapolis (now southwestern Turkey), while James died for the faith in Jerusalem—where, one tradition holds, he served as bishop. Their relics, in a stone sarcophagus under the high altar, which is decorated with a relief of the multiplication of loaves and fishes, testify to the Church's universal mission.

The immense crypt surrounding the tomb was constructed by Luigi Carimini between 1869 and 1871 during the fall of the Papal States: while Pius IX went into exile within the walls of the Vatican, the memory of the apostolic martyrs' sacrifice was being renewed here. Other martyrs' relics surround Philip and James: some were brought here in 886, when Pope Stephen IV, walking barefoot, carried them from the catacombs on his shoulders. Shortly after he removed the relics, the ancient Christian burial sites were closed; other relics were interred in the basilica in 1871, after the modern rediscovery of the catacombs.

The crypt decoration reflects the fascination with Roman catacombs spurred by Giovanni Battista de Rossi, whose richly illustrated *Roma Sotterranea Cristiana [Underground Christian Rome]* was published in three volumes between 1864 and 1877. The designs invoke the early Christian imagery of the Good Shepherd, a major Christological symbol. Derived from the Greco-Roman representation of philanthropy, the shepherd image bespoke one man taking on another's financial or civic burdens. Christians adapted the image to illustrate Christ's shouldering the burden of the world's sin. The shepherd's youthful countenance, in turn, alluded to Christ's divinity, his Apollonian features suggesting the Light of the world. Thus the Gentiles, unlettered in the biblical worldview, could contextualize Christ within their own cultural experience.

The Epiphany, another important early Christian image, is also part of the crypt decoration. Judaism prohibited images; thus, paleo-Christians were deeply uncomfortable with the idea of "portraying" God and the stories of salvation history. But the Epiphany proclaimed two essential facts about the Christian dispensation. First, the God who made himself known through deeds and words in the Old Testament had entered history in the person of his Son, the image of the Father; the New Covenant in Jesus Christ would therefore discover the importance of images-of-the-image, which opened new possibilities for Christian art. The second essential fact of the Epiphany (often symbolized by the peaked caps of the foreign Magi) was the universality of God's will to save: salvation is for everyone, Jew and Gentile alike. [E.L.]

St. Mary "at the Martyrs" (Pantheon): High altar with relics

FRIDAY WITHIN THE OCTAVE OF EASTER

Station at St. Mary "at the Martyrs"

Holy Mass
Acts 4.1–12
Psalm 118
John 21.1–14

Office of Readings
1 Peter 3.18–4.11
Jerusalem Catecheses: Mystagogica 3

TODAY'S STATION CHURCH and its Parisian counterpart suggest the cultural tensions for twenty-first-century pilgrims who walk to Galilee in response to the Risen Lord's command—and then go out to the ends of the earth, in response to the Great Commission.

Originally built by Marcus Agrippa in honor of all the gods of Rome—hence the name, *Pantheon*—and rebuilt by Hadrian in the early second century, this massive structure, with its colossal dome, became a Christian church in honor of the Virgin Mary and the martyrs in the seventh century. And while it shelters the tombs of great figures from later Italian history, most notably the artist Raphael, the Pantheon remains, manifestly, a *church*.

The story of the Panthéon in Paris reverses this historical trajectory. Originally built by King Louis XV as a *votum*, or thanksgiving offering, for his having survived an illness, the Church of St. Geneviève was seized by the Assembly during the French Revolution and turned into a secular shrine to the greats of France, many of whom are buried there. Among these national heroes is Voltaire, whose battle cry, *Écrasez l'infâme!* [Destroy the infamy!], was a declaration of war against Christianity, the last traces of which have been quite thoroughly erased from Louis XV's *votum*.

The Roman Pantheon-turned-church and the Church of St. Geneviève-turned-secular-mausoleum embody two conflicting stories of the role of biblical religion in the rise of the modern West. Today's *statio* illustrates one storyline: the civilization of the West grew out of the fruitful interaction of biblical religion, Greek rationality, and Roman law. The Parisian shrine illustrates an alternative understanding of the Western civilizational project: the God of the Bible had to be overthrown so that men and women could be truly free. The stational celebration at the Roman Pantheon during the Octave of Easter proposes that the God of the Bible came into history as a liberator who calls humanity into communion with him by love, and who demonstrated that love in the Paschal Mystery. A different kind of celebration took place in Paris in 1940: then and there, the Panthéon witnessed the triumphal march of a militant totalitarianism that, having declared war against the God of the Bible, also declared war against reason and law, leaving vast human suffering in its wake.

A tale of two cities; a tale of two pantheons; a tale to be pondered in imagining the human future.

The station of St. Mary *ad martyres* also prompts a reflection on martyrdom, a subject not unrelated to this tale of two cities.

Martyrdom does not figure prominently in the spiritual imagination of many, perhaps most, twenty-first-century Christians in the developed world. Christians who live along the often-bloody fault lines between Christianity and Islam in the Middle East, Africa, and Asia have lived a powerful experience of martyrdom in the late twentieth and early twenty-first centuries, as have the Christians of China. But for the Christian communities of the West, "martyrdom" is something that happened centuries, even millennia, ago. Yet the twentieth century was, statistically, the greatest century of martyrdom in Christian history. A commission on contemporary martyrs formed by Pope John Paul II in preparation for the Great Jubilee of 2000 concluded that more Christians had given their lives for Christ in the twentieth century than in the previous nineteen centuries of Christian history combined. Industrial-style mass murder, of the sort practiced by Nazis and communists, took a toll of Christian lives in the twentieth century that reached into the millions, and likely tens of millions.

Whatever Voltaire and those of his rationalist persuasion imagined in the eighteenth century, as they fought for a new political order that would over-throw the old regimes and their altar-and-throne arrangements, the twentieth century demonstrated in an ocean of blood that ultramundane political systems have been the most lethal threat to human freedom—and human decency—in the recorded history of humanity. When the God of the Bible was jettisoned, the result was not a strengthening of reason and the rule of law, but their severe attenuation—and, ultimately, the rule of brute force. Christians were not, of course, the only victims of the two great twentieth-century totalitarian projects: everyone suffered. But these two vast machines of oppression in the service of secular utopia produced, among their other depredations, the greatest harvest of martyrs in Christian history.

To stand, today, in this station *ad martyres* is to stand amid a great crowd of witnesses, many of them the contemporaries of twenty-first-century pilgrims.

The witness of martyrs, who are the seed of the Church, is also a reminder that the Resurrection inaugurated a new age, which is the final age of the world. For the first disciples, who were steeped in the messianic expectations of their time, the surprise was not that the "end times" had come. The surprise was that this inbreaking of a new historical epoch had taken place within history: it did not end history. Here and now, the Resurrection and its promise of a life-beyond-death that is eternal and untouched by decay displayed God's intentions for the end of history, such that men and women of Easter faith lived in a *now* that had been transformed radically by the revelation of the promised future. That revelation brought a new depth of courage into the *now* of Christian life, demonstrated by the witness of the martyrs. As the First Letter of Peter reminds pilgrims today, it should also bring a new serenity to quotidian life:

> The end of all things is at hand; therefore keep sane and sober for your prayers. Above all hold unfailing your love for one another, since love covers a multitude of sins. Practice hospitality ungrudgingly to one another. As each has received a gift, employ it for one another, as good stewards of God's varied grace: whoever speaks, as one who utters oracles of God; whoever renders service, as one who renders it by the strength which God supplies; in order that in everything God may be glorified through Jesus Christ. To him belong glory and dominion for ever and ever. Amen.

Not all the baptized are called to martyrdom—which, in the Christian view of things, is a privilege and a grace. But all the baptized are called to live the life of the Kingdom here and now. And all are called to live so that "in everything God may be glorified through Jesus Christ." Enabling the people of the New Covenant to live that way is how the grace of God equips "the saints" to be the kind of men and women who can live happily forever within the light and love of the Trinity.

St. Mary "at the Martyrs" (Pantheon): *Madonna of Mercy with Sts. Francis and John the Baptist* (Lazio/Umbrian School, fifteenth century)

THE PANTHEON, Rome's bid to outdo Egypt's pyramids, was dedicated to "all the gods": it was a huge, domed temple celebrating Roman conquests, engineering, and inventiveness, which the Romans understood to be signs of divine favor. The Pantheon also proclaimed a new entry into the parade of Roman deities: the Romans themselves. For with Julius Caesar's deification in 28 B.C., Rome declared that men could become gods, harnessing heaven to earth through their will. That conceit would be falsified when God became man—and the Pantheon would in turn become a Christian church.

While the first Pantheon was built on this site in 27 B.C. by Marcus Vispanius Agrippa, the building as we know it was a gift of the emperor Hadrian (117–138)—a building meant to evoke wonder. The rectangular façade, preceded by a portico, seemed, at first glance, like other squared temples omnipresent in the empire, if very large. Yet, the porch itself gave the pagan pilgrim pause, for supporting the massive space were sixteen granite columns, thirty-nine feet high and five feet in diameter, each weighing sixty tons, quarried in Egypt and transported over river and sea to Rome. The marble-encrusted walls and the bronze plates covering the wood and tile roof bore further evidence that no expense had been spared.

But true amazement came on entering the interior, where the building's essential form revealed itself. The giant dome, spanning 142 feet, was twice the size of anything built before. Nothing in the empire prepared a Roman for this space, as the perfect harmony of the building's diameter and height equalized the vertical line of heaven and the horizontal line of earth. Every surface was embellished with bronze or precious stone. At the center, under the oculus, sat the emperor: at the heart of the cosmos with a direct line to the heavens, in a colossal space that embodied the fundamental tenets of Roman religion in architecture.

After the fall of the Roman Empire, the Pantheon was still held in high regard, but as the city expanded into the Campus Martius, the building became more vulnerable to looting. Pope Boniface IV persuaded the Byzantine emperor Phocas to give the Pantheon to the Church, and on May 13, 609, Rome's greatest pagan shrine was reborn as a Christian church. The old idols were destroyed, but the building was always respected; thus, the Pantheon remains Rome's most intact temple. At the same time, the remains of many martyrs were transferred here from the catacombs, giving the building its ecclesiastical name: St. Mary "at the Martyrs."

The interior is ringed with altars. Renaissance efforts to capture the building's spatial harmony may be found in Melozzo da Forlì's stately *Annunciation* and the *Madonna of Mercy with Sts. Francis and John the Baptist*. A century later, Baroque exuberance led to more altarpieces and statues—and a pair of twinned bell towers often attributed to Gian Lorenzo Bernini, dubbed "donkey ears" and mercifully removed in the eighteenth century.

A nineteenth-century restoration returned the Pantheon as close to its original state as possible, and the building is now a monumental tomb for many of Italy's most notable sons. The great Raphael, Urbino's gift to Renaissance painting, was entombed here in 1520. He was later joined by other artists, including Baldassare Peruzzi and Annibale Carracci. The first kings of united Italy are also interred here. [E.L.]

St. John Lateran: *St. Matthew* (Camillo Rusconi, 1718)

SATURDAY WITHIN THE OCTAVE OF EASTER

Station at St. John Lateran

Holy Mass

Acts 4.13–21

Psalm 118

Mark 16.9–15

Office of Readings

1 Peter 4.12–5.14

Jerusalem Catecheses: Mystagogica 4

THROUGHOUT THE OCTAVE OF Easter, stational pilgrims have been reminded that the sacrament of Baptism confers responsibilities. Today's Mass readings stress the evangelical dimension of those responsibilities.

The gospel reading, taken from the extended ending to St. Mark, records the Risen Lord's instructions to the eleven disciples: "Go into all the world and preach the Gospel to the whole creation." The testimony of Peter and John from the Acts of the Apostles shows that this command was taken seriously; after being told by the elders of the Temple "not to speak or teach at all in the name of Jesus," the two apostles reply, "we cannot but speak of what we have seen and heard."

When he first came to today's *statio* as the Successor of Peter on May 7, 2005, Benedict XVI spoke from his *cathedra* as Bishop of Rome about the evangelical responsibility of every member of the Church: "All Christians in their own way can and must be witnesses of the Risen Lord." All must feel compelled to "speak of what [they] have seen and heard." This responsibility falls in a special way on those ordained to the ministry of the Word. But evangelism is not a matter for the ordained only. It is a common obligation, conferred by Baptism and reaffirmed by the gift of the Holy Spirit in Confirmation. That second sacrament of initiation, Benedict suggested, has much to do with the *how* and the *what* of every Christian's call to be an evangelist:

> The Lord promises the disciples his Holy Spirit . . . [who] will give "power" to the disciples . . . and guide them to the whole truth. As the living Word of God, Jesus told his disciples everything, and God can give no more than himself. In Jesus, God gave us his whole self, that is, he gave us everything. . . . In him, in the Son, all has been said, all has been given. . . .
>
> The Holy Spirit, therefore, is the power through which Christ causes us to experience his closeness. . . . [For the] Risen Christ needs witnesses who have met him, people who have known him immediately through the power of the Holy Spirit: those who have, so to speak, actually touched him can witness to him.
>
> It is in this way that the Church, the family of Christ, "beginning at Jerusalem" . . . speaks to the very ends of the earth. It is through witnesses that the Church was built.

This emphasis on witness and evangelism—every Christian's responsibility to testify to "what we have seen and heard"—is a twentieth-century development in the Catholic Church, although it clearly draws on the most ancient Christian traditions. In a 1991 essay analyzing Blessed John Paul II's consistent emphasis on evangelism, Cardinal Avery Dulles, SJ, traced the full emergence of this theme (which had been anticipated in certain streams of theological exploration in the first half of the twentieth century) to the Second Vatican Council

(1962–1965). The First Vatican Council (1869–1870), the cardinal noted, used the Latin word *evangelium* [gospel] only once, and as a synonym for the four canonical gospels in the New Testament. By contrast, Vatican II spoke of "the Gospel" 157 times, of the imperative to "evangelize" 18 times, and of "evangelization" 31 times. Beginning with his homily in Santo Domingo in 1992, on the fifth centenary of the planting of the Gospel in the Western Hemisphere, John Paul II put the "New Evangelization," and every Christian's responsibility to participate in it, at the center of the Catholic Church's self-understanding. And this, Cardinal Dulles commented, marked a dramatic shift that presaged a new Catholic approach to evangelical mission in the twenty-first century and the third millennium:

> For centuries, evangelization had been a poor stepchild. Even when the term was used, evangelization was treated as a secondary matter, the special vocation of a few priests and religious. And even these specialists were more concerned with gaining new adherents for the Church than in proclaiming the good news of Jesus Christ. Today, we seem to be witnessing the birth of a new Catholicism that, without loss of its institutional, sacramental, and social dimensions, is authentically evangelical.

In the 1991 encyclical *Redemptoris Missio* [The Mission of the Redeemer], John Paul II taught that the Church does not *have* a mission, as if "mission" were one among many things the Church does; the Church *is* a mission. Mission is the essence of the Church; mission is the reason for the Church; and the responsibility for mission, for witnessing to "what we have seen and heard," falls on everyone in the Church.

That is why John Paul II and Benedict XVI both stressed the importance of deepening one's personal relationship with the Lord Jesus—in Benedict's preferred terminology, deepening "friendship with Jesus." Only those who know the Lord can be his witnesses. Only those who have "seen and heard" on a regular basis can testify to the things they have witnessed. The deepening of personal faith is essential to empowerment for mission.

The New Evangelization that John Paul called for is global in range. It involves the re-evangelization of those parts of the world that once heard the Gospel but have grown soft and slack in their faith; it involves bringing the Gospel to those parts of the world that have been traditionally resistant to it, like much of Asia; it involves strengthening the faith where it is vibrant; and it means bringing the Gospel to the worlds of economics, politics, culture, and the mass media. Lay witnesses to "what we have seen and heard" are particularly important in this fourth part of the New Evangelization.

In John Paul II's mind, both the Second Vatican Council and the Great Jubilee of 2000 were aimed at this evangelical revitalization of the Church. Blessed John XXIII imagined Vatican II as a "new Pentecost"; that new Pentecost was to enflame the Church with an urgent sense of mission. Blessed John Paul II had a similar view of the Great Jubilee of 2000, which he often called the "key" to his pontificate: the Church spent an entire year marking the 2,000th anniversary of the Incarnation in order to ready itself, with renewed vitality, for a third millennium of evangelization.

As the station church road from Ash Wednesday to Divine Mercy Sunday draws to an end, stational pilgrims who have passed through the "annual catechumenate" of the Forty Days, and who have heard the Risen One's command to bring the Gospel to all nations during the Easter Octave, might well reflect on how, in going to Galilee and beyond, the imperative to tell of "what we have seen and heard" will be met: in marriages and families, in neighborhoods and parishes, in business and the professions, in public life, and in culture. Will this year's stational pilgrims bring others to the living waters of Baptism, or to the renewal of baptismal promises, a year from now?

St. John Lateran: Angels

THE ANCIENT baptistery of the Papal Archbasilica of St. John Lateran was the world's first legally constructed baptismal space: a gift of Constantine, like the basilica next door. In 432, the building was redecorated by Pope Sixtus II, who transformed it into a showcase of the first sacrament.

Constantine's architect employed an octagonal scheme, the eight sides evoking the seven days of Creation and the Eighth Day of the Christian Sabbath, the day of Resurrection. The exterior's simple brick, matching the Constantinian basilica's, evoked the humble materials through which sacramental grace flows: water, oil, and salt in Baptism; bread and wine in the Eucharist.

Today's entrance is opposite the original, reflecting the city's metamorphosis over time. In Constantine's day, pilgrims entered through the narthex, the porch at the building's far end. Porphyry columns, a sign of imperial patronage, articulated this entrance, where the catechumens awaited the day of their Baptism. The façade's wall retains traces of some of the baptistery's oldest decoration: inlaid veneers of antiquity's most prized stones form graceful arabesques; in the right apse, a mosaic decoration of delicate tendrils rests against a lapis blue background. These fragments illustrate patristic Christianity's commitment to marking the magnificence of baptismal regeneration with glorious décor.

The baptismal space was substantially restored by the Barberini pope, Urban VIII. The center contains the former baptismal basin, which was used for full-immersion "christening." (As the building was constructed atop the baths of an old Roman villa, the flow and drainage of water was a simple affair.) Constantine donated a porphyry and silver urn for the basin and a gold statue of the Lamb of God—treasures long since lost to looters. Today's green basalt urn and bronze cover were crafted in the seventeenth century. The eight porphyry columns framing the font were a gift of Sixtus II, as was the white marble architrave above. Frescoes recounting stories of Constantine date from Urban VIII's redecoration and were executed by the rising stars of Roman Baroque, Andrea Camassi and Carlo Maratta.

Side chapels were added shortly after Pope Sixtus's time. The two smaller chapels projecting from the central hall—dedicated to the basilica's Johannine patrons,

(*continues*)

(continued)

the Baptist and the Evangelist—were fifth-century additions by Pope Hilarius. The larger Blessed Sacrament Chapel was added in the seventh century by Pope John IV, who began the transfer of martyrs' relics from the catacombs to Roman churches and brought the remains of Sts. Venantius, Anastasia, and Marus here. The rich golden decoration was added a few years later by Pope Theodore I.

Sixtus II also contributed poetry to the baptistery. Inscribed around the architrave surrounding the font are distiches describing the glories of Baptism. These are believed to have been composed by Sixtus's deacon, who later became Pope St. Leo the Great:

Here springs the fount of life by which the entire world is laved
    since from Christ's wound it takes its origin and source.

Await the heavenly kingdom, who are reborn in this font;
    eternal life does not accept those who are born but once.

Though his sins be many or grievous, let none draw back afraid;
    reborn from out this stream, a Christian he shall be.
[E.L.]

St. Pancras: Coffered ceiling (seventeenth century)

THE SECOND SUNDAY OF EASTER (DIVINE MERCY SUNDAY)

Station at St. Pancras

Holy Mass

[A]	[B]	[C]
Acts 2.42–47	*Acts 4.32–35*	*Acts 5.12–16*
Psalm 118	*Psalm 118*	*Psalm 118*
1 Peter 1.3–9	*1 John 5.1–6*	*Revelation 1.9–11a, 12–13, 17–19*
John 20.19–31	*John 20.19–31*	*John 20.19–31*

Office of Readings

Colossians 3.1–17

St. Augustine: Sermon 8 in the Octave of Easter

T HE GOSPEL ACCOUNT OF "Doubting Thomas," read on this Sunday throughout the three-year Lectionary cycle, aptly sums up the Church's Easter Octave reflection on the trials of coming-to-Easter-faith. What God has wrought in the Resurrection is so utterly new that, as pilgrims have seen all week—and as anyone who meets the Risen One discovers—trying to comprehend the personal, historical, and cosmic meanings of that encounter stretches the human capacity for belief beyond its natural limits. To meet Jesus Christ, crucified and risen, is an experience that changes one's understanding of human possibilities—for here is one who shares in our humanity and yet lives in a new mode of existence. To meet Jesus Christ, crucified and risen, is also an experience that changes our understanding of God, for Christ reveals both the full truth about our humanity and the face of the merciful Father, who can and does bring life out of death.

That merciful Father also respects human freedom, and this is perhaps one of the deeper meanings of the familiar story of Thomas "the Twin" and his skepticism. Thomas, Lenten pilgrims will remember, is the disciple who courageously challenges his brethren to follow Jesus to Jerusalem so that "we may die with him" [John 11.16]. But after the Lord's death, Thomas, who has fled the scene of catastrophe with everyone else (save the holy women and the Beloved Disciple), has at least as much difficulty as the others, and perhaps more difficulty, believing that death has not had the final word. In this, he may stand for all those who struggle with faith—who make progress slowly (and sometimes from crisis to crisis) along the itinerary of conversion, growing from partial belief to the fullness of Easter faith.

The Church, in the persons of the other disciples, proclaims the Good News of Easter: "We have seen the Lord." But, for Thomas, the evidence of what others "have seen and heard" is not enough. So, from the very beginning, the Church is called to exercise patience as it waits for the often perplexing processes of human freedom to resolve themselves, with the help of grace, in favor of the act of Easter faith. The divine assistance and the divine mercy display themselves in a dramatic way when the Risen One appears to Thomas and the others and invites the doubter to pass over from skepticism to belief, and the encounter is so life-transforming that it leads the skeptic to make the strongest profession of Christological faith in the gospels: "My Lord and my God!" Thus does Thomas, the paradigm of growth-in-faith, provide a confessional bookend to the Christological confession at the beginning of John's gospel: "In the beginning was the Word, and the Word was with God, and the Word was God, . . . and we have beheld his glory, glory as of the only Son of the Father" [John 1.1, 14b].

The drama of Thomas is preceded in today's gospel reading by what biblical scholars call the "Johannine Pentecost": the gift of the Holy Spirit by the

Risen One to the disciples gathered in the Upper Room. The gift of the Spirit is for mission: for it is in the power of the Spirit that the Lord sends the disciples forth, even as the Son was sent by the Father, and it is through the Spirit's power in the sacraments that the Risen One will remain present to his brothers and sisters. That empowering Presence is the power to offer both the forgiveness of sins and the New Life—it is, as ever, power for mission.

O n April 30, 2000, during the Mass at which Sister Mary Faustina Kowalska was canonized as the first saint of the Church's third millennium, Pope John Paul II announced that the Octave of Easter would henceforth be celebrated as Divine Mercy Sunday throughout the Church. Sister Faustina's mystical visions had given the Church the Chaplet of Divine Mercy, a special mode of prayer; John Paul believed that the revelation of the divine mercy to this obscure Polish nun had been a providential gift to a world badly in need of an experience of mercy. The horrors of the mid-twentieth century, John Paul believed, had shredded the moral fabric of humanity; the message of divine mercy given to Sister Faustina was, the pope preached, "a gift of special enlightenment that helps us live the Gospel of Easter more intensely, to offer it as a ray of light to the men and women of our time." Those who accepted the message would see the face of the merciful Father with new clarity; they would also be enabled to look in a new way upon their brothers and sisters, "with an attitude of unselfishness and solidarity." The embrace of divine love and mercy, John Paul II concluded, was an antidote to the possibility that the third millennium might replicate (or even intensify) some of the most horrific experiences of the second millennium:

> It is this love which must inspire humanity if it is to face the crisis of the meaning of life, the challenges of the most diverse needs, and, especially, the duty to defend the dignity of every human person. Thus the message of divine mercy is also implicitly a message about the value of every human being. Each person is precious in God's eyes; Christ gave his life for each one; to everyone the Father gives his Spirit and offers intimacy.

This consoling message is addressed above all to those who, afflicted by a particularly harsh trial or crushed by the weight of the sins they have committed, have lost confidence in life and are tempted to give in to despair. To them the gentle face of Christ is offered; those rays from his heart [which Sister Faustina had seen in her visions] touch them and shine upon them, warm then, show them the way and fill them with hope.

The journey from Ash Wednesday through the Easter Octave is now complete—as is the stational pilgrimage through the history and geography of sanctity in Rome. Today's station, at which the Church venerates a youthful martyr, is a powerful reminder of a theme preached by Benedict XVI at the Mass marking the public beginning of his service as Bishop of Rome: "The Church is young!" Young and old share in the vitality of the Church, which is the gift of the Holy Spirit at work changing lives and history. At the end of this itinerary of conversion, St. Paul reminds us, in today's Office of Readings, that the Christian must not only look ahead, but also look up: "If then you have been raised with Christ, seek the things that are above, where Christ is, seated at the right hand of God. Set your mind on things that are above. . . . For you have died, and your life is hidden with Christ in God. When Christ who is our life appears, then you also will appear with him in glory." That glory has been made possible by the Cross, which is at the center of history and at the center of the cosmos. This is what pilgrims along the stational itinerary of conversion "have seen and heard"; this is the great truth to which they must testify:

He is the image of the invisible God, the first-born of all creation; for in him all things were created, in heaven and on earth, visible and invisible, whether thrones or dominions or principalities or authorities—all were created through him and for him. He is before all things, and in him all things hold together. He is the head of the body, the Church; he is the beginning, the first-born from the dead, that in everything he might be pre-eminent. For in him all the fullness of God was pleased to dwell, and through him to reconcile to himself all things, making peace by the blood of his cross [Colossians 1.15–20].

St. Pancras: Reliquary
of St. Pancras

THE BASILICA OF ST. PANCRAS is atop the Janiculum Hill, named for the Roman deity of beginnings and endings and designated protector of the ancient border between Roman and Etruscan territory. The Roman fear of finality was transformed by the cult of the martyrs and the conviction that death for the sake of Christ was the beginning of the fullness of life. Pancras, a young martyr, embodied this belief in a striking personal story.

A native of Phrygia (today's central Turkey) and an orphan, he was raised among the Roman aristocracy by an uncle. His conversion to Christianity at age fourteen incurred the wrath of Diocletian, who tried to cajole the youngster to return to the observances of his forefathers: "You are still a child and easily misled. . . . Give up this madness and I will treat you as my own son." Pancras's answer—"I may be a child in body but . . . by the power of the Lord Jesus Christ in me, your terror means no more to me than the idol we are looking at"—sealed his fate. The enraged emperor had the boy beheaded here on the Via Aureliana; he was buried by the Roman matron Octavilla in a nearby catacomb, which subsequently took its name from the young saint.

Memorials to St. Pancras began with a small oratory on the ancient Via Aurelia, which was transformed by Pope Symmachus (498–514) into a larger structure. Symmachus donated a silver altar to St. Pancras and added a bath structure for the clergy who ran the church as a Roman parish. A century later, after the Gothic wars, the church was restored and equipped with new features, including a transept and an annular crypt, to allow pilgrims to approach the relics of St. Pancras, which were brought from the catacombs and placed under the main altar.

Medieval embellishments, including Cosmatesque ambos and candelabra, were frequently lost during periods of neglect. In the first decades of the seventeenth century, Cardinal Cosimo del Torres, under the auspices of the Borghese pope, Paul V, restored St. Pancras in then-fashionable Baroque style. The ancient columns were incorporated into piers and decorated with festive plaster garlands; Antonio Tempesta added a cycle of frescoes. The church's cream color offered a luminous contrast to the darkness of the catacombs below. Carmelites, given charge of the church in 1662, added the charming reliefs of frolicking cherubs, but the church was heavily damaged by the French invasion of 1797. The struggles of the *Risorgimento* caused further damage; the basilica's last restoration took place in 1959.

Today's church is striking for its Baroque patina, but the floors and apse decoration are modern. There are hints of the site's many vicissitudes: the first pier boasts elements of the lost Cosmatesque decorations, while the third pier includes a marker noting the site of Pancras's martyrdom on May 12, 304; there is an image of his death above, while stairs lead to his first place of burial along the Via Aurelia, one of the roads that facilitated the Christian conversion of the ancient world. [E.L.]

ACKNOWLEDGMENTS

My son, Stephen, and I spent Lent and Easter Week in Rome in 2011. There, with Elizabeth Lev, a brilliant guide to Rome's art and architecture, we made the Lenten station church pilgrimage in full, working with Liz and many friends and colleagues so that others might, through this book, share this unique spiritual and aesthetic experience. Before, during, and after Lent 2011, the three of us incurred many debts, which it is my privilege to acknowledge gratefully.

The faculty, staff, and students of the Pontifical North American College were the kindest of hosts to Stephen and me and the most congenial of fellow-pilgrims. The College's rector, Msgr. James Checchio, was an enthusiastic supporter of the project from the beginning; both Msgr. Checchio and the College *Economo*, Msgr. Daniel Mueggenborg, were unfailingly helpful throughout the entire pilgrimage. Sister Rebecca Abel, O.S.B., helped me navigate the riches of the College library, while Sister Susan Hooks, O.S.B., the College comptroller, facilitated some of the financial aspects of the project. Virtually every member of the College faculty had a helpful suggestion along the 2011 Lenten pilgrimage trail, and the College staff and student body were constantly supportive of Stephen's and my work in their home.

In June 2010, when I first discussed with Liz Lev the possibility of our doing a station churches book with Stephen as the project photographer, Liz wisely said that we needed a "fixer": someone who would get things organized before Stephen and I arrived in Rome, run interference for us while we were there, and cope with this, that, or the other quirk of a given church or those responsible for its care. Ashley Noronha, whom Liz recommended, was the best possible choice for the job and an invaluable colleague throughout Lent 2011, maintaining a preternatural calm amidst sometimes trying circumstances. Ashley's husband, John, was another welcome member of our project family.

Several of my former students, who were in residence at the North American College in Lent 2011, were particularly helpful with logistics, counsel, and research: Fr. Ryan Connors, Fr. Nicholas Desimone, Fr. Peter Heasley, and Fr. Justin Huber.

Gregory DiPippo gave me an insightful tutorial on the history of the Roman station church pilgrimage and pointed me toward important scholarly resources on this ancient tradition. Msgr. Thomas Fucinaro of the Holy See's Congregation for Divine Worship and the Discipline of the Sacraments was helpful at the other end of history, so to speak.

Ideas culled from various friends and colleagues helped shape my reflections on the liturgical texts of Lent and the Easter Octave: Fr. Peter John Cameron, O.P., Fr. Joseph Carola, S.J., Fr. Brian Christensen, Fr. Raymond J. de Souza, Archbishop Joseph Augustine DiNoia, O.P., Msgr. Joseph Hanefeldt, Fr. Denis Heames, Fr. Brendan Hurley, S.J., Msgr. John Macfarlane, Fr. Matthew Monnig, S.J., Fr. George W. Rutler, Cardinal James Francis Stafford, and Fr. Jonathan Wallis.

Virginia Coda Nunziante, Cardinal James M. Harvey, Dr. Roberto de Mattei, Dr. Marcello Pera, Cardinal Camillo Ruini, and Msgr. Peter B. Wells helped my partners and me navigate the rocks and shoals of ecclesiastical and governmental bureaucracy in Rome. Dr. Lucia Di Maro, Director General of the *Fondo Edifici di Culto* of the Italian Ministry of the Interior, was a gracious facilitator of our work in the churches under FEC's authority.

Several ambassadors to the Holy See were in regular attendance at the station church Masses of 2011 and were cordial companions afterward at a variety of Roman coffee bars: Ambassador Miguel Díaz of the United States, Ambassador J. Noel Fahey of Ireland, Ambassador Tim Fischer of Australia, Ambassador Anne Leahy of Canada, and Ambassador Hanna Suchocka of Poland.

On the Basic Books team, Katherine Streckfus strengthened the manuscript with her insightful queries and exceptional copy-editing skills, Brent Wilcox was a masterful designer, Katy O'Donnell kept things moving in New York, and Michelle Welsh-Horst brought everything together as senior project editor. Best thanks, too, to Lara Heimert, for seeing *Roman Pilgrimage* as a Basic Books book.

My colleagues at the Ethics and Public Policy Center, my professional home since 1989, are a steady source of insight and good cheer as we work, in our various ways, to strengthen the moral-cultural foundations of the West. Special thanks are due to Edward Whelan, the Center's president, for his support of this project and the rest of my work, and to Stephen White, my colleague in the Center's Catholic Studies program, for keeping the program humming during my absence in Spring 2011. The Catholic Studies program's generous donors help set the foundation on which projects like *Roman Pilgrimage* can be pursued, and they deserve a very sincere and public word of thanks.

And while the pleasure of making these acknowledgments falls to me, the work of bringing the Roman station church pilgrimage to life in this book has been a joint effort throughout. Thus *Roman Pilgrimage* is as much Elizabeth Lev's and Stephen Weigel's as it is mine. We dedicate it in homage "to the martyrs, then and now."

G. W.
Easter 2013

INDEX OF COLOR ILLUSTRATIONS

Cover: St. Peter: Interior of the dome (Giuseppe Cesari, 1590)

INSERT 1

INSERT 2

ILLUSTRATION CREDITS

All the photographs in *Roman Pilgrimage* were taken by Stephen Weigel.

Permission from the following to conduct photography is gratefully acknowledged:

Basilica of St. Clement

Basilica of St. George in Velabro

Basilica of St. Mark

Basilica of St. Sabina

Basilica of St. Stephen on the Caelian Hill

Basilica of St. Susanna

Basilica of the Twelve Holy Apostles

Basilica of St. Vitalis

Fondo Edifici di Culto, Ministry of the Interior

Pontifical Council for Social Communications

Vicariate of Rome

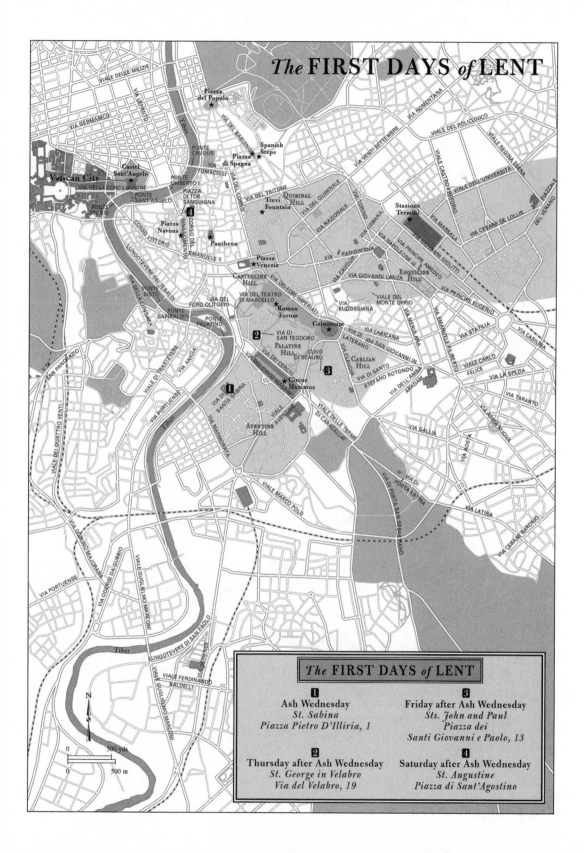

The FIRST DAYS of LENT

1
Ash Wednesday
St. Sabina
Piazza Pietro D'Illiria, 1

2
Thursday after Ash Wednesday
St. George in Velabro
Via del Velabro, 19

3
Friday after Ash Wednesday
Sts. John and Paul
Piazza dei
Santi Giovanni e Paolo, 13

4
Saturday after Ash Wednesday
St. Augustine
Piazza di Sant'Agostino

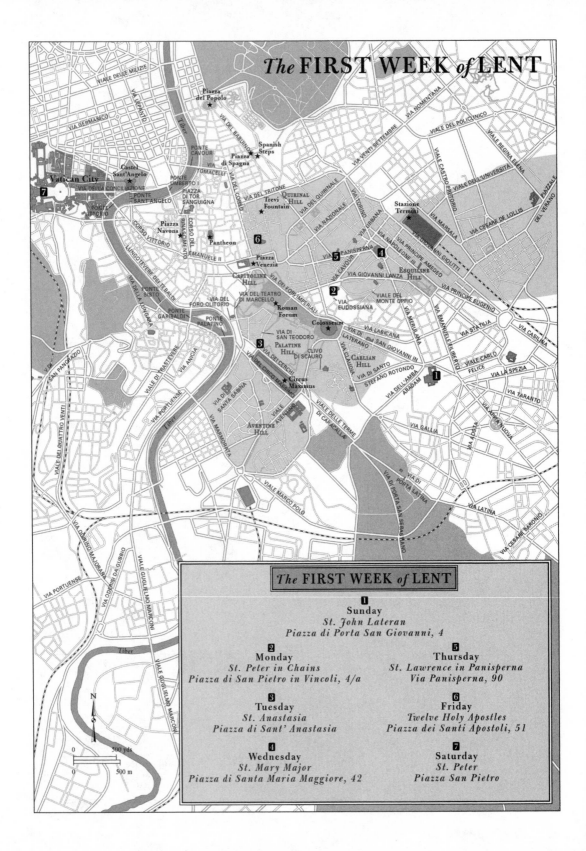

The FIRST WEEK of LENT

The FIRST WEEK of LENT

1
Sunday
St. John Lateran
Piazza di Porta San Giovanni, 4

2
Monday
St. Peter in Chains
Piazza di San Pietro in Vincoli, 4/a

3
Tuesday
St. Anastasia
Piazza di Sant' Anastasia

4
Wednesday
St. Mary Major
Piazza di Santa Maria Maggiore, 42

5
Thursday
St. Lawrence in Panisperna
Via Panisperna, 90

6
Friday
Twelve Holy Apostles
Piazza dei Santi Apostoli, 51

7
Saturday
St. Peter
Piazza San Pietro

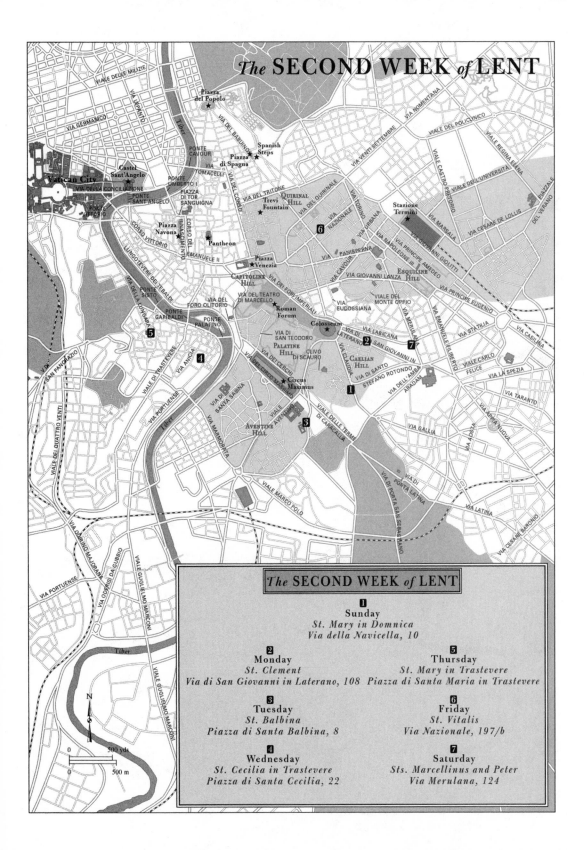

The SECOND WEEK of LENT

Piazza del Popolo ★

Spanish Steps ★

Piazza di Spagna ★

Castel Sant'Angelo

Vatican City

Trevi Fountain ★

Quirinal Hill

Stazione Termini

Piazza Navona

Pantheon ★

6

Piazza Venezia ★

Capitoline Hill

Esquiline Hill

Roman Forum

Colosseum

2

7

Palatine Hill

Caelian Hill

5

4

1

Circus Maximus ★

Aventine Hill

3

---

0   500 yds

0   500 m

N

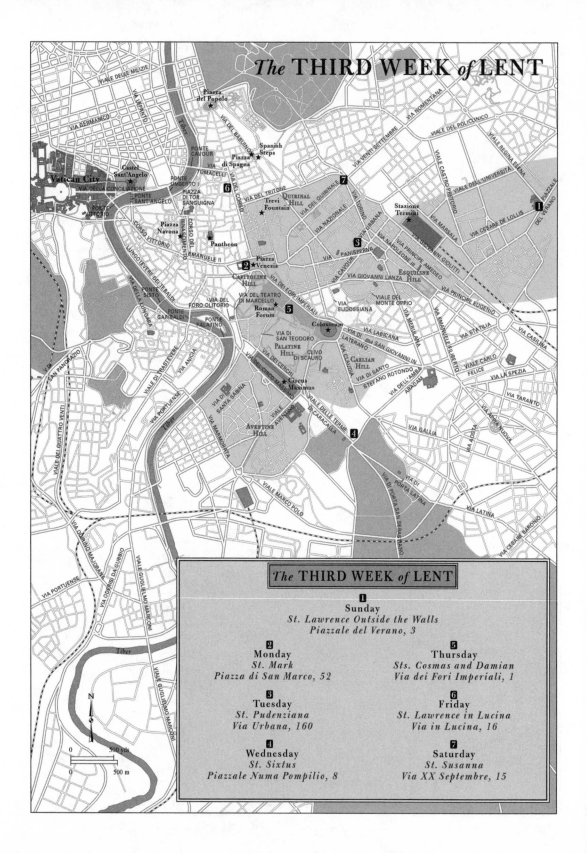

The THIRD WEEK *of* LENT

The THIRD WEEK *of* LENT

1
Sunday
St. Lawrence Outside the Walls
Piazzale del Verano, 3

2
Monday
St. Mark
Piazza di San Marco, 52

3
Tuesday
St. Pudenziana
Via Urbana, 160

4
Wednesday
St. Sixtus
Piazzale Numa Pompilio, 8

5
Thursday
Sts. Cosmas and Damian
Via dei Fori Imperiali, 1

6
Friday
St. Lawrence in Lucina
Via in Lucina, 16

7
Saturday
St. Susanna
Via XX Septembre, 15

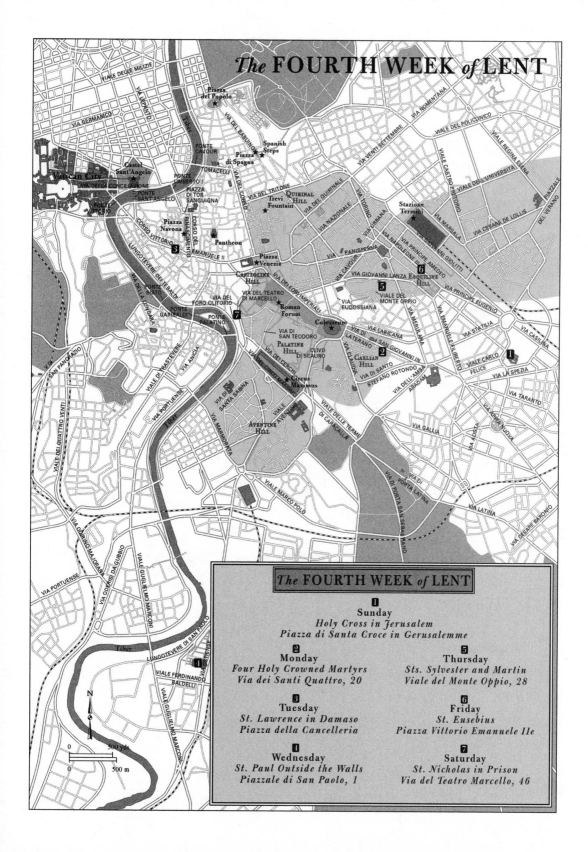

The FOURTH WEEK *of* LENT

The FOURTH WEEK *of* LENT

❶
Sunday
Holy Cross in Jerusalem
Piazza di Santa Croce in Gerusalemme

❷
Monday
Four Holy Crowned Martyrs
Via dei Santi Quattro, 20

❸
Tuesday
St. Lawrence in Damaso
Piazza della Cancelleria

❹
Wednesday
St. Paul Outside the Walls
Piazzale di San Paolo, 1

❺
Thursday
Sts. Sylvester and Martin
Viale del Monte Oppio, 28

❻
Friday
St. Eusebius
Piazza Vittorio Emanuele IIe

❼
Saturday
St. Nicholas in Prison
Via del Teatro Marcello, 46

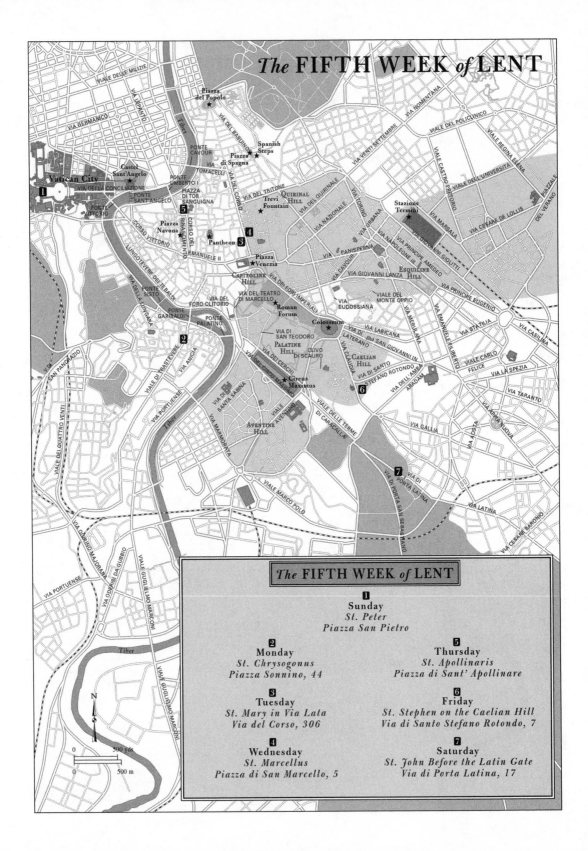

The FIFTH WEEK of LENT

The FIFTH WEEK of LENT

1
Sunday
St. Peter
Piazza San Pietro

2
Monday
St. Chrysogonus
Piazza Sonnino, 44

3
Tuesday
St. Mary in Via Lata
Via del Corso, 306

4
Wednesday
St. Marcellus
Piazza di San Marcello, 5

5
Thursday
St. Apollinaris
Piazza di Sant' Apollinare

6
Friday
St. Stephen on the Caelian Hill
Via di Santo Stefano Rotondo, 7

7
Saturday
St. John Before the Latin Gate
Via di Porta Latina, 17

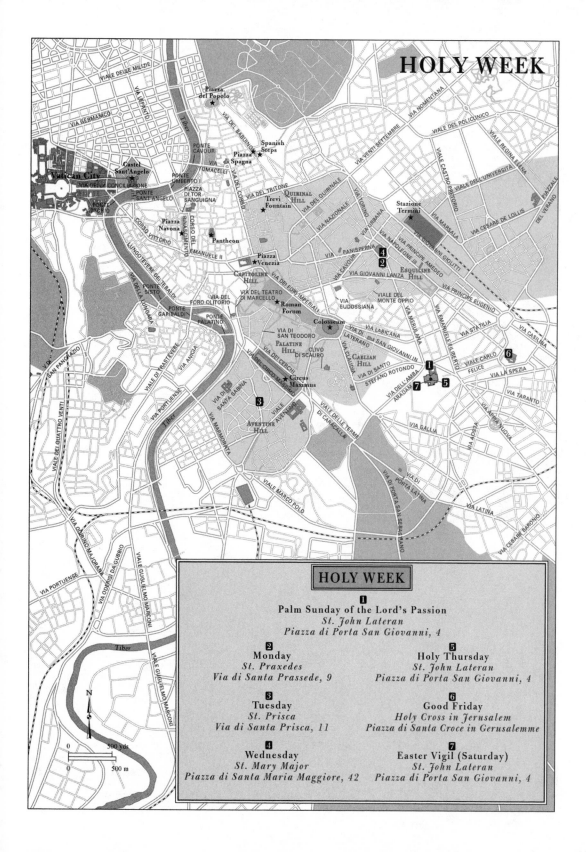

HOLY WEEK

HOLY WEEK

1
Palm Sunday of the Lord's Passion
St. John Lateran
Piazza di Porta San Giovanni, 4

2
Monday
St. Praxedes
Via di Santa Prassede, 9

5
Holy Thursday
St. John Lateran
Piazza di Porta San Giovanni, 4

3
Tuesday
St. Prisca
Via di Santa Prisca, 11

6
Good Friday
Holy Cross in Jerusalem
Piazza di Santa Croce in Gerusalemme

4
Wednesday
St. Mary Major
Piazza di Santa Maria Maggiore, 42

7
Easter Vigil (Saturday)
St. John Lateran
Piazza di Porta San Giovanni, 4

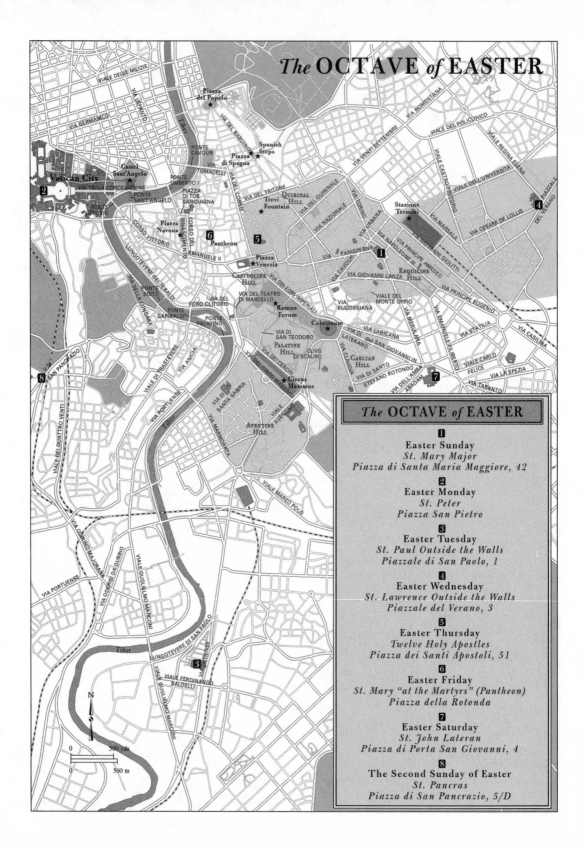

The OCTAVE of EASTER

The OCTAVE of EASTER

1
Easter Sunday
St. Mary Major
Piazza di Santa Maria Maggiore, 42

2
Easter Monday
St. Peter
Piazza San Pietro

3
Easter Tuesday
St. Paul Outside the Walls
Piazzale di San Paolo, 1

4
Easter Wednesday
St. Lawrence Outside the Walls
Piazzale del Verano, 3

5
Easter Thursday
Twelve Holy Apostles
Piazza dei Santi Apostoli, 51

6
Easter Friday
St. Mary "at the Martyrs" (Pantheon)
Piazza della Rotonda

7
Easter Saturday
St. John Lateran
Piazza di Porta San Giovanni, 4

8
The Second Sunday of Easter
St. Pancras
Piazza di San Pancrazio, 5/D